The political economy of
conflict and appropriation

Traditional economic analysis has concentrated on production and trading as the only means by which individual agents can increase their welfare. But both the history of industrialized countries and the current experience of many developing and transition economies suggest a major alternative: the appropriation of what others have produced through coercion, rent seeking, or influence peddling. Appropriation was how nobles, bandits, and kings used to make a living. The same is true nowadays for mafia bosses, army generals, lobbyists, and corrupt officials.

The essays in this volume integrate conflict and appropriation into economic analysis. In the first of two sets of essays, the actual or potential use of force is a primary determinant of aggregate outcomes. In the second set, appropriation takes subtler forms and is mediated by the political process of modern states. Collectively the essays indicate how, once appropriation is taken into account, some central properties of traditional economic analysis, as well as the presumption that they hold in reality, can break down. The contributions are part of the recent trend of reintroducing politics into economics, a trend that is having a growing impact on political science as well as on economics.

The political economy of conflict and appropriation

EDITED BY

MICHELLE R. GARFINKEL
University of California–Irvine

STERGIOS SKAPERDAS
University of California–Irvine

CAMBRIDGE
UNIVERSITY PRESS

Published by the Press Syndicate of the University of Cambridge
The Pitt Building, Trumpington Street, Cambridge CB2 1RP
40 West 20th Street, New York, NY 10011-4211, USA
10 Stamford Road, Oakleigh, Melbourne 3166, Australia

First Published 1996

Printed in the United States of America

Library of Congress Cataloging-in-Publication Data
The political economy of conflict and appropriation / edited by
    Michelle R. Garfinkel, Stergios Skaperdas.
       p.   cm.
    Papers presented at a conference held at the University of
California-Irvine in May 1994.
    ISBN 0-521-56063-2 (hc)
    1. Economics – Political aspects – Congresses. 2. Power (Social
sciences) – Economic aspects – Congresses. I. Garfinkel, Michelle
R., 1961–   . II. Skaperdas, Stergios.
HB74.P65P656   1996
330 – dc20   95-45578
                                                              CIP

A catalog record for this book is available from the British Library

ISBN   0-521-56063-2   Hardback

Contents

List of contributors

Lee J. Alston
Department of Economics
University of Illinois at
    Urbana–Champaign
Urbana, IL 61801

Nakgyoon Choi
Korea Institute for Economics
    and Trade
Seoul, Korea

Robert T. Deacon
Department of Economics
University of California-
    Santa Barbara
Santa Barbara, CA 93106

Ronald Findlay
Department of Economics
Columbia University
New York, NY 10027

Herschel I. Grossman
Department of Economics
Brown University
Providence, RI 02912

Jack Hirshleifer
Department of Economics
University of California–Los
    Angeles
Los Angeles, CA 90024

Minseong Kim
Department of Economics
Brown University
Providence, RI 02912

Gary D. Libecap
Department of Economics
University of Arizona
Tucson, AZ 85721

Susanne Lohmann
Department of Political Science
University of California-Los Angeles
Los Angeles, CA 90024

Stephen P. Magee
Department of Finance
University of Texas–Austin
Austin, TX 78712

Robert Schneider
World Bank
Washington, D.C.

Constantinos Syropoulos
Department of Economics
Pennsylvania State University
University Park, PA 16802

Acknowledgments

This volume consists of revisions of a number of papers presented at a conference held at the University of California–Irvine in May 1994. Funding provided by the Focused Research Program in Public Choice, the School of Social Sciences and the Academic Senate, all at the University of California–Irvine, is gratefully acknowledged.

We also wish to thank Linda Cohen, Jaewoo Lee, Martin McGuire, James Rauch, Robert Rider, Peter Rosendorff, Charles Stuart, and Murray Wolfson for their extensive comments on the papers presented at the conference; Karen Sandler for her invaluable help with the organizational aspects of the conference; and especially Amihai Glazer for his encouragement and participation in various stages of the process. Finally, we are indebted to Scott Parris and Linda Johnson for helping us to put this volume together.

Acknowledgements

CHAPTER 1

Introduction: Conflict and appropriation as economic activities

Michelle R. Garfinkel and Stergios Skaperdas
University of California, Irvine

> An American businessman, recently arrived in Moscow to open an office, was met at his hotel by five men with gold watches, pistols and a print-out of his firm's net worth. They demanded 7% of future earnings. He took the first flight to New York, where muggers are less sophisticated. (*The Economist*, 1994)

Although crime, conflict, and appropriation are common activities in all societies, the regularly reported incidents like the one just described from Moscow and other post-Soviet localities surprise even Westerners (who have been hardened by tales of muggings in New York and celluloid violence). The source of the surprise, at least from the perspective of most economists, is simply the failure of apparently rational individuals to engage in mutually advantageous trade spontaneously. In the absence of external or internal restraints, however, an individual with easy access to a pistol might find it more convenient to take what he wants from others outright by threatening to use force than to obtain what he wants through peaceful trade. As a general principle, resources can be used not only for production but also for appropriative purposes such as for theft and warfare. Individuals and groups can either produce and thus create wealth or seize the wealth created by others.

Although this might appear to be an obvious assessment of human behavior, the *Homo economicus* of traditional economic analysis has been assumed to behave rather differently. While completely rational and self-interested when it comes to truck, barter, and trade, they are also saints of sorts, obeying a stronger version of the ten commandments: They will not simply take what does not belong to them, even when it is in their interest to do so. They will not maim and kill. Often they will not even lobby for favorable taxation or trade protection. This rather schizophrenic predisposition of economic man could possibly be considered a reasonable approximation for societies with stable institutions, social norms, and beliefs (e.g., for the Western industrial-

We would like to thank Art DeVany, Herschel Grossman, Jaewoo Lee, and three anonymous referees for their helpful comments on a preliminary version of this introduction.

ized countries in the postwar period). A number of casual observations, though, cast some doubt on this approximation.

First, history clearly indicates that periods of stability have continually alternated with periods of instability, turmoil, and conflict. Just looking at Western Europe over the last two centuries – the period of unprecedented innovation and material progress – a sample of upheaval and conflict includes:

- The French revolution and numerous other revolutions and revolts.
- The Napoleonic wars, the two world wars, and many other less generalized wars.
- The building and dissolution of colonialism, which was accompanied by worldwide projection of military power.
- The construction of nations and the emergence of nation-states, sometimes out of the ashes of previously seemingly invincible empires.
- The control of sectors or geographic regions in several countries by mafias and gangs.

Each of these instances has had significant, and often overwhelming, economic impact. The French revolution, for example, abolished centuries-old institutions and inaugurated the building of new ones that have had very different ramifications for the conduct of economic activity. Besides the change in institutions that had long-term impact, the revolution and the upheaval following it had immediate effects on the production and distribution of commodities.

Second, much of the rest of the world now (not to speak of the past) would seem even more disorderly. According to some reports, local small businesses in Russia have to pay 30 to 50 percent of their profits to racketeers, not just the meager 7 percent demanded from the American businessman (Geyer, 1994; see also Handelman, 1994). Some countries are run by unconstrained kleptocrats. In other countries with some semblance of a rule of law and some limits on the ability of governments to enforce their will, anarchic conditions can prevail. For instance, beyond the regular stories of ethnic and religious conflict coming out of India, the following conditions have been reported from the state of Bihar:

> Atrocities continue with nauseating regularity. Most often they are the work of small landowners trying to make untouchables work their fields without payment. … What peace Bihar does enjoy is the peace of a mafia neighborhood, in which everyone pays for protection and disputes are settled by the gun. (*The Economist*, 1991)

Finally, even within stable, industrialized societies conflict and appropriation with or without overt violence permeate the economy. Police who clash with French farmers and youths or British striking coalminers are just tips of icebergs of distributional conflicts that are usually conducted through more normal political channels, but that nevertheless have many similarities with more overt forms of conflict.

Can the activities of the Bihari landowners, the police, the French farmers, the British coalminers, and the possible responses of other constituencies be exempt from study by economists? Going through an economics principles text or scanning the literature of the past century would suggest a positive answer. But surely this answer must not have been the result of a perception that conflict and appropriation have no relevance for economic welfare. Rather the absence of conflict and appropriation in mainstream economic writing appears to have its origins in late nineteenth-century Britain – starting with the marginalists and culminating in Marshall – with the purpose of making political economy analytically more tractable in accordance with a principle of division of labor in the social sciences. Tractability in the field of "political economy" was conveniently achieved by ignoring anything that smacked of politics, including conflict. To make the transformed discipline more respectable in the scientific circles of their time and to signify the break with the past, these gentlemen gave it a new name: economics.

This is not to say that discourse on conflict in economics was completely silenced. Many prominent economists have written on war and peace (Keynes, 1920, Pigou, 1939) while others have emphasized the trade-off between production and appropriation (Pareto, 1966). Yet such works have had minimal impact on the framework of analysis used by economists and the way they think about the economy. Pigou is known for his welfare economics, Keynes for his macroeconomics, and Pareto for his notion of efficiency, not for anything related to appropriation. Such an assessment can also be confirmed by leafing through an economics principles text, starting with the first modern one, that of Marshall's.

To be sure, not all facets of economic activity are directly affected by conflict and appropriation; we can be confident that the next breakthrough in understanding the market for pork bellies will not come from that direction. Although individual events like a sudden reduction in the supply of crude oil can influence the prices and quantities in a given market, the laws governing the day-to-day operations of markets are unaffected by conflict. Those laws, however, presuppose the existence of well-functioning markets, of endowments that are perfectly secure, of traders who will not steal from each other.

Incorporating conflict and appropriation into economic analysis can be seen as a quest for characterizing outcomes when traders can steal from one another, when endowments are insecure, or when well functioning markets are absent. A central objective of this quest is the discovery and characterization of regularities in individual and aggregate economic behavior under such conditions. Such regularities would certainly be at least as helpful as the laws of supply and demand in understanding, for example, the "market" for unskilled agricultural workers in Bihar, in which the untouchables participate with an apparently precarious ownership of their own labor. As for a worldwide market, the ownership and control of crude oil are at least partly and periodically disputed among governments and private entities, often with significant economic impact on the immediately concerned parties. (Recent examples of such disputes include the Iraq war and Russia's disputes with other post-Soviet republics over the control of oil reserves as well as over other matters.) The establishment of a market itself and the rules that will govern its functioning are usually hotly contested, not just through the political maneuvering that takes place in a Western country but also through the threat or the exercise of force as in the goods markets of today's Moscow. In other words, day-to-day economic activity as well as the institutions that shape this activity are influenced at least to some extent by force and conflict, by the appropriative or predatory use of resources.

The articles contained in this volume depart from the conventional economic paradigm by taking into account the appropriative use of resources. The first four articles (by Hirshleifer, Findlay, Grossman and Kim, and Skaperdas and Syropoulos) are part of an emerging literature on conflict and appropriation. In this work the use of force or the threat of using force is a primary determinant of aggregate outcomes; appropriative activities are swords, bombs, or guns. These articles primarily explore different facets of the emergence of order and restraints on individual behavior out of conditions without any or few restraints. The next two articles (by Choi and Magee and by Lohmann) suppose the existence of some institutions and examine behavior given the slack that emerges from incompletely specified institutions. These articles are part of the wider revival of political economy in recent years with appropriative activities taking subtler forms: influence peddling, lobbying, and rent seeking. The last two articles in this book (by Allston, Libecap, and Schneider and by Deacon) empirically examine the role of conflict and other determinants of secure institutions.

The perspective of the papers in this volume, though related, differs from several other literatures in economics and political science.[1] First, there is the field of defense economics that has been concerned with conflict among nations (for a survey, see McGuire, 1995). Some of the papers in the volume, especially the theoretical ones, can be applied to conflict among nations; but their perspective is more generic, aimed at understanding the economic implications of the trade-off between production and appropriation in contexts that

---

[1] Actually, each referee of this volume pointed out at least one literature, different from the others, that we had failed to mention. That made us realize both our ignorance and also the need for such an integrative survey and more generally for far more communication across the different fields and literatures that have dealt with conflict.

can go beyond those that have nations as the primary actors, without the normative content of much work in defense economics. Second, the field of international relations also concerns itself with conflict among nations and how economic considerations play a role therein (see, e.g., Keohane, 1986). While some work in this area (in particular, Powell, 1993) is methodologically similar to several of the papers in this volume, again the concerns of this literature are not the economic consequences of conflict and appropriation in general. The third related literature, largely in political science, is concerned with domestic political conflict (see, for example, Przeworki, 1991, and the survey by Lichbach, 1992). Substantively, this literature might also be the most closely related literature to the papers in this volume. Yet, as indicated by Lichbach (1992) who uses cross-citation evidence, that literature is very fragmented with little communication among its contributors, a condition that renders the term "literature" to the contributions in this area a bit immature. At any rate, despite substantive overlapping themes with those three literatures, there are important differences. The articles contained in this volume take a general equilibrium approach emphasizing the implications of conflict for economic outcomes and the effects of political institutions that shape that conflict.

In what follows, we will discuss the articles in this volume in terms of two general themes: conflict in history and controlled conflict in modern states. Along the way, we also hope to further clarify and justify our view of the importance of conflict and appropriation for economic activity that we tried to convey earlier on. (For complementary arguments, we suggest Hirshleifer, 1994.) Our discussion revolving around the first theme attempts to interpret and, to the extent possible, synthesize the findings in the articles of the volume as they relate to general historical development. As with any academic exercise that looks at the past, understanding the present is a primary objective. History, however, never exactly repeats itself and our understanding of the present, although enhanced by knowledge of the past, cannot solely rely on it. Today's governance structures are as complex as ever and continuously evolving, with conflict and appropriation taking subtler and often less violent forms now than in the past. Our discussion of the second theme attempts to extract from the papers in the volume lessons for today's more complex economies and societies in which conflict is often mediated through modern constitutions, legal systems, and liberal democratic politics.

1   On conflict in history

Conflict in human history became a serious problem with the advent of agriculture about 10,000 years ago. Earlier, most hunters and gatherers enjoyed a rather tolerable existence. Food was usually plentiful and easy to collect, leaving much time for leisure activities. High protein intake reduced the risk of disease, and low population densities slowed the spread of epidemics. Thus there was little scope for organized fighting over economic resources (see, e.g., Stavrianos, 1989 or Smith, 1993). While there were exceptions to this trend, one can hardly deny the contrast with what came later on.[2] Agriculture allowed for much higher population densities but at the expense of lower protein intakes and higher risks of disease, epidemics, and starvation due to crop failure. More directly related to our own topic, the necessary sedentarization of life coupled with the greater storability of grains provided outsiders with an easy target for plunder or enslavement. The agricultural community then had to defend itself by arming or, given its lack of comparative advantage in such activities, by hiring another band of outsiders, who would often turn out to be more dangerous than those they were supposed to defend against. Regardless of the particulars, with the spread of agriculture the appropriative use of resources became generalized and the associated risks were often as high as those from weather and plague. For long stretches of time and for many human beings, life became "poor, nasty, brutish and short."

The name given to that condition by political and moral philosophers was "state of nature" (a somewhat misleading characterization as it evokes a pre-agricultural state). Among economists, the term *anarchy* is the name often given to such "a social arrangement in which contenders struggle to conquer and defend durable resources, without effective regulation either by higher authorities or social pressure" (Hirshleifer, this volume).[3]

As argued by Hirshleifer, protracted conflict in anarchy or the state of nature can be a stable system. He finds that an important condition for the sustainability of anarchy is the existence of diminishing returns to fighting effort (or, according to Hirshleifer's terminology, when conflict is not decisive). In this circumstance, no one can completely overtake others and, at the same time, there are some incentives to devote resources to production so that the participants can survive. As examples of such stable anarchy, Hirshleifer points to tribal warfare in New Guinea up to relatively recently, the persistence of many city-states in ancient Greece before the Athenian hegemony, and others. By contrast, under increasing returns to fighting effort (or equivalently when conflict is more decisive), there is a tendency for one side – usually the one that can devote more resources to warfare – to prevail and thus render anarchy unstable. Although Hirshleifer does not examine what occurs under

---

[2] For an inspired interpretation of Genesis as a myth of conflict between the agricultural and hunter-gatherer ways of life, attributed to Hamblin (1987), see Smith (1993).

[3] An early model of anarchy is found in Bush and Mayer (1974). Tullock (1974) also examined conflict and appropriation from an economic perspective. However, to our knowledge the earliest formal model of conflict was developed by Haavelmo (1954, pp. 91–7). If the state of nature is taken to be conflictual, anarchy can be considered its superset, since anarchy does not have to be conflictual.

such circumstances, he conjectures reasonably that a Hobbesian "vertical" contract, in which the winning side imposes autocratic or dictatorial rule, is most likely to arise. Increasing returns to fighting effort also reduces political fragmentation and heightens the tendency for larger political units. The generalized introduction of cannon warfare, for instance, in early fifteenth-century Europe appears to have been instrumental in reducing the number of independent principalities. Although the remaining political units greatly increased their arms expenditures as a result of this and other innovations in the succeeding centuries, the effect of a smaller number of political units – conditional on the technology of conflict – is to reduce arming. Thus the long-run effect of technological change in warfare on fighting intensities, and therefore on the proportion of resources devoted to production for consumption purposes, cannot be determined unambiguously.

While Hirshleifer's paper is concerned with the stability of anarchy, the paper by Findlay examines the limits and stability of empires, which are in a sense the antithesis of anarchy (and, as conjectured by Hirshleifer, a likely outcome when anarchy is unstable). Findlay introduces a novel spatial model in which the limits of empire and the land that can be used for production are determined by the ability of its rulers to project military power. Such power, as in other work in this volume, has an opportunity cost in the production of final output. Findlay artfully weaves in numerous historical examples that fit his basic model and its various extensions: from the Roman and Chinese empires to the Burmese kings and the Zulus under Shaka.

Empires impose stability, but in the long run they come and go. As Findlay comments in his concluding section, the fall of empires could be attributed to the gradual loss of cohesion and solidarity of the originally conquering tribe or nation – in the words of the great Arab Historian Ibn Khaldun, to the dissolution of the bonds of *assabiya*. The mirror image of loss of solidarity is the gain of particularistic interests, as elaborated in Olson (1982) and examined more precisely in the articles by Lohmann and by Choi and Magee. However, another complementary factor in the fall of empires may be, surprisingly, the economic success itself brought about by stability and internal peace. In the Findlay model, for example, improvements in the production technology have ambiguous effects on the level of arming and consequently on the extent of empire. This occurs because increasing worker productivity increases the opportunity cost of soldiering and may therefore lead to a reduction in the resources that maintain the size of empire. On the other hand, the nomads and mountaineers of the fringe "rimland," who are accustomed more to plunder than to production and who are waiting in the wings while they improve their riding techniques and sharpen their knives, are more prepared to go after the larger prize implied by an empire's higher productivity. Such an inverse relationship between productive capacity and military power may have been a significant factor in the dissolution of empires as well as of other historical and economic change. The Grossman and Kim article also demonstrates how the empire's large resource capacity – not necessarily its productivity – can turn potential predators to pure predators who become completely specialized in plunder.

The often long periods of instability brought about by conquering nomadic tribes have had immediate effects on welfare through reduction in production and trade. In addition there are other long-term effects on the economy and the environment, as examined in Deacon's article. In particular, Deacon provides historical and quantitative evidence on the effects of political instability on deforestation and investment, with the quantitative evidence showing consistently increased deforestation and reduced investment as a result of increased political instability. The review of historical evidence from the Mediterranean basin also appears consistent with this hypothesis. Deacon, parenthetically, also points out that nomads contribute much more than agriculturists to deforestation and land degradation (presumably, even after taking account of the greater numbers that can be supported by agriculture).

Besides (stable) anarchy and empire, there are of course other possibilities, either with states smaller or less stable than empires or without a state but with some type of horizontal (and not necessarily explicit) contracting. Regardless of the organizational or contractual form of the arrangement, however, the parties involved will usually have to devote resources to policing and monitoring and to have the capacity to defend themselves in case the arrangement fails. Grossman and Kim, in their own predator-prey model, show that a nonaggressive arrangement can develop when the effectiveness of offense against defense is low and conflict is sufficiently destructive. In such a nonaggressive environment, resources are devoted only to defense by the prey, whereas the potential predators refrain from any attacks. Consequently, the prey can be thought of as having a secure property right over its resources without the presence of a third party, like a government, to validate this right.

The absence of third parties with enforcement power will likely induce everyone to devote at least some of their resources to arming. For there always exists something of value to dispute, whether a piece of land or the fruits of land and other productive inputs. The Skaperdas and Syropoulos article indicates how the presence of a disputed resource can make arming and conflict compatible with trading, as has often been the case in history, especially during the reign of colonial Western European powers. That paper also provides an additional rationale for trade restrictions, based on anarchic relations among states. In the presence of anarchy, there may exist sizable economic resources that are disputed by rival states; to settle those disputes, states arm and often enter into conflict. At the same time, as it has often happened in history, citizens of the same adversary states engage in ordinary competitive trade. With trade, however, the benefits to the winners of disputed resources may induce much more arming than when trade is restricted, so that the ordinary benefits to trade could be outweighed by the additional cost of arming. That is, one or more states could have an ex ante interest not to trade and, to do that, they could impose trade restrictions that are difficult to undo.

2 On controlled conflict in modern states

As Hirshleifer mentions at the end of his article, the reduction or elimination of conflict at one level may sharpen conflict at another level. The termination of dissent within a tribe may bring conflict against other tribes. The consolidation of power within any two states may mean that they are now able to devote more resources to fighting each other. That is, there is a hierarchy of levels of anarchy starting from very small political units, say the individual or family, to very large ones. The breakdown of empires indicates that history does not inexorably evolve toward ever larger political units.

However, the cessation of open, violent conflict as the normal means of settling disputes and the development of a social contract within a level of this hierarchy does not also imply the disappearance of the potential for violent conflict within that level. There is still occasional violence within families, within neighborhoods, and within the borders of any state, including the use of force by the police. And the great variation in the type of government provided – from a teetering kleptocratic dictatorship to a stable democracy – implies great variation in frameworks within which economic activity is conducted, yielding a wide variety of economic results.

Deacon's cross-sectional evidence on the effects of political instability (measured in various ways) on investment and deforestation is complemented by the micro-, time-series evidence in the Allston, Libecap, and Schneider article. In particular, the latter examines the assignment of property rights and the role of violence in two states in Brazil: one in the South that developed early and the other in the Amazon, which is still largely undeveloped and whose land values are low. In their qualitative assessment of the evidence concerning the assignment of property rights, the authors find that violence among competing claimants occurred most often in cases in which multiple government agencies or different levels of government (state versus federal) became involved in assigning tenure to the same land. Government infrastructure programs that unexpectedly and sharply raised rents and insufficient budgetary resources to process and police title are also cited as having sparked conflict among claimants. It would be interesting to probe further into the different constituencies that might have been behind the competing agencies, levels of government, and infrastructure programs – perhaps an overly ambitious endeavor given the lack of documentary evidence. In the same article, the effect of violence on the percentage of landholders with titles to their land is studied econometrically. In the Southern state the effect is negative, but statistically insignificant, whereas in the Amazonian state the more limited evidence does not show the expected effect.

In Brazil and elsewhere, however, violent conflict remains mostly in the background, as a distant threat and, more frequently, it has been completely supplanted by more civilized and controlled forms of conflict in the legal and political sphere. Within the modern state, and especially in prosperous countries, we don't observe the assembly of rival armies of soldiers. Rather, we observe the lining up of lawyers aided by assistants and expert witnesses or of lobbyists, mass mailers, and campaign consultants. This controlled conflict within modern states has many formal similarities with conflict under anarchy, models of which, appropriately reinterpreted, could be used to understand many facets of the political economy of modern states.

The possibility of an inverse relationship between production potential and power, which as mentioned earlier surfaces in many models of conflict, can appear within the modern economy as well. Firms, for instance, face a trade-off between productive investment and lobbying for favorable taxation or regulation. Firms with weak productive potential are likely to find lobbying to be a more effective means of maintaining their profits. Depending on the degree to which state institutions respond to lobbying, the actual profitability of such firms could turn out to be higher than those of more productive and efficient firms.

In fact, the Choi and Magee paper represents a variation on this theme. In standard neoclassical trade models, the returns to fixed factors of production – capital, land – are decreasing or constant. Admitting the opportunity for lobbying to obtain trade protection may reverse this result. Within a variant of the Findlay-Wellisz (1982) trade model of endogenous lobbying intended to capture developing countries in which there is a conflict between manufacturers and landowners, Choi and Magee derive conditions under which there exist increasing returns to factors of production (labor and capital), the Magee-Young theorem previously derived within the Heckscher-Ohlin model. In developing countries, a larger capital endowment induces more lobbying for the protection of domestic manufactures. The resultant increased domestic price of manufactures may more than offset the decreasing physical returns to capital and therefore increase the rate of return on capital, leading to "rapid industrialization and above average growth." Conversely, in developing countries with low capital endowments the landowners experience increasing returns, but at the expense of sluggish industrialization and low growth.

Beyond restrictions on trade, interest groups in modern liberal democracies lobby to receive many other types of favorable treatment or simply to avoid unfavorable treatment. Yet, everyone recognizes the inefficiency of this state of affairs; if all voters and politicians could credibly commit not to engage in lobbying and influence activities, they would all be better off (with the possibility of compensatory transfers). This is certainly not unlike the problem of cooperation in the state of nature, but of course at a different level. Given the abundance of experience in the history of man, there are many apparent difficulties in solving this problem in modern democracies. Or, to paraphrase Lohmann, why does a political entrepreneur, who stands for election to eliminate all the perks enjoyed by special interests, not get elected unanimously?

Lohmann's article, which uses the apt name of "demosclerosis" for this phenomenon, offers a possible explanation that is complementary to that of Olson (1982).[4] The problem according to Lohmann is informational: Voters cannot effectively ascertain whether candidates who promise to eliminate favorable treatment toward special interests will keep their promises once they reach office. Organized special interests, which are supported by at least some voters, can monitor politicians better than those who are not organized. But by their nature, the mission of organized special interests is to seek favorable treatment. The greater informational asymmetry there is between voters and organized special interests and the more office-motivated the politicians are, the greater is the problem of the policy bias toward special interests.

Lohmann's assessment of the prospects for overcoming the problem is rather grim, since the underlying informational asymmetries are not easily remedied, especially in the short run. In fact, the attitude of voters as maximizers of a narrow self-interest may have intensified over the past twenty years or so in liberal democracies, and the number of special interest groups has, at the same time, grown considerably. However, these trends need not persist in the long run. Social pressures or genuine concern for the public interest, whatever this is perceived to be, could bring about a change in the tide that now looks insurmountable.

Cooperation at any level of the hierarchy of anarchy may be modeled as an equilibrium in a supergame; but to overcome the fragility of such equilibria, the "hard-wiring" of the strategies that support cooperation as good in themselves appears to have been common in history. The sharing of an ideology that serves to emphasize the common good is, to say the least, well correlated with the achievement and perpetuation of cooperation. Whether it was the public spiritedness of classical Athenians and the Romans of the early republic, Ibn Khaldun's *assabiya,* the single god of the Jews, Christians, and Moslems, or the myths and realities of nationhood in its early stages, beliefs in the common good of the tribe, city, nation, or coreligionists fostered cooperation among its members and often expanded that membership at the expense of others who were less able to cooperate. Although typically economists are reluctant to talk about ideology and the origins of preferences of eco-

---

[4] The term *demosclerosis* was coined by Rauch (1994).

nomic agents, the issue is no longer a taboo. (See, for example, North, 1990 or Guttman, Nitzan, and Spiegel, 1992.) Until liberal democracies find an ideology that unifies their citizens – an entrepreneurial "special interest" group with the general interest and more in mind – demosclerosis, lobbying and counter-lobbying, and political fragmentation along narrow lines will likely continue.

3   Concluding comments

Bringing the study of conflict and appropriation back to economics is part of the larger trend or reintroducing politics into economics, after an absence of nearly a century. Once conflict and appropriation are taken into account, some central properties of traditional neoclassical economic models, as well as the presumption that they hold in reality, often break down. More abundant factors of production can boost their actual returns, despite a reduction in their marginal productivity, and technical improvements in production can make those who undertake them relatively worse off. Instead, those who do better may be those who have a comparative advantage in violence or, under controlled conflict, in lobbying and influence; nomads of the fringe can tax or destroy productive peasants; generals and lieutenants can treat whole countries as their personal fiefdoms; and lobbyists and other influence peddlers in industrialized democracies can have an impact that, although difficult to assess, is far from insignificant. Clearly, under such circumstances, the incentives for investment and innovation that would be normally present in an ideal economy are undermined, thus retarding and in some circumstances even reversing growth.

Whereas some of the qualitative effects of conflict and appropriation are easy to assess, their quantitative impact is uncertain, especially given the dearth of empirical work that takes into account those factors. The evolution of cooperation, or regression to conflict, within any level of the hierarchy of anarchy is also a very difficult issue. Aside from the importance of long-term relationships, partly learned from the study of repeated games, economists have little to say.

Beyond the bells and whistles of academic models, there is a real need for understanding better the sources of conflict and its effects on the economy and society. For, at this point, humanity appears to be in the midst of two opposing trends with sharply different implications for its destiny, at least for the medium run. One trend is toward unprecedented and widening prosperity, fueled by the spreading applications of advances in information and other technologies over the past twenty years [dubbed the "third industrial revolution" by Jensen (Hirshleifer et al., 1994)]. The second trend, which is largely a reaction to the forces of creative destruction of the first one, is toward increasing violent and political conflict among ethnicities, nations, social classes, and other groups, each trying to find its bearings within the whirlwind of change. We would expect the forces of prosperity to prevail eventually. In the meantime, the transition is, and will continue to be, painful for billions of human beings and of an uncertain length. Mainstream economic thought can no longer continue to ignore the effects of this second trend.

References

Bush, Winston C. and Lawrence S. Mayer, "Some Implications of Anarchy for the Distribution of Property," *Journal of Economic Theory,* August 1974, 8, 401–12.

Economist, The, "The Bihari Disease," April 6, 1991, 36.

Economist, The "The High Price of Freeing Markets," February 19, 1994, 57–8.

Findlay, Ronald and Stanislaw Wellisz, "Endogenous Tariffs, the Political Economy of Trade Restrictions, and Welfare," in J. N. Bhagwati (ed.), *Import Competition and Response,* Chicago: University of Chicago Press, 1982, 223–34.

Geyer, Georgie Anne, "Will the Criminals Take Over in Russia?" *Orange County Register,* August 10, 1994.

Guttman, Joel M., Shmuel Nitzan, and Uriel Spiegel, "Rent Seeking and Social Investment in Taste Change," *Economics and Politics,* March 1992, 3, 31–42.

Haavelmo, Trygve, *A Study in the Theory of Economic Evolution,* 1954, Amsterdam: North-Holland.

Hamblin, Dora J., "Has the Garden of Eden Been Located at Last?" *Smithsonian,* May 1987, 18, 127–35.

Handelman, Stephen, "The Russian 'Mafiya,'" *Foreign Affairs,* March/April 1994, 73 (2), 83–96.

Hirshleifer, Jack, "The Dark Side of the Force," *Economic Inquiry,* January 1994, 32, 1–10.

Hirshleifer, Jack, Michael C. Jensen, Robert E. Hall, Andrei Shleifer, and William H. Meckling, "Economics and Organizational Innovation," *Contemporary Economic Policy,* April 1994, 12, 1–21.

Keohane, Robert (ed.), *Neorealism and Its Critics,* 1986, New York: Columbia University Press.

Keynes, J. M., *The Economic Consequences of Peace,* 1920, New York: Harcourt, Brace and How.

Lichbach, Mark, "Nobody Cites Nobody Else: Mathematical Models of Domestic Political Conflict," *Defence Economics,* 1992, 3, 341–57.

McGuire, Martin C., "Defense Economics and International Security," 1995, forthcoming in K. Hartley and T. Sandler (eds.), *Handbook of Defense Economics,* New York: North Holland.

North, Douglass C., *Institutions, Institutional Change and Economic Performance,* 1990, Cambridge: Cambridge University Press.

Olson, Mancur, *The Rise and Decline of Nations,* 1982, New Haven: Yale University Press.

Pareto, Vilfredo, *Les Systemes d'Economie Politique,* in S. E. Finer (ed.), *Vilfredo Pareto Sociological Writings,* 1966 (1902), New York: Praeger.

Pigou, A. C., *The Political Economy of War,* 1939, New York: Macmillan Company.

Powell, Robert, "Guns, Butter, and Anarchy," *American Political Science Review,* March 1993, 87, 115–32.

Przeworski, Adam, *Democracy and the Market,* 1991, New York: Cambridge University Press.

Rauch, Jonathan, *Demosclerosis: The Silent Killer of American Government,* 1994, New York: Times Books.

Smith, Vernon L., "Humankind in Prehistory: Economy, Ecology, and Institutions," in T. L. Anderson and R. T. Simmons (eds.), *The Political Economy of Customs and Culture: Informal Solutions to the Commons Problem,* 1993, Lanham, Md.: Rowman & Littlefield.

Stavrianos, Leften S., *Lifelines from Our Past,* 1989, New York: M. E. Sharpe.

Tullock, Gordon, *The Social Dilemma: The Economics of War and Revolution,* 1974, Fairfax, Va.: The Center for the Study of Public Choice.

CHAPTER 2

Anarchy and its breakdown

Jack Hirshleifer
University of California, Los Angeles

What do the following have in common?

1. International struggles for control of the globe's resources.
2. Gang warfare in prohibition era Chicago.
3. Miners versus claim jumpers in the California gold rush.
4. Animal territoriality.
5. Male elephant seals who fight to sequester "harems" of females.

Answer: These are all anarchic situations.

Anarchy is not chaos. At least potentially, anarchic relationships can constitute a stable system. But not all environments are capable of sustaining an anarchic order. Anarchy can break down, to be replaced by another pattern of relationships.

Anarchy is a natural economy (Ghiselin, 1978), or spontaneous order in the sense of Hayek (1979). Various forms of spontaneous order emerge from resource competition among animals, including territoriality and dominance relationships.[1] As for humans, while associations ranging from primitive tribes to modern nation-states are all governed internally by some form of law, their external relations one with another remain mainly anarchic. Yet intertribal or international systems also have their regularities and systematic analyzable patterns.[2]

The term "anarchy" in ordinary usage conflates two rather different situations that the biological literature carefully distinguishes: "scramble" versus "interference" competition (Nicholson, 1954) – or, in an alternative terminology, "exploitation" versus "resource defense" (Krebs and Davies, 1987, p. 93). Under scramble competition, which might be termed *amorphy*[3] (absence of

Journal of Political Economy, Vol. 103, no. 1, 1995. Copyright © 1995 by The University of Chicago. All rights reserved. Reprinted with permission. For helpful comments I thank David Hirshleifer, Jay Y. C. Jen, John Pezzey, Alan Rogers, Stergios Skaperdas, Charles Stuart, Earl Thompson, Dan Usher, Michael Waldman, Don Wittman, and Murray Wolfson, as well as two anonymous referees of this journal.

[1] As surveyed in Wilson (1975), especially Chs. 11–13.

[2] See, e.g., Waltz (1954), Snyder and Diesing (1977), Bernholz (1985).

[3] Not a new coinage on my part: *The Shorter Oxford Dictionary* (3rd ed., 1955 revision) cites a use by Jonathan Swift (1704).

form), resources are not sequestered but consumed on the move. In the open sea, for example, resources are so fugitive that fish do not attempt to defend territories. Rousseau evidently had amorphy in mind when he described man in the "state of nature" as:

> ... wandering up and down the forests, without industry, without speech, without home, an equal stranger to war and to all ties, neither standing in need of his fellow-creatures nor having any desire to hurt them. ... (Rousseau, *A Discourse on the Origin of Inequality*)

Although amorphic competition poses a number of interesting modeling issues, the present analysis is limited to environments where durable resources, like land territories or movable capital goods, are captured and defended by individuals or by groups. (I will generally treat *groups* as unitary actors that have somehow managed to resolve the internal collective action problem.) So, as defined here, anarchy is a social arrangement in which contenders struggle to conquer and defend durable resources, without effective regulation either by higher authorities or social pressures.[4]

Given the possibility of sequestering resources, anarchic competitors have to divide their efforts between two main types of activities: (1) productive exploitation of the assets currently controlled, and (2) seizing and defending a resource base. Correspondingly, there are two separate technologies: a *technology of production* and a *technology of appropriation, conflict, and struggle* (Hirshleifer, 1991a). There are ways of tilling the land, and quite a different set of ways of capturing land and securing it against intruders.

While I will be using military terminology like "capturing" and "fighting," these are to be understood as metaphors. Falling also into the category of interference struggles are political campaigns, rent-seeking maneuvers for licenses, and monopoly privileges (Tullock, 1967), commercial efforts to raise rivals' costs (Salop and Scheffman, 1983), strikes and lockouts, and litigation – all being conflictual activities that need not involve actual violence.

A decision maker's chosen balance between productive and conflictual efforts may be influenced in the peaceful direction by an element of productive complementarity. Management and labor, since they need one another, are less motivated to engage in destructive struggles within the firm. Similarly, mutual interdependence within the polity may moderate international, region-

---

[4] Since regulation can vary from total to zero effectiveness, anarchy is typically a matter of degree. In gold rush California the U.S. Army, though decimated by desertion to the goldfields, maintained a limited presence [Sherman, 1990 (1885), Chs. 2–3]. And during the bootlegging wars in prohibition era Chicago (Allsop, 1968), the local police, while notoriously corrupt, were still a factor. In fact, an element of anarchy persists even in the most normal of times: Law and order being imperfect, some provision for self-defense of person and property is almost always advisable.

al, and other interest group conflicts.[5] Exchange relationships, in particular, increase mutual interdependence and thus partially harmonize diverging interests. But I will be assuming here a starker environment in which productive opportunities are entirely disjointed and the exchange option is excluded, so that competitors have to fight, or at least be prepared to fight, if they are to acquire or retain resources.[6]

The economic theory of conflict, like economic modeling generally, involves two analytical steps:

1. *Optimization:* Each competitor chooses a preferred balance of productive effort and conflictual effort.
2. *Equilibrium:* On the social level, the separate optimizing decisions interact to determine levels of production and the extent of fighting activity, together with the distribution of product among the claimants.

While the economic literature on conflict theory remains relatively sparse, in recent years a number of models employing such an analytical structure have been offered. But, as far as I know, none of these earlier writings have analyzed the viability of anarchy as a spontaneous social order.[7]

Among the specific issues to be considered here are:

1. *A stable anarchic solution:* Under what conditions can two or more anarchic contestants retain viable shares of the socially available resources in equilibrium? Or put the other way, in what circumstances does the anarchic system "break down" in favor of amorphy on the one hand, or alternatively, in favor of tyranny or some other form of social control?
2. *Equilibrium allocations of effort:* Assuming a stable anarchic equilibrium, what fractions of resources will be devoted to fighting? What levels of incomes will be attained?

[5] For analyses of conflict as moderated by a cooperative element in production, see Hirshleifer (1988) and Skaperdas (1992).

[6] Fighting is of course Pareto-inefficient. All parties could always benefit from an agreed peaceful resolution, but under anarchy there is no superior authority to enforce any such agreement. (In some cases *threats* may suffice to deter conflict, but that possibility is not modeled here.)

[7] To briefly review some related analytical contributions: (1) In Bush and Mayer (1974) production is costless (manna-like), but competitors may also *steal,* generating a "natural equilibrium." (2) Skogh and Stuart (1982) allowed for three types of activities: production, transfers (i.e., stealing, or offensive activity), and protection against transfers (defensive activity). (3) Usher (1989) modeled an alternation between despotism and anarchy. In anarchy there are two professions: farmers and bandits. The possible anarchic equilibria include a mixed population of farmers and bandits, an all-farmer outcome, and a (nonviable) all-bandit outcome. (4) Closest to the present paper in terms of modeling approach are Hirshleifer (1988, 1991b), Skaperdas (1992), and Grossman and Kim (1994). However, in these articles agents have inalienable resource endowments – or, at most, only a one-time reallocation is allowed. In contrast, the *continuing* struggle for resource endowments is the central phenomenon addressed in the present paper.

3. *Numbers:* If the number of contenders N is exogenously given, how are the equilibrium fighting efforts and attained income levels of income affected as N changes? Alternatively, if N is endogenous, how many contenders can survive?

4. *Technology and comparative advantage:* How do the outcomes respond to parametric variations, one-sided or two-sided, in the technology of production or in the technology of struggle?

5. *Strategic position:* How do the outcomes respond to positional asymmetries, for example where one side is a Stackelberg leader?

This analysis employs standard (though possibly still highly arguable!) economic postulates like rationality, self-interested motivations, and diminishing returns. Certain other assumptions are designed to achieve analytical simplicity in ways familiar to economists; for example, only steady-state solutions are considered. But to push ahead I have also at times made more special modeling choices – such as about the conflict technology. Whenever possible I will try to flag the results of such "nongeneric" assumptions and discuss the analytical implications.

For the simplest symmetric case of two competitors ($N = 2$), Section 1 describes the conditions for a stable anarchic equilibrium, while Section 2 analyzes the optimizing decision and final outcomes. Section 3 considers both exogenous and endogenous variation in the number of contenders N, and Section 4 examines the consequences of various types of asymmetries between the rival parties. Section 5 relates the analysis to important features of animal and human conflict. Section 6 summarizes the results and limitations. Finally, Section 7 asks "After anarchy, what?"

1 Stability of conflict equilibrium (N = 2)

Each of two rival claimants aims solely to maximize own-income. Neither benevolent nor malevolent preferences play a role, nor is there any taste for leisure or other nonincome-generating activity.

At any moment of time each contender $i = 1,2$ divides his or her current resource availability R_i between *productive effort* E_i (designed to extract income from resources currently controlled) versus *fighting effort* F_i (aimed at acquiring new resources at the expense of competitors, or repelling them as they attempt to do the same):[8]

$$R_i = a_i E_i + b_i F_i \qquad (2\text{-}1)$$

$R \equiv R_1 + R_2$, the aggregate resource base, is assumed constant and independent of the parties' actions.[9] The a_i and b_i can be interpreted as unit conversion

---

[8] I do not distinguish here between offensive and defensive activities. On this see Skogh and Stuart (1982) and Grossman and Kim (1994).

costs (assumed constant) of transforming resources into productive effort or into fighting effort, respectively. Making use of a military metaphor, b_i is a *logistics cost coefficient* quantifying the resource burden per fighting unit supported. Similarly a_i, the *production cost coefficient,* measures the resources required to maintain a worker or machine in civilian production.[10] In the decades preceding the American Civil War, inventions like the steamboat and railroad sharply reduced a_i (since workers could be fed and machines built more cheaply) and also b_i (since supplies could more easily be delivered to fighting troops). In consequence, vastly larger armies were able to take the field in the Civil War, as compared with the Revolutionary War or the War of 1812.

It will sometimes be more convenient to deal with the corresponding "intensities" e_i and f_i:

$$e_i \equiv E_i/R_i \quad \text{and} \quad f_i \equiv F_i/R_i \tag{2-2}$$

The e_i and f_i will be the crucial decision variables on each side, subject of course to:

$$a_i e_i + b_i f_i = 1 \tag{2-3}$$

Assuming steady-state conditions, each side makes an optimal once-and-for-all choice of e_i and f_i.[11]

In interpreting the model, the steady-state fighting intensity f_i can allow for time-averaging. A tribe choosing an f_i such that half its resources are devoted to fighting need not have half its human and material capital engaged in war night and day, season in and season out. More likely, the tribe as a whole will be alternating between periods of war and peace. Similarly, although a labor union may alternate between periods of strike and work, its long-term strategy could be interpreted as choice of a steady-state average fighting intensity f_i.

Symbolizing income to side i as Y_i, let the production function take the simple form:

$$Y_i = E_i^h = (e_i R_i)^h \qquad \text{Production function} \tag{2-4}$$

Resource control is achieved only by fighting, the outcome being the *success fractions* p_1 and p_2 (where of course $p_1 + p_2 = 1$). Thus:

---

[9] This crucial assumption – implying that fighting, while a diversion of resources, is non-destructive – will be discussed further in Section 6.

[10] Taking the a_i and b_i as constants implies a constant marginal rate of substitution between productive effort and fighting effort. Diminishing returns enter at another stage: the translation of productive effort E_i into income and of fighting effort F_i into contest success.

[11] More generally, instead of a once-and-for-all choice of f_i and the implied e_i, side i's choice could vary with the level of resources on hand. For example, it might pay to devote a larger fraction of one's resources to fighting when you're poor and a smaller fraction when rich (Hirshleifer, 1991b). However, finding the optimal function $f_i(R_i)$ as a best reply to the opponent's corresponding $f_j(R_j)$, and vice versa, poses a fearsome analytic problem that I do not attempt to address here.

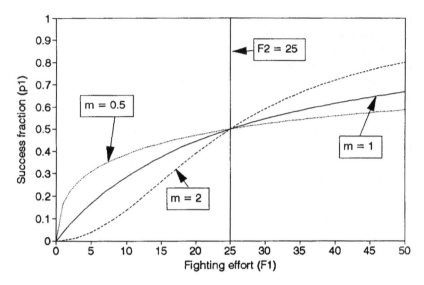

Figure 2-1. Contest success function (CSF)

$$R_i = p_i R \qquad \text{Resource partition equation} \qquad (2\text{-}5)$$

The technology of conflict is summarized by the contest success function (CSF), which in the form employed here determines the success ratio p_1/p_2 as a function of the ratio of the fighting efforts F_1/F_2 and (what plays a crucial role in the analysis) a *decisiveness parameter $m > 0$*:

$$p_1/p_2 = (F_1/F_2)^m \qquad \text{Contest success function (CSF)}^{12} \qquad (2\text{-}6a)$$

Or equivalently:

$$p_1 = F_1^m/(F_1^m + F_2^m) \quad \text{and} \quad p_2 = F_2^m/(F_1^m + F_2^m) \qquad (2\text{-}6b)$$

Figure 2-1 illustrates how, with F_2 held fixed, the success fraction p_1 responds to changes in fighting effort F_1. Evidently, the sensitivity of p_1 to F_1 grows as the decisiveness parameter m increases.

In military struggles, low m corresponds to the defense having the upper hand. On the western front in World War I, entrenchment plus the machine gun made for very low decisiveness m. Throughout 1914–18, attacks with even very large force superiority rarely succeeded in doing more than move the front

---

[12] This form of the CSF, in which the success fractions are determined by the *ratio* of the fighting efforts, was proposed in Tullock (1980). If instead the outcome were to depend on the *difference* between the fighting efforts, the CSF would be a logistic function (Hirshleifer, 1988). The question of the appropriate form for the CSF will arise again later.

lines back a few miles, and that at enormous cost in men and materiel. But in World War II the combination of airplanes, tanks, and mechanized infantry allowed the offense to concentrate firepower more rapidly than the defense, thus intensifying the effect of force superiority.[13] On the other hand, high decisiveness on the battlefield does not necessarily translate into correspondingly high decisiveness in a war as a whole. In 1870 Prussia won complete battlefield supremacy over France. But, whereas Rome razed Carthage to the ground, Prussia settled for very moderate peace terms: France had only to pay an indemnity and surrender the frontier provinces of Alsace and Lorraine. Prussian moderation was presumably due, in part at least, to fear of a guerrilla resistance, against which her battlefield supremacy would be much less decisive.

The decisiveness factor is by no means limited to strictly military struggles. In democratic constitutions, features like separation of powers and bills of rights reduce the decisiveness of majority supremacy, thereby tending to moderate the intensity of factional struggles. If the political system were winner-take-all, decisiveness m would be very high and all politics would be a fight to the death.[14]

From Eqs. (2-5) and (2-6a):

$$R_1/R_2 = (F_1/F_2)^m = (f_1R_1)^m/(f_2R_2)^m$$

This reduces to:

$$f_1^m R_1^{m-1} = f_2^m R_2^{m-1} \tag{2-7a}$$

So, finally:

$$p_1/p_2 = (f_1/f_2)^{m/(1-m)} \qquad \text{Equilibrium success ratio (steady-state)} \tag{2-7b}$$

Equations (2-7a) and (2-7b) describe the logically required steady-state relationships between the parties' chosen fighting intensities f_i and the equilibrium success ratio p_1/p_2 or resource ratio R_1/R_2. Figure 2-2 is a plot for different values of m. Note that as $m \to 1$, the curve approaches a limiting step function such that $p_1/p_2 = 0$ for all $f_1 < f_2$, jumping to $p_1/p_2 = \infty$ when $f_1 > f_2$. Without explicit proof, it will be evident that *for an interior stable equilibrium, the decisiveness parameter must lie in the range $0 < m < 1$.*

The preceding discussion has brought out one way in which anarchy could break down: An excessively large decisiveness parameter m leads to dynamic instability, i.e., movement toward a corner solution (see Numerical Example 1 in the Appendix). A second source of breakdown is *income inadequacy.*

---

[13] Of course, differences in *ability to employ* newer technologies are also often crucial, e.g., the German victory over France in 1940. (This and other asymmetries will be addressed in Section IV.)

[14] "Constitutions that are observed and last for a long time are those that reduce the stakes of political battles." (Przeworski, 1991, p. 36)

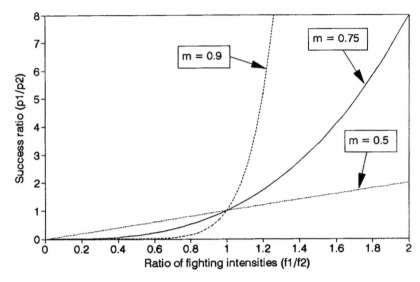

Figure 2-2. Fighting intensities and success ratio

Supposing that some minimum income y is required for an individual actor to sustain life, or for a group to preserve its institutional integrity, anarchy cannot be stable if the equilibrium of the dynamic process implies income $Y_i < y$ for either contender. To summarize:

> **Result 1:** The conditions for sustainability of a two-party anarchic system include (1) a sufficiently low decisiveness parameter m and (2) sufficiently high attained incomes Y_i:
>
> $m < 1$ Condition for dynamic stability
>
> $Y_i \geq y$ $(i = 1,2)$ Condition for viability   (2-8)

Note that these are *necessary,* not sufficient conditions for anarchy to be sustained. As will be seen, anarchy may be fragile even when the conditions are satisfied.

2   Optimization and equilibrium in symmetrical conflict ($N = 2$)

Figure 2-2 did not illustrate the *solution* of the anarchic system for $N = 2$, only the relations that must hold, in equilibrium, among the dependent variables R_1 and R_2 and the decision variables f_1 and f_2. The actual solution involves optimizing behavior on each side. Using the traditional Cournot assumption, each contender i chooses between steady-state e_i and f_i on the assumption that the opponent's corresponding choices will remain unchanged. In aiming to maximize income Y_i, a larger fighting effort f_i captures more resources or territory, while a larger productive effort e_i generates more income from the territory controlled. Thus, player 1's optimal f_1 is given by:

$$\max Y_1 = E_1^h = (e_1 R_1)^h = (e_1 R p_1)^h = [e_1 R f_1^M/(f_1^M + f_2^M)]^h \qquad (2\text{-}9)$$

subject to

$$a_1 e_1 + b_1 f_1 = 1$$

and defining for compactness

$$M \equiv m/(1-m)$$

Straightforward steps then generate player 1's reaction curve RC_1, showing his optimal f_1 as the opponent varies her f_2.[15] A corresponding analysis leads the opponent to her reaction curve RC_2:

$$f_1^M/f_2^M = M/(b_1 f_1) - (M + 1) \qquad \text{Reaction curve } RC_1 \qquad (2\text{-}10a)$$

$$f_2^M/f_1^M = M/(b_2 f_2) - (M + 1) \qquad \text{Reaction curve } RC_2 \qquad (2\text{-}10b)$$

RC_i, the reaction curve for player i, depends only on the decisiveness parameter m and on the decision maker's own logistics cost coefficient b_i. From the analytical form of the equations, and as illustrated in Figure 2-3, the reaction curves have positive slopes throughout. Thus, if player 1 chooses higher f_1, it pays player 2 to respond with higher f_2. And note that, as required for stability, in the neighborhood of equilibrium the matching is less than 1:1.

Equations (2-10a) and (2-10b) may be solved for f_1 and f_2, thus determining the equilibrium of the entire system. Unfortunately, there is no convenient general analytic solution. However, this section deals with the *symmetric* case where $a_1 = a_2 = a$ and $b_1 = b_2 = b$. Hence $f_1 = f_2$ at equilibrium, and Eqs. (2-10a) and (2-10b) reduce to:

$$f_1 = f_2 = M/[b(M + 2)] = m/[b(2 - m)]$$
Symmetrical conflict equilibrium $(N = 2)$ $\qquad (2\text{-}11)$

---

[15] The first-order conditions, where λ is the Lagrangian multiplier, are:

$$h(e_1 p_1 R)^{h-1} \frac{R f_1^M}{(f_1^M + f_2^M)^2} - \lambda a_1 = 0$$

$$h(e_1 p_1 R)^{h-1} \frac{e_1 R M f_1^{M-1} f_2^M}{(f_1^M + f_2^M)^2} - \lambda b_1 = 0$$

Routine steps lead to Eq. (2-10a), the reaction curve for player 1.

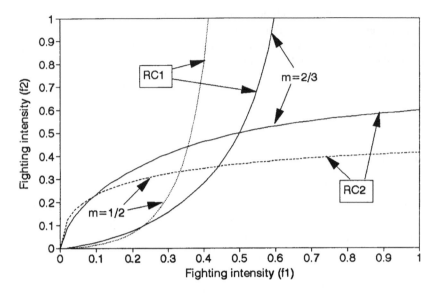

Figure 2-3. Reaction curves ($m = 1/2$ and $m = 2/3$)

Symmetrical solutions for $b = 1$ are illustrated by the intersections of the paired RC_1, RC_2 curves in Figure 2-3. If $m = 1/2$, the inner pair of curves apply, and the solution is $f_1 = f_2 = .333$. With a higher decisiveness parameter $m = 2/3$, the intersection occurs at $f_1 = f_2 = .5$.

The next result follows from the form of Eq. (2-3):

> **Result 2:** Assuming that the conditions for dynamic stability and viability both hold, in symmetrical conflict larger values of the *decisiveness parameter m* imply higher equilibrium fighting intensities f_1 and f_2, and thus higher fighting levels F_i and F_2. And similarly, the lower is the common value b of the *logistics cost coefficient,* the greater will be the equilibrium f_i and F_i.

For the underlying intuition recall that, as m increases, any given disparity between the fighting efforts F_1 and F_2 comes to have an increasingly powerful effect on the partition of resources. So, as m grows, each side is motivated to "try harder" – to choose a higher fighting intensity f_i than before. Similarly for the logistics cost coefficient: A reduction in b makes fighting effort cheaper; hence more of it comes to be generated on each side.

What is possibly disturbing is that Eq. (2-11) implies that f_i cannot be zero in equilibrium. There can be no peace in the sense of devoting no resources at all to conflict. This is a nongeneric result, since there are alternate forms of the CSF that could be consistent with total peace (Hirshleifer, 1988, Skaperdas,

1992). On the other hand, the implication might be regarded as quite realistic in many or most anarchic contexts.

Since $p_1 = p_2 = 1/2$ in the symmetrical conflict situation, direct substitutions lead to the equilibrium per-capita incomes:

$$Y_i \equiv (e_i p_i R)^h = \left[\frac{1 - m}{a(2 - m)} R \right]^h \tag{2-12}$$

Result 3: In the symmetrical conflict situation, assuming the conditions for dynamic stability and viability both hold, the incomes achieved (1) *rise* in response to increases in aggregate resource availability R and the productivity parameter h, but (2) *fall* in response to increases in the decisiveness parameter m and the production cost coefficient a.[16]

(See also Numerical Example 2 in the Appendix.)

3   Number of competitors – exogenous vs. endogenous variation

Exogenously varying N

Suppose that a fixed number of competitors N engage in a melee – a Hobbesian struggle of each against all, coalitions being ruled out.[17] The Cournot solution has each contender i choosing a fighting intensity f_i on the assumption that every opponent j will be holding f_j fixed. Generalizing Eq. (2-7a):

$$f_1^m R_1^{m-1} = f_2^m R_2^{m-1} = \ldots = f_N^m R_N^{m-1} \tag{2-13a}$$

Or, equivalently:

$$p_1{:}p_2{:} \ldots {:}p_N = (f_1{:}f_2{:} \ldots {:}f_N)^M \tag{2-13b}$$

Once again, for dynamic stability it is necessary to have $M > 0$, that is, $m < 1$. Of course, the viability condition $Y_i \geq y$ must also hold.

---

[16] A possibly puzzling feature of Eq. (2-12) is that, although a lower logistics cost coefficient b was shown above as increasing the fighting efforts f_i, the ultimate incomes Y_i end up independent of b. The reason: Lower b has two countervailing effects. On the one hand it implies lower e_i, smaller productive efforts on each side. But on the other hand, a smaller b means that the opportunity cost burden of any given f_i is less. That these two effects exactly cancel out is, however, also a "nongeneric" feature of the model and hence not insisted on. (Specifically, explorations indicate that the result would not be robust to changes in the form of the CSF that would make it sensitive to the *differences* in the respective fighting efforts.)

[17] "During the time men live without a common power to keep them in awe, they are in that condition which is called war; and such a war as is of every man against every man." (Hobbes, *Leviathan*, Ch. 13)

Contender 1's optimizing problem is

$$\max Y_1 = (e_1 R_1)^h = (e_1 p_1 R)^h = [e_1 R f_1^M/(f_1^M + f_2^M + \ldots + f_N^M)]^h \qquad (2\text{-}14)$$

subject to

$$a_1 e_1 + b_1 f_1 = 1$$

The analog of Eq. (2-10a), the generalized reaction curve for the first among N competitors, is:

$$f_1^M/(f_2^M + \ldots + f_N^M) = M/(b_1 f_1) - (M + 1) \qquad \text{Reaction curve } RC_1 \qquad (2\text{-}15)$$

And similarly for the other decision makers from the second on.

Assuming symmetrical logistics cost coefficients $b_i = b$ and productive cost coefficients $a_i = a$, and using the fact that in symmetrical equilibrium all the f_i are equal, the solution is:

$$f_1 = f_2 = \ldots = f_N = \frac{M/b}{M + 1 + 1/(N-1)} = \frac{m(N-1)}{b(N-m)}$$

$$\text{Symmetrical conflict equilibrium (general } N) \qquad (2\text{-}16)$$

As before, the fractions of resources devoted to fighting increase as the decisiveness parameter m rises and as the logistics cost coefficient b falls. And we see now that these fighting intensities also increase with larger numbers. That is, as N rises parametrically, each contender has to waste more effort in fighting even to retain his new (reduced) pro-rata share. The equilibrium incomes are:

$$Y_i = (e_i p_i R)^h = \left(\frac{1 - m}{a(N - m)} R \right)^h \qquad (2\text{-}17)$$

provided as always that $m < 1$ and $Y_i \geq y$.

> **Result 4A** *(parametrically varying* N*, fixed* R*):* Assuming that the conditions for sustainability of anarchy hold, with symmetrical production cost coefficients $a_i = a$ and logistics cost coefficients $b_i = b$, if aggregate resources remain fixed, then as N rises exogenously the equilibrium fighting intensities f_i increase. Individual incomes fall as N rises, owing to (1) smaller pro-rata resource shares $p_i = 1/N$ and (2) larger f_i.

It follows immediately that, as N increases, the attained incomes under anarchy are not only smaller *per capita* but smaller *in aggregate*.

Now consider instead a more friendly environment in which the aggregate resource base is not fixed but grows in proportion to the number of claimants. We can imagine that each entrant brings in a resource quantum r, so that $R \equiv$

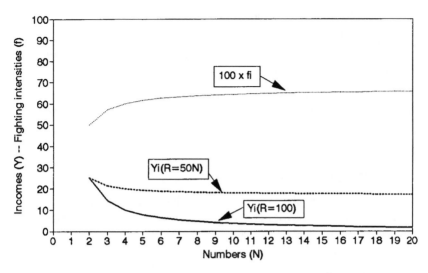

Figure 2-4. Effect of rising numbers (*N*)

Nr. Evidently, the expanding resource base exactly cancels out the adverse effect of increased *N* associated with the reduced pro-rata share. But the adverse effect of the larger fighting efforts f_i remains. Under this more optimistic assumption the equilibrium incomes become:

$$Y_i = (e_i p_i R)^h = \left(\frac{1-m}{a(N-m)} Nr \right)^h$$

(2-18)

Result 4B *(R and N rising in proportion):* Even if aggregate resource availability *R* increases in proportion to numbers *N*, individual incomes still fall as *N* rises, owing to the higher equilibrium fighting intensities f_i.

Figure 2-4 illustrates how fighting intensity f_i rises with numbers *N*, and the implications of that fact for per-capita income $Y_i = (e_i p_i R)^h$ under both the more and the less favorable assumptions about the relation of aggregate resources to the number of contenders. (The parameter values for the diagram are as stated in Numerical Example 3 in the Appendix.)

Endogenous N

If population numbers are subject to Malthusian increase/decrease or to immigration/emigration, the equilibrium *N* will be determined by the viability limit *y*, a kind of zero-profit condition:

$$Y_i(N) = y \qquad \text{Condition for equilibrium } N \qquad\qquad (2\text{-}19)$$

Once again, the actual viable population will depend on whether aggregate resources R are fixed or alternatively grow in proportion to N. (See Numerical Example 4 in the Appendix.)

> **Result 5:** If N is endogenously determined, a zero-profit condition will establish the viable number of contestants. That number is of course smaller when aggregate resources remain constant, larger when each added entrant brings in a resource increment.

4   Three types of asymmetries

So far only symmetrical solutions have been analyzed. In this section three different kinds of asymmetries are considered: cost differences, functional differences, and positional differences.

Cost differences

A lower production cost coefficient ($a_1 < a_2$) or logistics cost coefficient ($b_1 < b_2$) would of course give side 1 a corresponding advantage. (Since these are absolute comparisons, it is quite possible for one side to have the advantage in both directions at once.)

Figure 2-5[18] shows that a reduced production cost coefficient a_1 for player 1 leaves all the equilibrium solutions unchanged except for raising 1's own income Y_1.[19] In contrast, as the logistics cost coefficient b_1 falls in Figure 2-6, contender 1's fighting intensity f_1 and income Y_1 both rise. And, since contender 2 will respond with a less than 1:1 increase in f_2, she suffers reduced income Y_2.

Functional differences

Equation (2-4) for the production function postulated a common productivity parameter h. More generally, there could be differing h_i. If $h_1 > h_2$, side 1 has a productive advantage yielding higher income $Y_1 > Y_2$. (No diagram is provided for this simulation, since, apart from a left-right reversal, such a picture would closely parallel Figure 2-5. So, a *rise* in h_1, with h_2 held fixed, is very like a *fall* in the productive cost coefficient a_1, with a_2 held fixed.) Similarly, Eq. (2-6)

---

[18] Figures 2-5 through 2-8 each represents a large number of simulations calculated in terms of variations of the base case parameters given in numerical example 2.

[19] This also needs to be flagged as one of the "nongeneric" results adverted to in Section 1. The special assumption most implicated here is the total disjointedness of the productive efforts on the two sides. Given a degree of productive interaction, a reduction in one side's production cost coefficient a_1 would generally affect the opponent's f_2, hence redound back on 1's optimal choice of fighting intensity f_1.

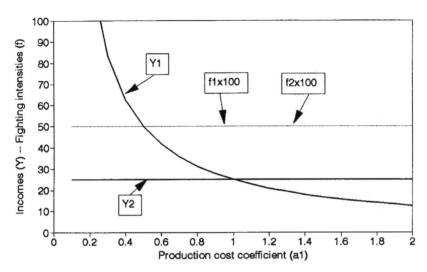

Figure 2-5. Effect of production cost asymmetry

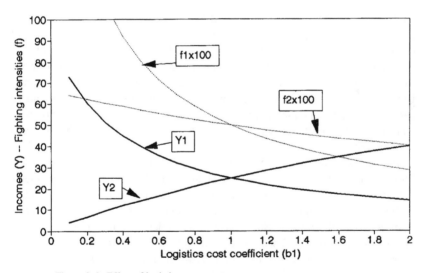

Figure 2-6. Effect of logistics cost asymmetry

could be generalized to allow for differing decisiveness parameters m_i. Figure 2-7 indicates that as m_1 rises, with m_2 held constant, side 1's optimal f_1 always increases. Side 2 at first replies with a smaller increase in f_2, but eventually she retreats from the unequal struggle and devotes more effort to production instead.

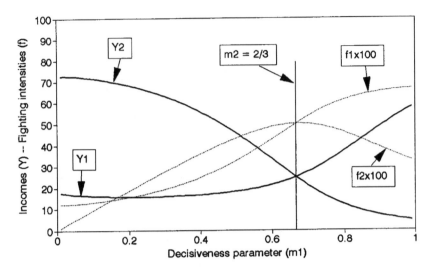

Figure 2-7. Effect of decisiveness asymmetry

Positional differences

Under the Cournot assumption, the parties are symmetrically situated. Among the many possible positional asymmetries, only the Stackelberg situation will be considered here. As first mover, the Stackelberg "leader" chooses a fighting intensity to which the opponent then optimally responds. Ability to move first is often advantageous, such as taking the high ground as a military tactic. But the second mover, able to optimize in the light of the opponent's known choice, always has a countervailing informational advantage. So it is not clear a priori whether, in the present context, a Stackelberg leader can be expected to come out ahead.[20]

Figure 2-8 shows that, in shifting from the Cournot to the Stackelberg equilibrium, the fighting efforts f_i become smaller and the incomes Y_i consequently higher on both sides. But note that the follower does better than the leader! Is this a general result? Recall that the reaction curves (see Figure 2-3) have positive slopes throughout. So if player 1 as leader were to choose a smaller-than-Cournot f_1, player 2 would respond with a smaller f_2, implying higher aggregate income for the two together. However, as already pointed out, in the neighborhood of equilibrium the best reply to an increase in the opponent's f_i

---

[20] A Stackelberg leader is quite different from a *hierarchical* leader. The latter is someone who, in order to influence a subordinate's behavior, can issue a credible prior threat and/or promise as to how he/she will react to the latter's choice. Thus the hierarchical leader is somehow able to *commit in advance to a reaction curve*, in the light of which it is up to the subordinate to make the first action move. See Thompson and Faith (1981), Hirshleifer (1988).

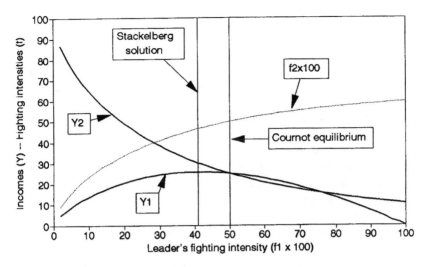

Figure 2-8. Stackelberg optimum

is always less than 1:1. So while the leader gains absolutely, he loses out rel-atively.[21] In international affairs, for example, suppose nation 1 were to take the initiative in a disarmament move, reducing f_1 in the hope that nation 2 will reciprocate. The model suggests that only partial reciprocation would occur, leaving the first disarmer at a relative disadvantage.

> **Result 6:** In the Stackelberg equilibrium, in comparison with the Cournot outcome, both sides' fighting efforts f_i are smaller and incomes Y_i higher. But the follower gains relative to the leader.

5   Discussion and applications

The model presented here, while more of a framework of analysis than a tight-ly specified theory, suggests new ways of understanding diverse yet logically parallel phenomena arising in entirely separate domains. I will illustrate its bearing for some observed patterns of animal territoriality and human warfare.

Animal territoriality[22]

The biologists' textbook approach to the problem of territoriality is termed the *economic defense model*. Ecological theorists ask when does it pay to defend

---

[21] More generally, in an otherwise symmetrical situation with sequential moves, if the reaction curves are positively sloped the relative advantage is always to the second mover (Gal-Or, 1985).

[22] Discussion based mainly on Wilson (1975, Ch. 12), McNaughton and Wolf (1973, Chs. 11–12), Morse (1980, Chs. 9–10), and Krebs and Davies (1987, Ch. 5).

territories? If it does pay, what are the determinants of territory size and the level of conflict? I will list only a few points of contact with the previous theoretical development.

1. If resources are unpredictable or nondefendable, organisms do not appropriate territories but compete by "scramble," i.e., the social system is amorphy rather than anarchy in the sense of this paper. Territoriality (anarchy) tends to emerge when resources are defendable and predictable, and also dispersed. When resources are predictable and defendable but are geographically concentrated instead, dominance hierarchies tend to replace territoriality. [*Explanation:* Struggles for the control of tightly concentrated resources approach winner-take-all battles (high decisiveness m). High m makes anarchy dynamically unstable (from Result 1), leading to dictatorship by the strongest.]

2. In a territorial system, increased population, even if sustainable in terms of the viability limit, reduces per-capita territory size (smaller p_i and R_i). Less obviously, larger N raises the intensity of aggressive interactions (higher f_i, from Result 4A). As population pressure increases further, proprietors have to spend so much time fighting off intruders that the system eventually breaks down. [Per-capita incomes Y_i fall below viability limit y (Result 1)]. Under these conditions territoriality is commonly succeeded by a dominance hierarchy, in which at least a few stronger animals retain access to the resource.[23]

3. While dominance systems lie outside the domain of the present model, the steepness of the hierarchical gradient – the disproportionality between incomes of dominants and subordinates – tends to be minimized when there are ecological opportunities for subordinates to exit the group, and when fighting abilities are not too dissimilar.[24] These conditions correspond to a low value of the decisiveness parameter (small m) and relatively modest decisiveness asymmetry (not too disparate m_i's). Thus, the same qualitative factors that are conducive to survival of anarchy also serve to mitigate the exploitive features of dominance systems.

Human warfare

The model here, with its necessarily severe simplifications, can hardly be expected to predict all the subtleties and complications of human social arrangements. Still, it sheds light on some patterns of human social conflict, of which warfare is the most obvious.

---

[23] Barash (1977, p. 262). An experiment with Norway rats indicates that, if overcrowding becomes extremely severe, even hierarchy can break down in favor of a "pathological" (i.e., amorphic) state. (Calhoun, 1962)

[24] See Vehrencamp (1983) and, for analogous results in terms of human hierarchical structures, Betzig (1992).

Among the Enga tribesmen of New Guinea, at least up to quite recently, warfare was the regular means of redistributing territories (Meggitt, 1977). Contrary to assertions that primitive war is largely a ritualized show with few casualties, warfare in New Guinea was a serious matter. Deaths in battle or from wounds accounted for around 35 percent of lifetime mortality among male adults.[25] The factor driving warfare has been increasing population density. [*Explanation:* As Malthusian pressures depress per-capita incomes, it comes to a choice between fight or starve. Yet, owing to low decisiveness m, no single tribe has been able to take over. The anarchic system appears to be stabilized by war casualties that bring per-capita incomes Y_i back in line with the viability limit y.]

In ancient Greece[26] the persistence of small city-states was associated with relatively indecisive warfare patterns [low m]. The phalanx was the dominant tactical formation, missile weapons were largely ineffective, and cavalry almost absent; these factors combined to preclude the deadly pursuit that makes victory truly decisive.

However, with advancing wealth and commerce, sea power became increasingly important. Naval conflict tends of its nature to be militarily more decisive; the stronger force gains command of the seas. Athens, the wealthiest state with a large and skilled navy, reduced many smaller city-states to dependencies within her empire. [*Explanation:* Higher decisiveness m implied higher fighting intensities f_i and thus a smaller number of militarily viable contenders N.] But Athens was ultimately defeated by a countercoalition led by Sparta (Aegospotami, 404 B.C.). Sparta in turn failed to achieve sole hierarchical dominance (Leuctra, 371 B.C.), and a period of shifting alliances followed. [The available conflict technology was characterized by a decisiveness parameter m *too high* for independent city-states to survive without allies, but *not high enough* for a single hegemon to defeat countercoalitions.]

Eventually Macedon gained military predominance (Charonea, 338 B.C.), owing in large part to Philip II's successful integration of cavalry, missile weapons, and siege apparatus with infantry in a disciplined force. [These military innovations led to higher m in land combat. And, of course, Macedon had the asymmetric advantage of being first in the field with them.] In the ensuing conflict between the united Greek forces under Alexander versus the Persian Empire, cavalry [high m] was again crucial to the decisive victory (Gaugamela, 331 B.C.). But none of Alexander's successors was able to achieve sole control.

---

[25] For the Yanomamo tribesmen of South America ("the fierce people"), Chagnon (1988) provides a similar estimate: 30 percent of adult male mortality is the result of violent conflict. An interesting comparison: for prohibition era Chicago, Allsop (1968, p. 41) reports 703 gangland fatalities in the course of 14 years. Given the number of active gangster-fighters, the proportion of deaths may not be too dissimilar.

[26] This discussion is based largely on Preston and Wise (1979, Chs. 1–2), Fuller (1954, Chs. 1–3), and of course Thucydides.

[Owing mainly to the huge land masses involved, conflict decisiveness m was still not high enough for hegemony.] Thus, an anarchic system returned in the form of a shifting pattern of three or four successor states, each based on combined sea and land power. This pattern lasted for some 150 years, ending when Rome finally did achieve hegemony in the Mediterranean (Pydna, 168 B.C.). [Rome benefited, it seems, from asymmetrically higher m due more to superior organization than to any special weaponry or tactics.]

A number of other historical periods or episodes also illustrate implications of our model.

1. *Cannon:* In the early fifteenth century, the introduction of cannon made it possible to batter down old-style castle walls, ending a long historical period of indecisive siege warfare. A major consequence was a sharp reduction in the number of independent principalities in western Europe. [Higher $m \rightarrow$ higher $f_1 \rightarrow$ smaller viable N.][27] Actually, this *technological* predominance of the offense was temporary, being shortly reversed by improvements in the art of fortification. But the *economic* effect remained much the same, because their enormous cost put modern fortifications beyond the reach of smaller political units.[28] [Asymmetrically lower logistic cost coefficient b favored the larger states, given returns to scale in producing and transporting cannons.]

2. *Gang wars:* In prohibition era Chicago, the Capone mob ultimately achieved hegemonic control, owing perhaps to superior ruthlessness as evidenced by the St. Valentine's Day massacre [asymmetrically higher m]. As movie and television viewers know, it took decisive intervention by an outside power, the federal government, to put Capone away.

3. *California gold rush:* In contrast, even though the official organs of law were impotent, no Capone-type hegemony over the forty-niners ever developed. Highly dispersed resources (widely separated goldfields in difficult mountainous country) made it difficult for a gang to achieve effective control [low decisiveness m]. Another factor, however, falls outside the model: Despite the collective action problems involved, mining camp communities were surprisingly effective in setting up "social contracts" for resisting invaders (Umbeck, 1981).

6   Conclusions and limitations

It will be convenient to summarize by responding briefly to the specific issues raised in the introduction.

---

[27] See Batchelder and Freudenberger (1983) and especially Parker (1988, Ch. 1). But also compare Anderson (1992).

[28] In 1553 the city of Siena undertook modernization of its fortifications. But the costs were so high that, when attack came, not only were the defense works still incomplete but funds to hire a supporting mercenary army or fleet were lacking. So in 1555 Siena surrendered to Florence and permanently lost its independence. (See Parker, 1988, p. 12.)

1. *A stable anarchic solution:* An anarchic system, to be sustained, must be *dynamically stable* and *viable*. The former condition holds when, most importantly, the decisiveness of conflict (measured by the parameter m in the model) is sufficiently low. Otherwise the most militarily effective contender would become a hegemon. Viability requires sufficiently high income Y_i for survival on the individual level or, in the case of larger contending units, for maintaining group integrity.

2. *Equilibrium allocations of effort:* In the symmetrical Cournot solution with $N = 2$ contestants, the crucial result is that, as the decisiveness parameter m rises, each side is forced to fight harder (f_1 and f_2 both increase). The consequences include reduced incomes on both sides.

3. *Numbers:* As N grows exogenously, equilibrium fighting intensities f_i rise. With fixed aggregate resources R, per-capita incomes Y_i fall for two reasons: *First,* because each party's pro-rata share $p_i = 1/N$ is less, and *second* because f_i is higher (that is, a contestant has to fight harder just to obtain a pro-rata share). This second reason continues to apply even in a more generous environment where resources grow in proportion to N. On the other hand, if N is *endogenous,* the equilibrium number of contenders is determined by the viability condition $Y_i \geq y$, that is, entry occurs up to the point of zero profit.

4. *Technology and comparative advantage:* An asymmetrical productive improvement (a decrease in the production cost coefficient a_i or increase in the productivity parameter h_i) increases own-income Y_i but within the model here does not otherwise affect any of the results. (However, I have flagged this as a nongeneric result deriving from special features of the model, in particular, the total disjointedness of productive opportunities.) On the conflict side, corresponding one-sided improvements, i.e., a reduction in the logistics cost coefficient b_i or an increase in the decisiveness parameter m_i, generally increase own-income while reducing opponent income.

5. *Strategic position:* The Stackelberg solution, as compared with the symmetric Cournot equilibrium, involves reduced fighting on both sides but the reduction is greater for the leader than the follower. This evidently tends to stabilize the anarchic system. Although all could gain from the change, each single participant is motivated to hold back and let the opponent become the leader.

The analytic results here depend on a particular way of modeling anarchy that omits many possibly important elements. To mention only a few:

1. Full information was assumed throughout, so that factors like deception have been set aside.[29]

---

[29] On this see, for example, Tullock (1974, Ch. 10) and Brams (1977).

2. Apart from opportunity costs in the form of foregone production, fighting was assumed nondestructive. (This assumption biases our results in the direction of conflict.)[30]
3. The effects of distance and other geographical factors[31] were not explicitly considered (though entering implicitly as determinants of the logistic cost and decisiveness parameters).
4. The steady-state assumption rules out issues involving *timing,* such as arms races, economic growth, or (on a smaller time-scale) signaling resolve through successive escalation.
5. Finally, I have not attempted to model the problems of group formation and collective action (but see following section).

The justification for these and other omissions is that one must begin somewhere. The model illustrates a method of analysis. In many contexts, for example, it might be unacceptable to omit the element of collateral damage (the preceding qualification 2). Still, that effect could be incorporated by means of an adjustment within our general analytical framework.

7   After anarchy, what?

Though this topic lies outside the bounds of the model, the analysis insistently suggests the question: Supposing that anarchy breaks down, what happens next?

Theoretical considerations, as well as the historical and other applications described in Section 5, combine to suggest that anarchic systems are fragile. Anarchy is always liable to "break down" into amorphy, or "break up" into organization! First of all, exogenous changes may lead to violation of the necessary conditions of Result 1. Military technology (very often, though not always) has moved in the direction of higher decisiveness m, threatening *dynamic stability.* And Malthusian pressures are at work to dilute per-capita incomes, threatening *viability.*

But even if the necessary conditions are met, making anarchy in principle sustainable, the system may be undermined by "the urge to merge." Benefits from group formation may include (1) reduced fighting within, (2) complementarities in production, and (3) enhanced ability to fight outsiders. The other side of the coin – the factor hampering mergers – is the collective action problem: how to get agreement on a social contract and, even more important, how to enforce it.

---

[30] The model of Grossman and Kim (1994) allows for damage due to fighting. The extent of "collateral damage" has been influenced by two opposed technological trends: greater destructive power and improved aiming precision. In a nonmilitary context, Becker's (1983) analysis of pressure group competition shows how incidental damage to the economy ("deadweight loss") tends to limit the extent of conflict.

[31] See, e.g., Boulding (1962, Chs. 12–13).

It is useful to distinguish *vertical* from *horizontal* social contracts. The vertical alternative, Hobbes' version, would be represented by arrangements like hierarchical dominance in the biological realm or dictatorship on the human level. Locke's version, the horizontal alternative, corresponds to more egalitarian arrangements in either sphere.[32]

Of the two major sources of breakdown – *dynamic instability* and *income inviability* – the former is likely to lead to a vertical social contract. An excessively high decisiveness coefficient m implies a range of increasing returns to fighting effort. At the extreme this may imply a "natural monopoly" in fighting activity, i.e., the struggle is likely to end with all the resources under one party's control. In contrast, the mere fact of low income under anarchy, since it may be the consequence of many different forces, of itself provides no clear indication as to what is likely to happen next.

Owing to closer sympathies, better monitoring of shirkers, etc., the collective action problem is more readily solved in small groups. But these small groups in turn come into anarchic competition at the group level. This of course provides a cascading motivation for unification one level higher up. In modern times this process has led to a sharp reduction in the number of independent states and principalities: In Europe alone, from hundreds or even thousands to around a dozen or two after the unifications of Germany and Italy. Still, there never has been an all-European state. Nor should we assume that the process can go only in the direction of agglomeration, as the fall of the Roman Empire and the recent dissolution of the Soviet Union demonstrate.

The upshot is that, even if anarchy breaks up into organization on one level, anarchic conflict may be sharpened on another level. If the clans within a tribe agree on a social contract, peace among the clans may be only the prelude to more violent struggles against other tribes.

Appendix: Numerical examples

All these numerical examples are connected, and can be read together as a running illustration of the model.

Numerical Example 1: Letting the decisiveness parameter be $m = 2/3$, Eqs. (2-7a) and (2-7b) simplify to:

$$p_1/p_2 = R_1/R_2 = (f_1/f_2)^2$$

---

[32] Chicago gangland history (Allsop, 1968) provides nice instances of both arrangements. Johnny Torrio, a "statesman-like leader," attempted to bring all the gangs together in a Lockian solution with profit sharing and allocation of territories. However, the intransigent South Side O'Donnells resisted confederation. Torrio's more ruthless successor Al Capone ultimately succeeded in imposing a vertical Hobbesian solution.

If the total resources available are $R = 100$ and the fighting intensities on each side have been chosen (not necessarily optimally) to be $f_1 = .1$ and $f_2 = .2$, respectively, then:

$$p_1/p_2 = (.1/.2)^2 = 1/4$$

implying that, in equilibrium, $R_1 = 20$ and $R_2 = 80$.

To illustrate convergence when $m = 2/3$, suppose the initial resource vector is set at $(R_1^\circ, R_2^\circ) = (60,40)$. The first-period conflict outcome is $p_1/p_2 = (6/8)^{2/3}$ $= .825$, implying an end-of-period revised resource allocation $(R_1', R_2') =$ $(45.2, 54.8)$. After one more period of conflict the resource allocation becomes $(R_1'', R_2'') = (35.7, 64.3)$. Evidently, the equilibrium $(R_1, R_2) = (20,80)$ is being approached asymptotically.

In contrast, for a decisiveness parameter in the range $m > 1$, say $m = 2$, starting from the same initial resource vector $(60,40)$, the first- and second-period reallocations would be $(36.0, 64.0)$ and $(7.3, 92.7)$. The process rapidly diverges in favor of the side with the higher f_i.

Numerical Example 2: In the previous numerical example, the contenders were arbitrarily assumed to have chosen fighting intensities $f_1 = .1$ and $f_2 = .2$, leading to the equilibrium resource distribution $R_1 = 20$ and $R_2 = 80$. But if the parties choose *optimally* instead under the Nash-Cournot assumption, with symmetrical logistics cost coefficients $b_1 = b_2 = b = 1$, from Eq. (2-11) the equilibrium choices are $f_1 = f_2 = .5$, implying an equal equilibrium resource division $R_1 = R_2 = 50$. From Eq. (2-12), and assuming production cost coefficients $a_1 = a_2 = a = 1$ and productivity parameter $h = 1$ (constant returns in production), the associated incomes are $Y_1 = Y_2 = 25$. (In contrast, had no conflict occurred – i.e., if the choices had been $f_1 = f_2 = 0$ – the per-capita incomes would have been 50 each.)

Numerical Example 3: With aggregate resources $R = 100$ and $N = 2$, equilibrium fighting intensities in the previous example were $f_1 = f_2 = .5$ yielding per-capita incomes $Y_1 = Y_2 = 25$. Using the same parameter values, and holding aggregate resources fixed at 100, for $N = 3$ the equilibrium fighting efforts rise to $f_1 = f_2 = .571$ while the per-capita incomes fall to $Y_i = 14.3$, approximately. (Note that the *aggregate* income is lower as well.) If on the other hand resources were to rise in proportion to numbers – specifically, if $R \equiv Nr$, where $r = 50$ – then in equilibrium $Y_i = 21.4$, approximately. Thus, even when the resource base expands with N, there is a per-capita income loss owing to the larger optimal f_i.

Numerical Example 4: With the same parameter values, for aggregate resources fixed at $R = 100$ suppose the viability threshold is $y = 4$. From Eq. (2-17), the equilibrium incomes are $Y_i = 4$ at $N = 9$. So this fixed resource magnitude will support a population of $N = 9$ competitors. If instead resources expand with population so that $R \equiv 50N$, the situation is much more favorable. In such an environment, Eq. (2-19) indicates that an equilibrium population of $N = 9$ could be supported even at a much higher viability threshold $y = 18$.

Numerical Example 5: Under the quantitative assumptions of numerical example 2, the Cournot equilibrium was $f_1 = f_2 = .5$ and $Y_1 = Y_2 = 25$. Using the same numerical assumptions, side 1 as Stackelberg leader does best by choosing a somewhat lower $f_1 = .41$, approximately, and his income rises slightly to about 25.7. The second mover optimally responds by cutting back her fighting intensity to only about .466, reaping a considerably higher income of around 30.1.

References

Allsop, Kenneth, *The Bootleggers,* new ed., 1968, New Rochelle, N.Y.: Arlington House.

Anderson, Gary M., "Cannon, Castles, and Capitalism: The Invention of Gunpowder and the Rise of the West," *Defence Economics,* 1992, 3,: 147–60.

Barash, David P., *Sociobiology and Behavior,* 1977, New York: Elsevier.

Batchelder, Ronald W. and Herman Freudenberger, "On the Rational Origins of the Modern Centralized State," *Explorations in Economic History,* 1983, 20, 1–13.

Becker, Gary S., "A Theory of Competition among Pressure Groups for Political Influence," *Quarterly Journal of Economics,* 1983, 98, 371–400.

Bernholz, Peter, *The International Game of Power,* 1985, Berlin: Mouton Publishers.

Betzig, Laura, "Of Human Bonding: Cooperation or Exploitation," *Social Science Information,* 1992, 31, 611–42.

Boulding, Kenneth E, *Conflict and Defense,* 1962, New York: Harper & Brothers.

Brams, Steven J., "Deception in 2×2 Games," *Journal of Peace Science,* 1977, 2, 171–203.

Bush, Winston C. and Lawrence S. Mayer, "Some Implications of Anarchy for the Distribution of Property," *Journal of Economic Theory* , 1974, 8, 401–12.

Calhoun, J. B., "Population Density and Social Pathology," *Scientific American,* 1962, 206, 139–8.

Chagnon, N. A., "Life Histories, Blood Revenge, and Warfare in a Tribal Population," *Science,* 1988, 239, 985–92.

Fuller, J. F. C., *From the Earliest Times to the Battle of Lepanto,* v. 1 of *A Military History of the Western World,* 1954, New York: Da Capo Press.

Gal-Or, Esther, "First Mover and Second Mover Advantages," *International Economic Review,* October 1985, 26, 649–53.

Ghiselin, Michael T., "The Economy of the Body," *American Economic Review,* May 1978, 68, 233–7.

Grossman, Herschel I. and Minseong Kim, "A Theory of the Security of Claims to Property," June 1994, Providence, R.I.: Brown University, Department of Economics, Working Paper 94–12.

Hayek, F. A., *The Political Order of a Free People,* v. 3 of *Law, Legislation, and Liberty,* 1979, Chicago: University of Chicago Press.

Hirshleifer, J., "The Analytics of Continuing Conflict," *Synthese,* 1988, 76, 201–33.

Hirshleifer, J., "The Technology of Conflict as an Economic Activity," *American Economic Review,* May 1991a, 81, 130–4.

Hirshleifer, J., "The Paradox of Power," *Economics and Politics,* November 1991b, 3, 177–200.

Krebs, J. R. and N. B. Davies, *An Introduction to Behavioural Ecology,* 1987, Oxford: Blackwell Scientific Publications.

Meggitt, Mervyn, *Blood Is Their Argument,* 1977, Palo Alto, Calif.: Mayfield Publishing Co.

McNaughton, S. J. and Larry Wolf, *General Ecology,* 1973, New York: Holt, Rinehart and Winston.

Morse, Douglass H., *Behavioral Mechanisms in Ecology,* 1980, Cambridge, Mass.: Harvard University Press.

Nicholson, A. J., "An Outline of the Dynamics of Animal Populations," *Australian Journal of Zoology,* 1954, 2, 9–65.

Parker, Geoffrey, *The Military Revolution: Military Innovation and the Rise of the West, 1500–1800,* 1988, Cambridge: Cambridge University Press.

Preston, Richard A. and Sydney F. Wise, *Men in Arms,* 4th ed., 1979, New York: Holt, Rinehart and Winston.

Przeworski, Adam, *Democracy and the Market,* 1991, Cambridge: Cambridge University Press.

Salop, Steven C. and David T. Scheffman, "Raising Rivals' Costs," *American Economic Review,* 1983, 73, 267–70.

Sherman, William Tecumseh, *Memoirs of General W. T. Sherman,* 1990, New York: The Library of America (edited reprint of the 2nd edition of 1885).

Skaperdas, Stergios, "Cooperation, Conflict, and Power in the Absence of Property Rights," *American Economic Review,* September 1992, 82, 720–39.

Skogh, Goran and Charles Stuart, "A Contractarian Theory of Property Rights and Crime," *Scandinavian Journal of Economics,* 1982, 84, 27–40.

Snyder, Glenn H. and Paul Diesing, *Conflict among Nations,* 1977, Princeton, N.J.: Princeton University Press.

Thompson, Earl and Roger L. Faith, "A Pure Theory of Strategic Behavior and Social Institutions," *American Economic Review,* 1981, 71, 366–80.

Tullock, Gordon, "The Welfare Costs of Tariffs, Monopolies, and Theft," *Western Economic Journal,* 1967, 5, 224–32.

Tullock, Gordon, *The Social Dilemma,* 1974, Blacksburg, Va.: University Publications.

Tullock, Gordon, "Efficient Rent-seeking," in *Toward a Theory of the Rent-seeking Society,* J. M. Buchanan, R. D. Tollison, and G. Tullock (eds.), 1980, College Station: Texas A&M University Press.

Umbeck, John, "Might Makes Rights: A Theory of the Formation and Initial Distribution of Property Rights," *Economic Inquiry,* January 1981, 19, 38–58.

Usher, Dan, "The Dynastic Cycle and the Stationary State," *American Economic Review,* December 1989, 79, 1031–44.

Vehrencamp, Sandra L., "A Model for the Evolution of Despotic versus Egalitarian Societies," *Animal Behavior,* 1983, 31, 667–82.

Waltz, Kenneth N., *Man, the State, and War,* 1954, New York: Columbia University Press.

Wilson, Edward O., *Sociobiology: The New Synthesis,* 1975, Cambridge, Mass.: Harvard University Press.

CHAPTER 3

Towards a model of territorial expansion and the limits of empire

Ronald Findlay
Columbia University

> The question of the size of political units never seems to attract among historians and sociologists the attention which it deserves. What determines why states and empires have expanded to the limits which they have historically achieved? What are the conditions under which it has been possible to maintain those frontiers? Why have the larger states normally broken up into fragments after a certain period of time? As a general problem – distinct from the specific question of why particular units have disintegrated – this is still largely unexplored territory.

Adding economists to historians and sociologists in the first sentence of this quotation from the eminent Sinologist, Mark Elvin (1973, p. 17) only enhances its salience. Insofar as they are considered at all in economics, the boundaries of a given economic system or "country" are generally regarded as given, along with the population living within those boundaries. Yet it is obvious that, however sanctified these boundaries may have become in international law, they were all at one time or another contested between rival claimants and determined ultimately by the balance of economic and military power between the contending parties. The process by which these boundaries are determined and defined clearly depends on the interplay of economic and military forces, which have, however, generally been regarded as independent factors.

Elementary textbooks frequently introduce the production possibilities frontier between "guns" and "butter" to illustrate the nature of the economic problem and the concept of opportunity cost. It is noteworthy, however, that they never, as far as I am aware, consider the question of how "guns" might be used in a predatory fashion to acquire resources from neighboring peoples or states

An earlier version of this paper was presented at a conference on "Conflict and Rent-Seeking" at the University of California, Irvine, in May 1994. I would like to thank the participants at that conference and at a Columbia University Political Economy Seminar in September 1994 for very helpful comments. Several friends and colleagues have also given me the benefit of their criticism. Though I cannot mention all of them, I must acknowledge in particular the comments of David Bloom, Alessandra Casella, Richard Clarida, Andrew Newman, Stanislaw Wellisz, and Murray Wolfson. All remaining defects are, of course, my own responsibility.

,and thus push out the production possibilities frontier of the society itself. As Jack Hirshleifer (1987, p. 297) points out in his brief but penetrating survey of the little that we have on "The Economic Approach to Conflict":

> The institutions of property and law, and the peaceful process of exchange, are highly beneficial aspects of human life. But the economist's inquiries should not be limited to such "nice" behaviors and interactions. Struggle, imposing costs on others, and downright violence are crucial phenomena of the world as we know it. Nor is the opposition between the "nice" and the "not nice" by any means total. Law and property, and thus the possibilities of peaceful exchange, can only persist where individuals are ultimately willing to use violence in their defense.

While the literature on violence and coercion as "rational" economic options, subject to the usual calculus of benefits and costs is scarce, it is by no means devoid of insightful contributions, upon which I attempt to build in this paper. Kenneth Boulding (1963) in a work entitled *Conflict and Defense: A General Theory*, has many wise and interesting things to say about the subject. I found his Chapters 12 and 13, on international conflict, particularly stimulating. Other important references are Bush and Mayer (1974), Friedman (1977), Thompson and Faith (1981), Usher (1989), Hirshleifer (1991), and Skaperdas (1992). An interesting alternative to the approach taken here, through coercion and violence as rational activities, is the "mergers and acquisitions" view of Wittman (1991).

1   The basic model

Consider, to begin with, a collective entity or "tribe" such as the Romans, Han Chinese, or Ottoman Turks. The primary resource owned by the tribe is their labor, which we will assume to be initially fixed. We also suppose that there is only a single final output, that we can identify with agriculture, although a second "crafts" or "manufacturing" sector will be introduced later. Production of the final output requires land or "territory," which is not simply given but has to be acquired and held against the tribe's enemies who surround it. To fix ideas, let us conceive of the labor of the tribe as concentrated at a single point on a "featureless plain" so beloved by the location theorists. We can think of this central point as its "home base." To secure and hold territory, the tribe must devote some of its labor force to fighting. We can call those so engaged the "army" of the tribe, with the remainder as the "workers."

Letting N denote the total size of the tribe, A the army, and L the workers we have the manpower constraint of the tribe as

$$L + A = N \qquad\qquad (3\text{-}1)$$

while the production function for final output, denoted Q, has labor and "territory," denoted T, as its arguments:

$$Q = Q(L,T) \tag{3-2}$$

We assume that the production function (3-2) exhibits constant returns to scale and diminishing returns to either factor with the other held fixed. The territory that the tribe can acquire and defend against its enemies, an undifferentiated mass of "barbarians," is given by the function

$$T = a\pi r(A)^2 \tag{3-3}$$

where r is the radius of a circle centered on the original point, the home base of the tribe, and a is a constant. We postulate that

$$r'(A) > 0, \qquad r''(A) < 0 \tag{3-4}$$

i.e., the larger the army, the greater is the radius of the tribe's "sphere of influence." But there is a diminishing returns effect of increases in the size of the army on the radius of the circular territory that it can control and defend. Since the area of the circle, $a\pi r(A)^2$, is a convex function of the radius, the territory occupied could still increase more than proportionately to the size of the army. We shall initially assume, however, that the absolute value of the negative second derivative in Eq. (3-4) is sufficiently high to give us T as a concave function of A, so that

$$\frac{d}{dA}\left(\frac{dT}{dA}\right) < 0 \tag{3-5}$$

What does the tribe want to maximize? Territory could conceivably be desired for its own sake, for the kind of pleasure that British schoolboys were supposed to get from seeing so much of the map of the world painted red in the days when the sun never set on their empire. However, let us suppose initially that the tribe is narrowly "rational" and desires territory only for its contribution to production. The economic problem of empire, then, is simply to maximize (3-2) subject to the manpower constraint (3-1) and the sphere of influence function (3-3). The obvious trade-off is that each man added to the army adds economically valuable land that raises final output but withdraws a man from the labor force that works on the land. Because of Eq. (3-5), the extra land added as the army is extended declines at the margin, while the marginal productivity of the falling labor force on the increased land obtained by the expanding army is rising. When the marginal productivity of a warrior is equal to that of a worker, we have the optimal size of the army and associated extent of territory, which maximizes final output.

The first-order condition for the optimal size of empire is

$$\frac{\partial Q}{\partial L} = \frac{\partial Q}{\partial T}\frac{dT}{dA} = \frac{\partial Q}{\partial T}\,2a\pi r'(A) \tag{3-6}$$

in which the left-hand side is the marginal productivity of a worker and the right-hand side the marginal productivity of a warrior. This condition can also be interpreted as stating that the marginal rate of substitution between land and labor in production is equal to the marginal product of a warrior in terms of territory, which is $2a\pi r'(A)$.

The sphere of influence function $r(A)$ clearly depends on the *relative* military proficiency of the tribe and the barbarians. Fluctuations in the relative military efficiency variable, brought about, say, by diffusion of weapons or tactics from one side to the other, would lead to pulsations in the size of the empire in response. Thus adoption of iron for weapons by the steppe nomads, brought about by contact with China, led to a rise in their relative military efficiency and hence made the holding of the size of the Chinese empire at its original level more difficult. Technology could, however, flow in the other direction also. As pointed out by Creel (1970), the sedentary Chinese were dependent on the steppe nomads not only for the provision of horses for cavalry, but also for techniques of riding and training these essential military assets for control of the frontier. Similarly the Germanic tribes north of the Roman frontier also learned from the imperial power, especially after many of them came to be employed as mercenaries in the Roman army.

Improvements in production technology, however, have an ambiguous effect on the size of the army and the empire. An additional acre of land is worth more, so that the marginal productivity of a warrior goes up, but so does his opportunity cost, which is the marginal productivity of a worker. Thus the effect of the technical improvement on the *relative* marginal products of land and labor in production is what determines the impact of the innovation on the size of the army and the extent of the empire.

By what means are resources allocated between farming and fighting, and how is the final output divided between warriors and workers on the one hand, and these and the "ruling elite" of chiefs, priests, and officials on the other? Here a variety of outcomes is possible. The territory could be allocated by the leader of the tribe to his relatives and other privileged individuals, who then hire labor in a free market to work on the land at the going wage rate. The army could recruit soldiers in the same labor market, and the optimal result defined by Eq. (3-6) could be brought about by giving just enough tax revenue to the army to hire the optimal A at the market-clearing wage w, equal to the marginal product of both warriors and workers. The taxes could be raised on rents of land distributed to the privileged elite or on the labor force as a whole, preserving efficiency in allocation. Taxes only on workers would equate the after-tax civilian wage to the army wage, implying too few civilian workers and too large an army.

At the other extreme we could imagine that all the land was the property of the tribe as a whole, with the surplus of output above subsistence for all distributed in some arbitrary fashion to the optimally determined members of the army and civilian workers and privileged elite. Since most historic empires had great difficulty collecting taxes, it could be that the optimal size of army could not be maintained because of a shortage of revenue. Thus the size of the empire would shrink below the optimal level just determined to whatever was possible, given the revenue constraint, minus luxury consumption by the elite. At the level of generality of the present paper, it would be a distraction to consider particular institutional alternatives in detail, though this would be an interesting subject for further research.

2   Absorption of subject populations

Up to now we have been assuming that it is only territory that the tribal army acquires. The alien population is either exterminated or expelled – "ethnic cleansing" as we have come to call it in our enlightened age. While such horrors have certainly not been unknown in the records of historic empires, reason, if not compassion, dictated that the conquered populations, and not only the land that they lived on, were valuable assets that could be enslaved, enserfed, or simply taxed, at higher rates than the members of the tribe themselves. Cultural assimilation to the language and customs of the conquerors could ultimately result in such enlightened outcomes as the extension of Roman citizenship to all the subjects of the empire. Conversion to the religion of the conquerors was, of course, another major avenue of assimilation, as in the cases of the early Arab and Ottoman Turk empires.

The model can be readily modified to take account of this important feature of all historic empires. We assume that the absorbed alien population increases as a function of the territory that the tribe acquires. Assuming complete assimilation for simplicity, we have N in the manpower constraint (3-1) as a positive function of the territory T, which of course is itself a positive but concave function of the size of the army. The marginal benefit of adding warriors is then not only the additional territory they bring in but the people along with it, valued at their shadow price, which is the marginal productivity of labor in production. The manpower constraint (3-1) now becomes

$$L + A = N[T(A)] \tag{3-7}$$

while the first-order condition (3-6) is now

$$\left\{ \frac{\partial Q}{\partial L} \frac{dN}{dT} + \frac{\partial Q}{\partial T} \right\} \frac{dT}{dA} = \frac{\partial Q}{\partial L} \tag{3-8}$$

The empire now not only has territory but an alien population absorbed within its borders as well. As already noted, there is a very wide array of different practices known to history about the manner in which the subject pop-

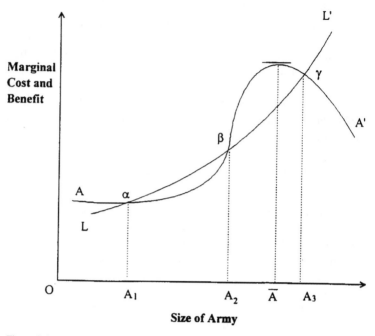

Figure 3-1.

ulation is treated relative to members of the original tribe. In the case of Sparta and the *helots,* the Spartans themselves did not follow any occupation other than warfare and the supervision of the *helots,* who did all the productive work. On the other hand we have the Mamelukes of Egypt and the Janissaries of the Ottoman Turks, exclusively alien-born military elites in the service of these realms.

3   Local and global optima

As we have seen the concave function $r(A)$ and the extent of the territory associated to it by the factor of $\pi r(A)^2$ can interact to make territory T either a concave or a convex function of the size of the army. While in the case of the basic model we assumed that it was concave throughout, it is interesting to consider the possible implications of the $T(A)$ function being convex over an initial range and concave only after a certain critical size is passed.[1]

In Figure 3-1, the monotonically positive relation LL' depicts the rising opportunity cost of additional warriors in terms of their marginal productivity

[1] See Wolfson (1994) for an interesting extension of my original analysis along these lines.

as workers with an increasing supply of land resulting from increases in the size of the army. The function AA', however, depicts the marginal productivity of warriors $\frac{\partial Q}{\partial T} \frac{dT}{dA}$ as first rising and then falling only after the level of $\overline{A}$ is reached. The AA' function cuts LL' at three points, denoted α, β, and γ corresponding to army levels of A_1, A_2, and A_3. It is apparent, from Figure 3-1, that α and γ are stable equilibria, while β is unstable. This is because to the left of α and γ the marginal product of a warrior exceeds his marginal opportunity cost while to the right it falls short of it. The opposite is the case with β.

If there are no constraints on the level of the army that a unified decision-making process can determine and there is full information about the relevant functions, the outcome will, of course, be the global optimum at A_3 and the corresponding $T_3 (A_3)$. If these conditions are not fulfilled, however, the situation could be analogous to the familiar "low-level equilibrium trap" of development economics. There will be no incentive to expand beyond A_1 if the decision makers are "myopic" and the equilibrium will therefore be at the locally stable point α in this case, with army level A_1 and associated territory $T_1(A_1)$. On the other hand, full information about the shapes of AA' and LL' might be available, but there could be a constraint on the possible size of the army at some point between A_1 and A_2, again leading to point α as the "normal" solution.

Suppose that the original historical equilibrium is at α. There will be no incentive to expand further if only small incremental changes take place in the size of the army. Suppose, however, that under some very special circumstances a unique, charismatic leader arises who can organize an expansion in the size of the army to A_2 or beyond. Once this initial feat is performed, success will be cumulative, since the marginal productivity of additional warriors will now exceed their marginal cost. Expansion can take place all the way to A_3, with the territory of the empire at the globally optimal level of $T_3(A_3)$.

Historical examples of such sudden explosive conquests are rare but not unknown. There are at least three of great interest and significance. The first is the establishment of the original Arab empire after the tribes of the Arabian peninsula had been united by the new religion of Islam preached by the Prophet. Ending their intensive feuding and banding together, and exercising spectacular mobility across the deserts, they conquered most of the land from Spain to India in a generation. Even more spectacular, though less long-lived, was the unification of the Mongols under Genghis Khan. Their historic equilibrium was a "tribal confederacy," a loosely knit association that subsisted on a parasitic relation with their more sedentary and wealthier neighbors. Genghis Khan, by a mixture of ruthlessness and daring, welded the various tribes into a centralized steppe kingdom before launching his whirlwind conquests of the civilized world from China to the borders of Poland. A final example is that of the Zulu chief Shaka early in the nineteenth century in Southern Africa, with his combination of military innovations and terror against rival chieftains. The fact that all three great conquests were difficult to sustain shows how hard it was to establish them initially, dependent as they were on the emergence of truly extraordinary personalities.[2]

4   A manufacturing sector

Up to now we have identified production with land and agriculture. How will the introduction of a manufacturing sector alter the determinants of the optimal size of territory and population? We will suppose that manufacturing does not require any land at all, only labor and a specific input capital. For simplicity, we will take this stock of specific manufacturing capital as fixed. The model will now have an additional production function for manufacturing:

$$M = M(L_M, \overline{K}) \tag{3-9}$$

where M is output of manufactures, $\overline{K}$ is the specific input of capital, and L_M is labor employed in manufacturing. The manpower constraint (3-7) is now

$$L_A + L_M + A = N[T(A)] \tag{3-10}$$

where L_A denotes labor in agriculture.

We suppose that the relative valuation of the two goods Q and M, with Q as the *numeraire*, is a constant p. This constant could be thought of either as a relative price on a world market in which our economic system is imbedded, or a constant marginal rate of substitution in a linear utility function. National income will be

$$Y = Q + pM \tag{3-11}$$

The augmented model thus corresponds closely to the familiar Ricardo-Viner model of international trade theory, expounded in Jones (1971) and Samuelson (1971). The significant difference of course is that the supplies of the specific input land T and the overall labor force N are both endogenous instead of fixed, as a result of our hypotheses in Eqs. (3-3), (3-4), (3-5), and (3-7).

The objective of the empire is now to maximize Eq. (3-11), subject to the technology and the resource constraints. The first-order condition now becomes

$$p \frac{\partial M}{\partial L_M} = \frac{\partial Q}{\partial L_A} = \left\{ \frac{\partial Q}{\partial L_A} \frac{dN}{dT} + \frac{\partial Q}{\partial T} \right\} \frac{dT}{dA} \tag{3-12}$$

which is the same as Eq. (3-8) except for the fact that the marginal productivity of labor must now be equal in *three* uses – the army, agriculture, and manufacturing – instead of just two as before.

---

[2] On the rise of Islam and Arab conquests, see Crone (1987), Chapter 10; on Genghis Khan and the Mongols, see Ratchenevsky (1991) and Barfield (1989); on Shaka and the Zulus, see Morris (1969) and Gluckman (1940).

It is apparent that the higher is the relative price p, holding N, A, and T initially constant, the larger will be L_M and M and the smaller will be L_A and Q, i.e., production and labor allocation will shift in favor of M and against Q. The marginal product of labor in agriculture will rise and the marginal product of land will fall. What will be the effect on the incentive to adjust the size of the army as a result of the rise in the relative price of manufactures?

If $\frac{dN}{dT}$ is small or negligible the effect will be to reduce the size of the army, since $\frac{\partial Q}{\partial T}$, the value of each additional acre won by the army, is now smaller. It pays instead to deploy some of the former warriors in manufacturing, and thus to sacrifice some territory. If $\frac{dN}{dT}$ is large, however, it pays to expand the army *not* to get more territory for its own sake, since land is now less valuable as an input, but to absorb more labor from subject populations into the workforce of the empire.

It is interesting to note in this connection that, in the fierce wars waged by the Burmese kings against Thailand from the sixteenth to the eighteenth centuries, the objective was not to take and hold territory but to bring back large numbers of the Thai population, particularly skilled craftsmen. Slave raiding for domestic use was also widespread in Africa and of course in the ancient world of Greece and Rome, especially the latter.

Very similar results will follow from an increase in the supply of capital. Combining these results, we can say that the more important the manufacturing sector is in the economic system, the less incentive will the empire have to expand its army and its territorial extent. An exception to this would be when labor is scarce within the existing borders of the empire but plentiful outside it, and there is furthermore a strong comparative advantage of military force relative to the "barbarians" beyond the borders.

A more important exception, however, would be the inclusion of manufactured output as an input, along with the army, in the conquest or sphere of influence function, so that instead of simply $r(A)$ in Eqs. (3-3) and (3-4), we have instead

$$T = a\pi r(A, M_A)^2 \tag{3-3'}$$

where M_A is manufacturing input, such as arms, that is complementary to the army A. The partial derivative of r with respect to M_A would be positive and the second derivative negative, analogous to the conditions regarding the relationship between r and A in Eq. (3-4). The cross partials of A and M_A are positive.

Introducing a "military-industrial complex" in this way clearly opens up many interesting and relevant considerations. Technical progress or capital accumulation in manufacturing now not only raises the opportunity cost of soldiers but potentially increases their marginal product as well. Thus, on balance, it would be possible to have manufacturing progress lead to an *extension* of conquest and aggression as a result of enhanced military effectiveness, par-

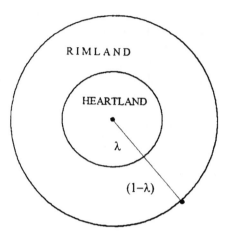

Figure 3-2.

ticularly if the improvement is confined, at least initially, to the empire itself. Such temporary but nevertheless long sustained monopolies of bronze or iron weapons, chariots, or firearms have been major factors in the annals of conquest and the rise of empires.

5   Reaction functions and the balance of power

The model has so far dealt with the opponents beyond the borders of the empire as an undifferentiated mass, without any conscious strategy of their own in response to that of the empire. In many historical cases, however, we have the clash of two or even more empires, each with a unified strategy relative to the opponents. Even with such examples as the Germanic tribes beyond the Roman frontiers, or the steppe nomads in the case of China, the "barbarians" frequently banded together to coordinate their offensive and defensive measures.

To analyze this problem let us consider the following highly stylized extension of our basic model. Suppose that the entire space with which the model is concerned is now finite, a circle with unit radius centered on the home base of our original tribe. The tribe strives to capture and hold a circular area centered on this point, with the fraction of the unit radius under its control determined by the relative sizes of its own army and that of its opponent. For any given disposition of the two forces, the original tribe holds the inner of two concentric circles, while the opponent retains the complementary area of the outer circle.

Let us call the area held by the tribe the Heartland and that held by its opponents the Rimland, in the evocative terminology of the great geopolitical theorist Sir Halford Mackinder, as depicted in Figure 3-2. Denoting the fraction

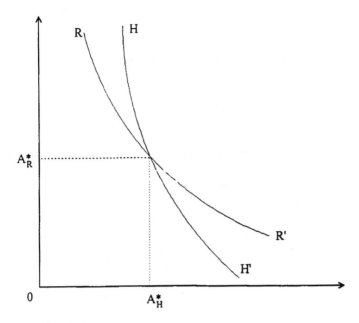

Figure 3-3.

of the unit radius held by the Heartland as λ, and A_H and A_R as the sizes of the two opposing forces, we postulate that

$$\lambda = \lambda(A_H, A_R)$$

$$\frac{\partial \lambda}{\partial A_H} > 0, \qquad \frac{\partial \lambda}{\partial A_R} < 0 \tag{3-13}$$

with negative second derivatives in each case.

Thus given A_R, we see that $\lambda(A_H)$ behaves exactly like our earlier function $r(A)$ in the basic model. An increase in A_R will reduce $\lambda(A_H)$ for any given value of A_H. Similar relations will hold for A_R, given A_H. With technology and resource endowments specified for each side, we can determine the optimum A_H for given A_R and vice versa. This enables us to derive the "reaction functions" HH' and RR'. These functions can be negatively sloped as shown in Figure 3-3. (Although outher configurations of the reaction functions are also possible, we do not examine them here.) If HH' is steeper than RR', the intersection of the two curves yields a stable equilibrium or "balance of power" with A_H^* and A_R^* as the optimal force sizes of the two opponents and T_H^* and T_R^* as the corresponding areas of the territories that they control.

What determines the fraction of the radius and hence the relative size of the territory that each side controls in this balance of power? It is clearly not just the relative military efficiency but the entire structure of the two economic systems and "ways of life." One obvious application of the model is to think of the Heartland as China, the Central Kingdom as it has been known to its inhabitants for millennia, and the Rimland as the domain of the pastoral nomads. The ratio of territory could be very much in favor of the latter, even though the compact central core might be much wealthier and more sophisticated with a flourishing industry that makes land, and therefore an army, not so essential except for strictly defensive purposes. Chinese culture has traditionally found military activities distasteful, reflecting this fact. For the nomads on the other hand with mobility a way of life that makes them take readily to war, a wide swathe of territory may be natural to acquire and hold.

An alternative interpretation of the model, however. would be to think of the Rimland as the more "developed" and "sophisticated" region, say because the outer land circle is surrounded by water, making transport around the rim and contact with the foreign lands across the sea much easier and therefore leading to an increase in wealth. The Heartland could then be the more pastoral and agricultural of the two regions, giving an incentive for a large army and pushing the Rimland back to a thin corridor around the boundary. It is natural to think here of Europe, with land-based kingdoms such as Prussia and Austria-Hungary in the central core and maritime Rimland nations like Portugal, Holland, England, and Italy drawing their wealth from industry and overseas trade rather than land and agriculture.

6   Comments on the literature

While economic factors are explicitly alluded to only incidentally in his stimulating book, *A History of Warfare,* the military historian John Keegan (1993) gives considerable attention to a concept developed by the sociologist Stanislaw Andreski (1968) called the military participation ratio (MPR), or the fraction of a population engaged in military activities. It is interesting to note that our model, instead of simply taking this MPR as given by some innate propensity for aggression, *derives* it from more basic structural parameters of resources and technology, though preferences could no doubt be made to play an additional role as well. Thus the fact that many of the great empires were established by nomadic peoples can be accounted for in terms of our model as reflection of what North (1981) calls a "comparative advantage in violence," arising from a low opportunity cost of peaceful activities because of a paucity of resources. combined with the externalities for military effectiveness generated by riding, hunting, and other such practices that are a natural part of nomadic life. Manufacturing and other peaceful arts, as we have seen, tend to raise the opportunity cost of maintaining armies and hence lower the MPR, though they can also enhance military efficiency through improving the technology of warfare.

Our model does also allow, however, for such cultural or social factors stressed by Andreski and Keegan as cohesion or solidarity of the conquering tribe or nation, what the great Arab historian Ibn Khaldun called *assabiya*. This factor is particularly important in the case of multiple equilibria analyzed earlier. Whether this factor is operative or not could determine whether or not the "high" equilibrium rather then the "low" one is determined. The more normal low state could be occasionally punctuated by great unifications and conquests brought about by charismatic leaders. After some time, however, as Ibn Khaldun points out, the bonds of *assabiya* tend to dissolve and the empire fragments or the dynasty loses the "mandate of heaven" as the Chinese saw it.[3]

Our analysis of reaction functions and the resulting balance of power is akin to the well-known mathematical model of "arms races" associated with the names of Lanchester and Richardson. The difference, however, is that we link the military sectors to the economic systems through the opportunity costs of allocating resource for war. Our model thus links the arms race itself into the wider context of the economy and society as a whole.

In an extensive recent comparative study of theories of empire, Doyle (1986) offers threefold classification into metrocentric, pericentric, and systemic, depending on whether the primary stress is laid on tendencies emanating from the center or metropolis in the first case, the dependent periphery in the second, or the relationship between both in some wider contextual space in the third. An example of the first would be the Hobson-Lenin theory of imperialism as the attempt by developed capitalist countries to offset a declining rate of profit at home investment in colonies. The approach of our original model of expansion by centralized entity against the resistance of "barbarians" would also fit this category, while our later analysis of competing empires through reaction functions establishing a balance of power would be an example of a systemic theory.

The sociologist, Michael Mann (1986) in a very ambitious and interesting work, subtitled *A History of Power from the Beginning to AD 1760,* makes a distinction between empires of domination, which exact tribute and exercise indirect control, and territorial empires, which conquer and administer directly. While our model is obviously entirely consistent with the second, it can also apply to the first, since the exaction of tribute and the exercise of control also require the allocation of resources to predatory rather than directly productive activities.

---

[3] On Ibn Khaldun see the selections from his major work translated and arranged, with a valuable introduction, by Charles Issawi (1950).

Both Doyle and Mann, not surprisingly, devote considerable space to the Roman Empire and its characterization. On this subject our model is entirely consistent with the view of the most eminent recent authority, William Harris (1979). Contrary to many earlier ancient historians, Harris considered the root of the Roman expansion to be the desire to accumulate land, slaves, and plunder, with the greatest political and economic rewards going to those members of the Roman upper classes most successful in waging war.[4] The emphasis on a rational, even though implicit, calculus of costs and benefits in extending the limits of the empire is also present in a subtle and penetrating study of the *Frontiers of the Roman Empire* by Whittaker (1994, p. 86), who points out that "Roman emperors had some awareness, however crude, of what we would call the marginal costs of imperialism."

In a central chapter on "Why Did the Frontiers Stop Where They Did?" Whittaker rejects the idea of "natural frontiers," such as mountain ranges and rivers like the Rhine, Danube, and Euphrates. Despite the authority of Tacitus and numerous subsequent authorities down to the present day, he argues that they were not impenetrable barriers or clear demarcation lines between Roman and barbarian. Rather, he adopts the view of the great student of the interaction between China and the steppe nomads of Inner Asia, Owen Lattimore (1940). Lattimore says "a major imperial boundary ... is not merely a line dividing geographical regions and human societies. It also represents the *optimal limit of growth* of one particular society (p. 40)." He defines the optimum limit as the point at which "centripetal gain, accordingly, was converted into centrifugal loss" (p. 242), which I find to be an elegant verbal equivalent to my more cumbersome mathematical first-order conditions.

What Paul Kennedy (1987) in his influential book calls "imperial overstretch," the tendency of empires to press beyond these rational limits, can also be illustrated in our model as a desire to hold territory as a point of honor or dynastic piety, rather than rationally cutting back consistently with resource availabilities. Thus the many examples such as the Habsburgs blindly persisting in wasting the riches of their overseas possessions in trying to hold Flanders and their other European patrimonies.

It would be easy to apply the model to various other historical examples and episodes, but I hope to have convinced the reader already about the relevance of this analysis to the fascinating questions posed in the opening quotation from Mark Elvin. Before closing, however, I would like to point to the strong formal resemblance between this model and those of the division of labor between "soldiers" and "workers" among the "social insects" such as ants and wasps, studied by means of very sophisticated optimizing techniques in the classic work of Oster and Wilson (1978). Here we have another striking example of the convergence of biological and economic theory.

---

[4] See also Rich and Shipley eds. (1993), for extended discussion of the Harris thesis.

References

Andreski, S., *Military Organization and Society,* 1968, Berkeley, Calif: University of California Press.

Barfield, T. J., *The Perilous Frontier,* 1989, Cambridge, Mass.: Blackwell.

Boulding, K. E., *Conflict and Defense: A General Theory,* 1963, New York: Harper.

Bush, W. C. and L. S. Mayer, "Some Implications of Anarchy for the Distribution of Property," *Journal of Economic Theory,* 1974, 8, 401–12.

Creel, H. G., "The Role of the Horse in Chinese History," in *What is Taoism? and Other Studies in Chinese History,* 1970, Chicago: University of Chicago Press.

Crone, P., *Meccan Trade and the Rise of Islam,* 1987, Princeton, N.J.: Princeton University Press.

Doyle, M. W., *Empires,* 1986, Ithaca, N.Y.: Cornell University Press.

Elvin, M., *The Pattern of the Chinese Past,* 1973, Stanford, Calif.: Stanford University Press.

Friedman, D., "A Theory of the Size and Shape of Nations," *Journal of Political Economy,* February 1977.

Gluckman M., "The Kingdom of the Zulu of South Africa," in M. Fortes and E. E. Evans-Pritchard (eds.), *African Political Systems,* 1979, Oxford, UK: Oxford University Press.

Harris, W. V., *War and Imperialism in Republican Rome 327–70 BC,* 1979, Oxford: Oxford University Press.

Hirshleifer, J., *Economic Behavior in Adversity,* 1987, Chicago: University of Chicago Press.

———, "The Technology of Conflict as an Economic Activity," *American Economic Review,* May 1991.

Issawi, C., *An Arab Philosophy of History,* 1950, London: John Murray.

Jones, R. W., "A Three-Factor Model in Theory, Trade and History," in J. Bhagwati et al. (eds.), *Trade, Balance of Payments and Growth,* 1971, Amsterdam: North-Holland.

Keegan, J., *A History of Warfare,* 1993, New York: Knopf.

Kennedy, P., *The Rise and Fall of the Great Powers,* 1987, New York: Random House.

Lattimore, O., *Inner Asian Frontiers of China,* 1960, New York: Beacon Press [first edition published by American Geographical Society, New York, 1940].

Mann, M., *The Sources of Social Power,* vol. 1, 1986, Cambridge: Cambridge University Press.

Morris, D. R., *The Washing of the Spears,* 1969, New York: Simon & Schuster.

North, D. C., *Structure and Change in Economic History,* 1981, New York: Norton.

Oster, G. F. and E. O. Wilson, *Caste and Ecology in the Social Insects,* 1978, Princeton, N.J.: Princeton University Press.

Ratchnevsky, P., *Ghengis Khan,* 1991, Cambridge, Mass.: Blackwell.

Rich, J. and G. Shipley (eds.), *War and Society in the Roman World,* 1993, London: Routledge.

Samuelson, P. A., "Ohlin Was Right," *Swedish Journal of Economics,* 1971, 73.

Skaperdas, S., "Cooperation, Conflict and Power in the Absence of Property Rights," *American Economic Review,* September 1992.

Thompson, E. and R. Faith, "A Pure Theory of Strategic Behavior and Social Institutions," *American Economic Review,* June 1981.

Usher, D., "The Dynastic Cycle and the Stationary State," *American Economic Review,* December 1989.

Whittaker, C. R., *The Frontiers of the Roman Empire,* 1994, Baltimore: Johns Hopkins University Press.

Wittman, D., "Nations and States, Mergers and Acquisitions, Dissolutions and Divorce," *American Economic Review,* May 1991.

Wolfson, M., "A Note on Growth, Politics and War," mimeo, 1994, Irvine: University of California.

CHAPTER 4

Predation and production

Herschel I. Grossman and Minseong Kim
Brown University

Although most economic agents allocate most of their resources to productive activities, sometimes individuals and groups live mainly or solely by appropriating from others. For example, at some stages of their histories the Vikings and the Mongols seem to have been pure predators. Other examples include individuals who specialize in being thieves and robbers. Under what conditions would an individual or a group choose to produce nothing and devote itself to preying on others?

Adam Smith (1776, Book V, Chapter 1, Part I) observed the relation between the relative wealth of nations and appropriative interactions.

> That wealth ... which always follows the improvements of agriculture and manufacture ... provokes the invasion of all their neighbors. An industrious, and upon that account a wealthy nation, is of all nations the most likely to be attacked ...

The wealth of a richer agent gives a poor agent an incentive to prey on the richer agent and, perhaps, even to be a pure predator. Jack Hirshleifer (1991) provides an interesting example in which, if the relative endowment of an agent is sufficiently small, then that agent allocates all its resources to predatory activities.

This paper develops a general equilibrium model of appropriative interaction between two agents, a potential predator and the prey. The prey allocates its resources to the production of consumables and to defensive fortifications that serve to protect its property. The potential predator allocates its resources either to the production of consumables, or to offensive weapons that the predator uses to appropriate the prey's property, or to both.[1]

We are especially interested in determining the conditions that yield different types of equilibria. In a nonaggressive equilibrium, the potential predator allocates no resources to predatory activity. In an equilibrium of pure predation, the predator allocates no resources to productive activity. In an equilibri-

---

[1] In biology, the terms "predator" and "prey" are used differently. In biology, the predator eats the prey. But, here, the predator is interested only in the resources of the prey, not in the prey itself.

um of part-time predation, the predator allocates positive amounts of resources both to predatory activity and to productive activity.

The present paper builds on the general equilibrium model of two-sided appropriative interaction developed in Grossman and Kim (1995). That model abstracted from the possibility of pure predation. It assumed that all agents allocate positive amounts of resources to productive activities. The model in the present paper relaxes this assumption to allow for the possibility that a poor agent might choose to specialize in predatory activity. To make this analysis tractable, we assume that only one of the agents is a potential predator.

We also analyze the welfare properties of the allocation of resources between appropriative and productive activities. This analysis shows how the welfare of the prey and the welfare of the potential predator are related to the security of the prey's property.

1   Appropriation and production

Consider the following one-period model of appropriation and production. There are two agents: z, the potential predator, and y, his prey. These agents can be either individuals or collectives, such as tribes or nation states. The prey and the potential predator have initial positive resource endowments, n_y and n_z. Because the property of the prey is subject to appropriation by the potential predator, the prey's property can be more or less secure. The security of the prey's property is determined endogenously.[2]

We want our model to capture the role of defensive fortifications as a deterrent to predation. For example, strong locks deter burglars and strong forts deter invaders. Accordingly, we assume that the agents allocate their initial endowments in the following sequence.

First, the prey allocates its initial endowment, n_y, to defensive fortifications h and productive capital k_y, with the constraints $h \geq 0$, $k_y \geq 0$, and $n_y = h + k_y$. Second, the potential predator allocates its initial endowment n_z to offensive weapons g and productive capital k_z, with the constraints $g \geq 0$, $k_z \geq 0$, and $n_z = g + k_z$.

---

[2] As already mentioned, this appropriative interaction is one-sided. The prey does not attempt to appropriate the property of the potential predator either because the potential predator is simply invulnerable or because its resources are useless for the prey. This analysis also does not explicitly address the possibility that a third party, like government, acts as the proximate enforcer of claims to property. In fact, in situations in which the claimants to property are groups like tribes or nations, third parties typically play no role in enforcing claims to property. Moreover, even if the claimants to property are individuals, third-party enforcement is not the historical basis for secure claims to property. As Vernon Smith (1993, p. 170) points out, "property rights ... precede the state. ..." In addition, incorporating third-party enforcement into the theory would require us to model the principal–agent relation between the claimants to property and the third party.

In this model, the allocations k_y and k_z to productive activities and either g or h to appropriative activities are rival uses of the endowment. The same unit of endowment cannot be allocated simultaneously to more than one of these activities.

The productive capital produces consumables. We assume, for simplicity, that the productive activities of the two agents are independent and that the two agents have the same production technology. Specifically, the two agents produce consumables of amounts αk_y and αk_z, where α is a positive productivity parameter.[3]

After the allocation of resources and production of consumables, the entire endowment of the prey, regardless of how it has been allocated, is subject to appropriation by the potential predator. In other words, the potential predator can capture the prey's defensive fortifications as well as the prey's productive capital. But we assume, again for simplicity, that, although the potential predator can appropriate the prey's endowment, the potential predator cannot appropriate consumables produced by the prey.

The fraction of its own endowment that the prey retains provides a measure of the security of its property. This fraction depends on the relative allocations of resources by the two agents to offensive weapons and defensive fortifications. Specifically, the prey retains the fraction p of its own endowment, where

$$p = \frac{1}{1+x} \quad \text{and} \quad x = \theta \frac{g}{h}. \tag{4-1}$$

In Eq. (4-1), x measures the offensive strength of the potential predator relative to the defensive strength of the prey, where θ is a positive parameter that indicates the effectiveness of offensive weapons against defensive fortifications.[4] Equation (4-1) implies that $0 \le p \le 1$ and that p is decreasing in x.

We also allow for the possibility that predation is destructive, by which we mean that the predator gains less than the prey loses. For example, perhaps the predator's gain is subject to deterioration during shipment or the predator's

---

[3] Other specifications of the technology would allow for cooperative production of consumables with the two agents as owners of complementary resources. With cooperative production, either consumables would go into a common pool subject to appropriation, as in the models of Hirshleifer (1991) and Skaperdas (1992), or the model would have to include some social arrangement such as a market, as in Grossman (1994, 1995), for determining income claims.

[4] In this formulation of the strength of offense relative to defense, x is a homogeneous function of degree zero in g and h and of degree one in the ratio g/h. A more general specification, used by some authors, would be that x is homogeneous of degree r in the ratio g/h, $r > 0$. Hirshleifer (1991) interprets r as a decisiveness parameter. Note that, although x is a positive function of θ, x could be either a positive or negative function of r depending on whether g is larger or smaller than h. An even more general specification – see, for example, Grossman (1991) – would be that x is homogeneous, but not necessarily of degree zero, in g and h and that x is not homogeneous in the ratio g/h.

gain needs to be processed to be usable.[5] Specifically, although the prey loses the fraction $1 - p$ of its endowment, the potential predator gains only the fraction $(1 - \beta)(1 - p)$ of the endowment of the prey, where $0 \le \beta \le 1$. The parameter β measures the destructiveness of predation.

With these specifications, the final wealth of the prey is

$$m_y = p\, n_y, \tag{4-2}$$

and the final wealth of the predator is

$$m_z = n_z + (1 - \beta)(1 - p)\, n_y. \tag{4-3}$$

In this one-period model, the objective of agent i, $i = y, z$, is to maximize the sum of its production of consumables and its final wealth, denoted by v_i, where

$$v_i = \alpha\, k_i + m_i. \tag{4-4}$$

The essential tradeoff that each agent faces is that an increase in the amount of its initial endowment that an agent allocates to either offensive weapons or defensive fortifications, rather than to productive capital, decreases that agent's production, but increases that agent's final wealth.

2   Resource allocation: The potential predator

To analyze the allocation of resources in this model, we begin by considering the second-stage choice of offensive weapons g and productive capital k_z by the potential predator. At this second stage, the potential predator takes h, the defensive fortifications of the prey, as given and chooses g and k_z to maximize v_z, subject to the constraints $g \ge 0$, $k_z \ge 0$, and $n_z = g + k_z$.

Equations (4-1), (4-3), and (4-4) imply either that v_z has an interior maximum at an interior value of g that satisfies

$$\frac{dv_z}{dg} = -(1 - \beta)\frac{\partial p}{\partial g}\, n_y - \alpha = 0 \quad \text{with} \quad 0 < g < n_z \tag{4-5}$$

or that v_z is maximized at a corner either with

$$\frac{dv_z}{dg} = -(1 - \beta)\frac{\partial p}{\partial g}\, n_y - \alpha \le 0 \quad \text{and} \quad g = 0 \tag{4-6}$$

or with

---

[5] Another possibility would be that predation involves violence and destruction. But, given complete information and the absence of stochastic factors, this model does not provide an internal explanation for violence and destruction. Dagobert Brito and Michael Intriligator (1985) address the question of whether appropriative conflict is resolved with or without violence and destruction, and emphasize the importance of incomplete information as a cause of violence.

$$\frac{dv_z}{dg} = -(1-\beta)\frac{\partial p}{\partial g}\,n_y - \alpha \geq 0 \quad \text{and} \quad g = n_z.$$
(4-7)

Conditions (4-5), (4-6), and (4-7) allow three possibilities. First, if the predator chooses an interior value for g, then g is such that the marginal cost of g equals the marginal benefit of g. The marginal cost of g is α, which is the production of consumables foregone by allocating a unit of the initial endowment to predation rather than to production. The marginal benefit of g is the marginal increase in the final wealth of the predator from appropriating a larger fraction of the prey's endowment.

Second, if the potential predator chooses g equal to zero, then at g equal to zero the marginal cost of g is equal to or larger than the marginal benefit. Third, if the predator chooses g equal to n_z, then at g equal to n_z the marginal cost of g is equal to or smaller than the marginal benefit.

Substituting for $\frac{\partial p}{\partial g}$ from Eq. (4-1), Conditions (4-5), (4-6), and (4-7) imply that

$$g = \begin{cases} g(h) & \text{for } h \in H = \{h \mid 0 < g(h) < n_z\} \\ 0 & \text{for } h \in \tilde{H} = \{h \mid h > 0 \text{ and } g(h) \leq 0\} \\ n_z & \text{for } h \in \bar{H} = \{h \mid g(h) \geq n_z\} \end{cases}$$
(4-8)

where

$$g(h) = \sqrt{(1-\beta)\frac{n_y}{\alpha}\frac{h}{\theta}} - \frac{h}{\theta}.$$

The set $\bar{H}$ is such that the constraint $k_z \geq 0$ is binding for any $h \in \bar{H}$. Solving the inequality $g(h) \geq n_z$, we see that

$$\bar{H} = \{h \mid \hat{h} \leq h \leq \hat{\hat{h}}\}$$

where

$$\hat{h} = \frac{\theta}{2}\left[(1-\beta)\frac{n_y}{\alpha} - 2n_z - \sqrt{(1-\beta)\frac{n_y}{\alpha}\left[(1-\beta)\frac{n_y}{\alpha} - 4n_z\right]}\right]$$

$$\hat{\hat{h}} = \frac{\theta}{2}\left[(1-\beta)\frac{n_y}{\alpha} - 2n_z + \sqrt{(1-\beta)\frac{n_y}{\alpha}\left[(1-\beta)\frac{n_y}{\alpha} - 4n_z\right]}\right].$$

For any value of h not smaller than $\hat{h}$ and not larger than $\hat{\hat{h}}$, Condition (4-7) obtains, and the predator chooses to allocate no resources to production. Note that the set $\bar{H}$ is nonempty if and only if $\frac{n_y}{n_z} \geq \frac{4\alpha}{1-\beta}$. In other words, the constraint $k_z \geq 0$ can be binding only if the ratio of the prey's initial endowment to the potential predator's initial endowment is sufficiently large relative to α and β.

g: offensive weapons

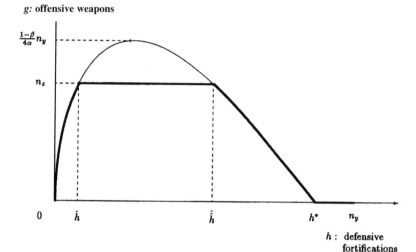

Figure 4-1. How the choice of offensive weapons depends on the defensive fortifications

The set $\tilde{H}$ is such that the constraint $g \geq 0$ is binding for any $h \in \tilde{H}$. Solving the inequality $g(h) \leq$ with $h > 0$, we see that

$$\tilde{H} = \{h \mid h \geq h^*\}$$

where

$$h^* = (1 - \beta)\theta \, \frac{n_y}{\alpha}.$$

For any value of h equal to or larger than h^*, Condition (4-6) obtains, and the potential predator chooses to allocate no resources to predation. Thus, h^* is the minimum allocation of resources by the prey to defense against predation necessary to deter the potential predator from engaging in predation. Note that h^* depends positively on the effectiveness of offensive weapons against defensive fortifications θ and depends negatively on the productivity of capital α and on the destructiveness of predation β. Also, h^* is proportionate to the prey's own endowment n_y, but it does not depend on the potential predator's endowment n_z.

The set H is such that the predator allocates positive fractions of its initial endowment both to production and predation for any $h \in H$. Solving the inequality $0 < g(h) < n_z$, we have

$$H = \{h \mid 0 < h < \hat{h} \text{ or } \hat{\hat{h}} < h < h^*\}.$$

Figure 4-1 shows how g depends on h. If $\frac{n_y}{n_z} < \frac{4\alpha}{1-\beta}$, then g is a hump-shaped function of h that peaks at $h = \frac{1}{4}(1 - \beta)\theta\frac{n_y}{\alpha}$. Otherwise, the functional relation between g and h becomes flat for $\hat{h} \leq h \leq \hat{\hat{h}}$ with $g = n_z$. In any case, g equals zero for $h \geq h^*$.

3 Resource allocation: The prey

We consider next the first-stage choice of defensive fortifications and productive capital by the prey. At this first stage, the prey chooses h and k_y to maximize v_y, subject to the constraints $h \geq 0$, $k_y \geq 0$, and $n_y = h + k_y$. In choosing h, the prey takes into account how the choice of g by the potential predator will depend on h.

Given Eq. (4-8) for g, Eq. (4-4) implies that, in the limit as h approaches zero, the derivative of v_y with respect to h becomes infinite. Accordingly, the constraint $h \geq 0$ is not binding. Also, we assume that the constraint $k_y \geq 0$ is not binding.

Combined with Eq. (4-8), Eq. (4-4) implies that v_y has either one or two local maxima. First, v_y can have a local maximum either at a value of h that satisfies

$$\frac{dv_y}{dh} = \left(\frac{\partial p}{\partial h} + \frac{\partial p}{\partial g} \frac{dg}{dh} \right) n_y - \alpha = 0 \quad \text{with} \quad h \in H \tag{4-9}$$

or at $h = h^*$ with

$$\frac{dv_y}{dh} = \left(\frac{\partial p}{\partial h} + \frac{\partial p}{\partial g} \frac{dg}{dh} \right) n_y - \alpha > 0 \quad \text{for all} \quad h \in H \tag{4-10}$$

Second, v_y can have another local maximum at a value of h that satisfies

$$\frac{dv_y}{dh} = \frac{\partial p}{\partial h} n_y - \alpha = 0 \quad \text{with} \quad h \in \bar{H} \tag{4-11}$$

Condition (4-9) says that, if the prey chooses $h \in H$, then h is such that the marginal benefit of h equals the marginal cost of h. The marginal cost of h is α, which is the production of consumables foregone by allocating a unit of resources to defensive fortifications rather than to production. The marginal benefit of h is the marginal increase in the prey's final wealth – that is, the marginal increase in the amount of its own endowment that the prey keeps. This increase results from both a direct effect of h on p and an indirect effect of h on p via $g(h)$. Condition (4-9) describes a local maximum if and only if $\left[2(1 - \beta)\theta > 1 \text{ and } \frac{n_y}{n_z} \lessgtr \alpha\theta \frac{4(1-\beta)\theta}{2(1-\beta)\theta-1} \right]$. If $\frac{n_y}{n_z}$ is too large relative to α, θ, and β, then $\hat{h}$ is so small and $\hat{\hat{h}}$ is so large that no value of $h \in H$ can satisfy Condition (4-9).

Condition (4-10) says that, if the prey chooses h equal to h^*, then the marginal benefit of h would exceed the marginal cost of h for all values of $h \in H$. Note that, because the marginal benefit is zero when h is larger than h^*, whereas the marginal cost is always equal to α, the prey never chooses $h > h^*$. Condition (4-10) describes a local maximum if and only if $[2(1 - \beta)\theta \le 1.]$

Condition (4-11) says that, if the prey chooses $h \in \bar{H}$, then h is such that the marginal benefit of h includes only the direct effect on p and equals the marginal cost. In this case, because the predator is allocating all its resources to offensive weapons, marginal changes in h do not affect g. Condition (4-11) describes a local maximum if and only if $\left[\frac{n_y}{n_z} \ge \alpha\theta\left(1 + \frac{1}{(1-\beta)\theta}\right)^2\right]$.

Substituting for $\frac{\partial p}{\partial h}$, $\frac{\partial p}{\partial g}$, and $\frac{dg}{dh}$ from Eqs. (4-1) and (4-8), with a comparison of two local maxima if necessary, Conditions (4-9)–(4-11) imply that the optimal choice of defensive fortifications is

$$
h = \begin{cases}
\dfrac{1}{4(1-\beta)\theta}\dfrac{n_y}{\alpha} \in H & \text{if and only if } \dfrac{n_y}{n_z} < N \text{ and } 2(1 - \beta)\theta > 1 \\[3ex]
h^* \in \tilde{H} & \text{if and only if } \dfrac{n_y}{n_z} < N \text{ and } 2(1 - \beta)\theta \le 1 \\[3ex]
\sqrt{\theta n_z \dfrac{n_y}{\alpha}} - \theta n_z \in \bar{H} & \text{if and only if } \dfrac{n_y}{n_z} \ge N
\end{cases}
\tag{4-12}
$$

where

$$
N = \begin{cases}
\alpha\theta\left[1 + \dfrac{1}{2\sqrt{(1-\beta)\theta}-1}\right]^2 & \text{for } 2(1 - \beta)\theta > 1 \\[3ex]
\alpha\theta\left[\dfrac{1+\sqrt{1-(1-\beta)\theta}}{(1-\beta)\theta}\right]^2 & \text{for } 2(1 - \beta)\theta \le 1.
\end{cases}
$$

Equation (4-12) says that, if $2(1 - \beta)\theta > 1$, then the prey chooses either $h \in \bar{H}$ or $h \in H$ depending on whether or not $\frac{n_y}{n_z} \ge N$.[6] Equation (4-12) also says that, if $2(1 - \beta)\theta \le 1$, then the prey chooses either $h \in \bar{H}$ or $h = h^*$ depending on whether or not $\frac{n_y}{n_z} \ge N$.[7]

In sum, the choice of h depends on relative endowments and on parameter values.[8] If the prey is sufficiently rich relative to the potential predator, then the prey chooses $h \in \bar{H}$. If the prey is not sufficiently rich relative to the poten-

---

[6] If $\frac{n_y}{n_z} \ge N$ and $2(1 - \beta)\theta > 1$, then Condition (4-11) describes the global maximum whether or not Condition (4-9) describes a local maximum. If $\frac{n_y}{n_z} < N$ and $2(1 - \beta)\theta > 1$, then Condition (4-9) describes the global maximum whether or not Condition (4-10) describes a local maximum.

[7] If $\frac{n_y}{n_z} \ge N$ and $2(1 - \beta)\theta \le 1$, then both Condition (4-11) and Condition (4-10) describe local maxima, and Condition (4-11) describes the global maximum. If $\frac{n_y}{n_z} < N$ and $2(1 - \beta)\theta \le 1$, then Condition (4-10) describes the global maximum whether or not Condition (4-11) describes a local maximum.

[8] In deriving Eq. (4-12), we assumed that the constraint $k_y \ge 0$ is not binding. The assumption that this constraint is not binding means that the chosen value of h satisfies $h \le n_y$. Equation (4-12) implies that the condition $h \le n_y$ obtains if and only if

tial predator, then there are two possibilities. First, if θ is small relative to β, then the prey chooses $h = h^* \in \tilde{H}$. A small θ or a large β implies that the deterrent effect of defensive fortifications is large. Second, if θ is large relative to β, then the prey chooses $h \in H$.

4 Equilibria and the security of the prey's property

Substituting Eq. (4-12) into Eq. (4-8), the equilibrium allocation of resources to offensive weapons by the potential predator is

$$
g = \begin{cases}
\dfrac{1}{2\theta}\left[1 - \dfrac{1}{2(1-\beta)\theta}\right]\dfrac{n_y}{\alpha} & \text{for } \dfrac{n_y}{n_z} < N \quad \text{and} \quad 2(1-\beta)\theta > 1 \\[3ex]
0 & \text{for } \dfrac{n_y}{n_z} < N \quad \text{and} \quad 2(1-\beta)\theta \le 1 \\[3ex]
n_z & \text{for } \dfrac{n_y}{n_z} \ge N.
\end{cases}
\tag{4-13}
$$

According to Eq. (4-13), the ratio of initial endowments, $\frac{n_y}{n_z}$, the effectiveness of offensive weapons against defensive fortifications, θ, the destructiveness of predation, β, and the productivity of capital, α, determine the type of equilibrium: nonaggression, part-time predation, or pure predation.

Figure 4-2 shows the relation between the type of equilibrium that obtains and the parameters and initial endowments. If and only if the initial endowment of the prey is sufficiently large relative to the initial endowment of the potential predator and θ is neither too large nor too small, then the potential predator allocates all its resources to offensive weapons and the equilibrium is pure predation. Note that, even if the prey is very rich relative to the predator, a value of θ that is either too large or too small rules out this equilibrium of pure predation. If θ is too large, then the offensive weapons of the predator are so effective against the defensive fortifications of the prey that a small allocation of resources to predation allows the predator to appropriate a large amount of the prey's endowment. If θ is too small, then the offensive

$$
\alpha \ge \begin{cases}
\dfrac{1}{4(1-\beta)\theta} & \text{for } \dfrac{n_y}{n_z} < N \quad \text{and} \quad 2(1-\beta)\theta > 1 \\[3ex]
(1-\beta)\theta & \text{for } \dfrac{n_y}{n_z} < N \quad \text{and} \quad 2(1-\beta)\theta \le 1 \\[3ex]
\dfrac{\theta n_z n_y}{(n_y + \theta n_z)^2} & \text{for } \dfrac{n_y}{n_z} \ge N.
\end{cases}
$$

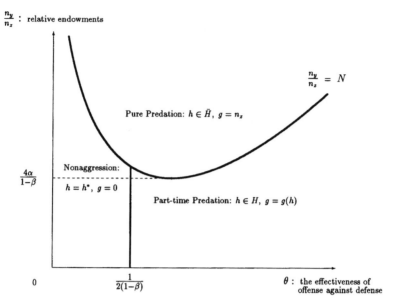

$\frac{n_y}{n_z}$: relative endowments

$\frac{n_y}{n_z} = N$

Pure Predation: $h \in \bar{H}$, $g = n_z$

Nonaggression:

$\frac{4\alpha}{1-\beta}$

$h = h^{*}$, $g = 0$

Part-time Predation: $h \in H$, $g = g(h)$

0

$\frac{1}{2(1-\beta)}$

θ : the effectiveness of offense against defense

Figure 4-2. Three regions of equilibria

weapons of the predator are so ineffective against the defensive fortifications of the prey that allocating much of its resources to offensive weapons is not worthwhile for the predator.

If the initial endowment of the prey is not large relative to the initial endowment of the potential predator, then the equilibrium is either nonaggressive or part-time predation. If also θ is sufficiently small, then a nonaggressive equilibrium obtains. In this case, offensive weapons are so ineffective that the potential predator is better off engaging only in production. But, if θ is sufficiently large, then the predator is better off engaging in some predation, and an equilibrium with part-time predation obtains.

The productivity of capital α does not affect whether the equilibrium is nonaggression or part-time predation. But α affects whether the equilibrium is pure predation. Other things being equal, an equilibrium with pure predation obtains for a sufficiently small α. The smaller is α, the smaller the return to resources allocated to production and the more likely that the constraint $k_z \geq 0$ is binding. In Figure 4-2, a smaller α results in a downward shift of the locus of $\frac{n_y}{n_z} = N$.

The destructiveness of predation β deters predation because the larger is β the smaller is the gain from predation. Thus, the larger is β the less likely is an equilibrium with pure predation and the more likely is a nonaggressive equilibrium. In Figure 4-2, a larger β results in a shift of the boundary between nonaggression and part-time predation to the right and in an upward shift of the locus $\frac{n_y}{n_z} = N$.

Substituting Eqs. (4-12) and (4-13) into Eq. (4-1) gives for the equilibrium value of the security of the prey's property p

$$p = \begin{cases} \dfrac{1}{2(1-\beta)\theta} & \text{for } \dfrac{n_y}{n_z} < N \quad \text{and} \quad 2(1-\beta)\theta > 1 \\[2em] 1 & \text{for } \dfrac{n_y}{n_z} < N \quad \text{and} \quad 2(1-\beta)\theta \le 1 \\[2em] 1 - \sqrt{\alpha\theta\,\dfrac{n_z}{n_y}} & \text{for } \dfrac{n_y}{n_z} \ge N. \end{cases} \qquad (4\text{-}14)$$

If $\frac{n_y}{n_z} < N$ and $2(1-\beta)\theta \le 1$, then p equals unity and the prey's property is fully secure. But, if $\frac{n_y}{n_z} < N$ and $2(1-\beta)\theta > 1$, then p is less than unity and the prey's property is less than fully secure. In this case, the security of the prey's property is inversely related to $(1-\beta)\theta$. The larger is $(1-\beta)\theta$, either due to greater effectiveness of offensive weapons against defensive fortifications or due to less destructive predation, the less secure is the prey's property. Note that, as long as $\frac{n_y}{n_z} < N$ and hence the equilibrium is not pure predation, p does not depend either on the initial endowments of the agents or on the productivity of capital. These results obtain because g and h are both proportionate to n_y and independent of n_z and because the productivity of capital is the same for both agents and is the marginal cost of both g and h.

If, alternatively, $\frac{n_y}{n_z} \ge N$ and hence the equilibrium is pure predation, then p depends positively on $\frac{n_y}{n_z}$ and negatively on α as well as negatively on θ. Now p depends on α because g equals n_z and is independent of α, whereas h still depends on α as the marginal cost. Also, p does not depend on β because h depends on β only through the effect of β on g, which is now independent of β.

Equation (4-14) also reveals that the equilibrium security of the prey's property is weakly decreasing in θ across different types of equilibria. For relatively low values of θ, it is worthwhile for the prey to allocate resources to defensive fortifications in order to secure its property fully. As θ increases, however, it takes more and more resources for the prey to completely deter predation. At some point, which depends on the value of $\frac{n_y}{n_z}$, it becomes better for the prey to lose a fraction of its endowment and produce more consumables by shifting resources from defensive fortifications to production. After that point, the larger is θ the less resources the prey allocates to defensive fortifications and the smaller is p.

5   Predation and economic welfare

We now analyze the effect of appropriative activities on the economic welfare of each agent. More specifically, we will see how the welfare of the prey and the welfare of the potential predator depend on the parameters α, θ, and β, and on the initial endowments n_y and n_z. We also see how the welfare of the prey and the welfare of the potential predator are related to the security of the prey's property.

These parameters and the initial endowments affect either the production of consumables of each agent, the final wealth of each agent, or both. Substituting into Eq. (4-4) the equilibrium values of k_y and k_z obtained from Eqs. (4-12) and (4-13), where $k_y = n_y - h$ and $k_z = n_z - g$, and the equilibrium values of m_y and m_z obtained from Eqs. (4-2), (4-3), and (4-14), we find that the prey's sum of production of consumables and final wealth is

$$
v_y = \begin{cases}
\alpha\left[n_y - \dfrac{1}{4(1-\beta)\theta}\dfrac{n_y}{\alpha}\right] + \dfrac{1}{2(1-\beta)\theta}\, n_y & \text{for } \dfrac{n_y}{n_z} < N \text{ and } 2(1-\beta)\theta > 1 \\[3ex]
\alpha\left[n_y - (1-\beta)\theta\,\dfrac{n_y}{\alpha}\right] + n_y & \text{for } \dfrac{n_y}{n_z} < N \text{ and } 2(1-\beta)\theta \le 1 \\[3ex]
\alpha\left(n_y - \sqrt{\theta n_z \dfrac{n_y}{\alpha}} + \theta n_z\right) & \\[2ex]
\quad + \left(1 - \sqrt{\alpha\theta\,\dfrac{n_z}{n_y}}\right) n_y & \text{for } \dfrac{n_y}{n_z} \ge N
\end{cases}
\tag{4-15}
$$

and that the predator's sum of production of consumables and final wealth is

$$
v_z = \begin{cases}
\alpha\left\{n_z - \dfrac{1}{2\theta}\left[1 - \dfrac{1}{2(1-\beta)\theta}\right]\dfrac{n_y}{\alpha}\right\} & \\[3ex]
\quad + n_z + (1-\beta)\left[1 - \dfrac{1}{2(1-\beta)\theta}\right] n_y & \text{for } \dfrac{n_y}{n_z} < N \text{ and } 2(1-\beta)\theta > 1 \\[3ex]
\alpha n_z + n_z & \text{for } \dfrac{n_y}{n_z} < N \text{ and } 2(1-\beta)\theta \le 1 \\[3ex]
n_z + (1-\beta)\sqrt{\alpha\theta n_y n_z} & \text{for } \dfrac{n_y}{n_z} \ge N.
\end{cases}
\tag{4-16}
$$

In Eqs. (4-15) and (4-16), the terms that are premultiplied by α are the production of consumables and the other terms are the final wealth for each agent.

Note that, if $\frac{n_y}{n_z} \geq N$, then the predator allocates all its initial endowment to predation and has no production of consumables.

In equilibria with part-time predation, either the larger is θ, the effectiveness of offensive weapons against defensive fortifications, or the smaller is β, the destructiveness of predation, the smaller is the equilibrium value of p, the security of the prey's property. Thus, the larger is θ or the smaller is β, the smaller is the final wealth of the prey and the larger is the final wealth of the predator. From Eqs. (4-15) and (4-16), we can confirm that these effects on final wealth dominate any offsetting effects on production of consumables. Consequently, in equilibria with part-time predation, the larger is θ or the smaller is β, the worse off is the prey and the better off is the predator.

In nonaggressive equilibria, the prey's property is fully secure and the final wealth of each agent equals that agent's initial endowment. Moreover, the potential predator's production of consumables depends only on its initial endowment. Thus, the welfare of the potential predator does not depend on either θ or β.

The prey, however, allocates the amount h^* out of its initial endowment to defensive fortifications to deter the potential predator from predation. Either the larger is θ or the smaller is β, the larger is h^* and the smaller is the prey's production of consumables. Consequently, in nonaggressive equilibria, the larger is θ or the smaller is β, the worse off is the prey.

In equilibria with pure predation, the larger is θ or the larger is $\frac{n_y}{n_z}$, the initial endowment of the predator relative to the prey, the smaller is the equilibrium security of the prey's property. Thus, the larger is θ, the smaller is the final wealth of the prey and the larger is the final wealth of the predator. Also, the larger is n_z the smaller is the final wealth of the prey, and the larger is n_y the larger is the final wealth of the predator.

Again, from Eq. (4-15), we can confirm that these effects on the final wealth of the prey dominate any offsetting effects on the prey's production of consumables. With pure predation the welfare of the predator depends only on its final wealth. Consequently, in equilibria with pure predation, either the larger is θ or the larger is n_z, the worse off is the prey, whereas either the larger is θ or the larger is n_y, the better off is the predator.

Overall, the welfare of the prey is decreasing in θ, weakly increasing in β, and weakly decreasing in n_z. The welfare of the potential predator is weakly increasing in θ, weakly decreasing in β, and weakly increasing in n_y.

6   Conclusions and extensions

This paper has developed a model of one-sided appropriative interaction between a potential predator and his prey. In this model, the type of the equilibrium – that is, how the potential predator allocates its resource endowment between predation and production – depends on how effective the offense of the potential predator is against the defense of the prey, how destructive predation is, and how rich the prey is relative to the potential predator. The model suggests an explanation for the behavior of potential predators, who can live by plundering, by producing consumables, or both.

If a potential predator is sufficiently poor relative to its prey, then the wealth of the prey can induce the predator to specialize in predation. Such pure predation also requires that the offense of the predator be neither too effective nor too ineffective against the defense of the prey. If the offense of the predator is too ineffective against the defense of the prey, then allocating all its resources to predation is not worthwhile for the predator. If the offense of the predator is too effective against the defense of the prey, then the predator can appropriate a large fraction of the prey's endowment with only a small amount of resources allocated to predation. In addition, the destructiveness of predation acts as a deterrent to predation. Thus, pure predation also requires that predation not be too destructive.

If a potential predator is not too poor relative to its prey, then it allocates at least a part of its resource endowment to the production of consumables. In addition, either if the offense of the potential predator is not sufficiently effective against the defense of the prey or if predation is sufficiently destructive, then the prey builds enough defensive fortifications to completely deter the potential predator from predation. In this case, the potential predator allocates all its resource endowment to producing consumables.

Although the analysis in this paper is static, it lays the foundation for a dynamic analysis of the interdependence between the evolution of the stock of resources and the evolution of the allocation of resources among four basic activities: consumption, investment, predation, and defense against predation. Associating predation with the distribution of endowments opens up a way to a dynamic analysis of the historical evolution of predators, like the Vikings and the Mongols, to producers. By also incorporating intertemporal decisions about saving and investment, such an analysis would identify conditions under which the wealth of the prey and the wealth of the potential predator grows or shrinks and conditions under which the wealth distribution between the prey and the potential predator diverges or converges.

References

Brito, Dagobert and Michael Intriligator, "Conflict, War, and Redistribution," *American Political Science Review,* 1985, 79, 943–57.

Grossman, Herschel I., "A General Equilibrium Model of Insurrections," *American Economic Review,* September 1991, 81, 912–21.

Grossman, Herschel I., "Production, Appropriation, and Land Reform," *American Economic Review,* June 1994, 84, 705–12.

Grossman, Herschel I., "Robin Hood and the Redistribution of Property Income," *European Journal of Political Economy,* 1995, 11.

Grossman, Herschel I. and Minseong Kim, "Swords or Plowshares? A Theory of the Security of Claims to Property," *Journal of Political Economy,* December 1995, 103.

Hirshleifer, Jack, "The Paradox of Power," *Economics and Politics,* November 1991, 3, 177–200.

Skaperdas, Stergios, "Cooperation, Conflict, and Power in the Absence of Property Rights," *American Economic Review,* September 1992, 82, 720–39.

Smith, Adam, *An Inquiry into the Nature and Causes of the Wealth of Nations,* 1776, reprinted 1976, Oxford: Clarendon Press.

Smith, Vernon L., "Humankind in History: Economy, Ecology, and Institutions," in Terry L. Anderson and Randy T. Simmons (eds.), *The Political Economy of Customs and Culture: Informal Solutions to the Commons Problem,* 1993, Lanham, Md.: Rowman & Littlefield.

CHAPTER 5

Competitive trade with conflict

Stergios Skaperdas
University of California, Irvine
Constantinos Syropoulos
Pennsylvania State University

1   Introduction

"If no Naval Force, no Trade," a British official commented in the eighteenth century.[1] Such an assessment is hardly unique to the beginnings of the British trading empire. Historically, trade, arming, and conflict have always gone hand in hand. The experience of all other European colonial powers can attest to that: the Spaniards, the Dutch, the French, the Russians. Earlier on, Venice and Genoa had similarly created their own trading empires, mostly within the Mediterranean, with the necessary help of strong navies. The Vikings who founded Kievan Russia in the ninth century were both traders and formidable warriors. Similarly, the expansion of Islam in its first century was spearheaded by merchant-warriors.[2]

How does trading affect arming? How do arming and conflict affect trading and the welfare of the interested parties? Such questions cannot be answered with the help of extant models of trade since, by construction, arming and conflict are ruled out. Therefore to begin thinking systematically about issues of conflict and trade, one needs a conceptual framework from which to start. The issue is not of concern just for historical reasons. Trade with overt conflict is pervasive even today but, probably more importantly, other less

We would like to thank Michelle Garfinkel and participants at Harvard's International Economics Workshop for comments on a preliminary draft of this paper and the National Science Foundation (grant no. SES-9210297) for financial support.
[1] The official was Charles Boone, the English Governor of Bombay (quoted in Chaudhuri, 1985, p. 3).
[2] An overview of the European colonial powers within the context of Western European history over the last five centuries can be found in Kennedy (1989). For Genoa and Venice in the sixteenth century see Braudel (1972). Obolensky (1971) discusses the admittedly uncertain history of early Kievan Russia. Chaudhuri (1985, Chapter 2) briefly reviews the early expansion of Islam and examines its contribution to the development of trading links in the Indian Ocean.

overt forms of conflict are in principle similar to overt arming and warfare.[3] Our first aim in this paper is to reconcile, in a general equilibrium economic setting, the simultaneous presence of arming, conflict, and trading and thus provide a framework within which such questions can be asked.

We start from a condition with absence of enforceable property rights over at least one economic resource; for example, a territory containing valuable oil, land used for pasture or agriculture, or fishing grounds. To put it differently, we relax the usual assumption in models of trade of secure ownership of all initial endowments by allowing the ownership of one economic good to be subject to dispute. The disputed resource is contested by adversaries who are prepared to use force. Force, however, requires the expenditure of other resources, which then become unavailable for production and consumption. Within such a setting, the adversaries first arm and then engage in open conflict, with one of them emerging as the winner of the disputed resource. The adversaries, interpreted as countries in the main body of the paper, can subsequently either produce and consume in autarky or engage in ordinary competitive trade with all their endowments becoming secure after the resolution of conflict. We thereby construct a model not only in which arming and ordinary useful production can coexist, but also in which open warfare and competitive trading can occur in succession.

We show how the prospects for conflict without subsequent trade (i.e., autarky) and for conflict with trade have often very different implications for the allocation of resources to war and for the welfare of the adversaries. We also examine how differences in initial secure endowments, the importance of the contested resource, the efficiency of arming and useful production, and other factors influence the final allocations and the welfare of the parties. Probably our least expected result is that one or all countries may ex ante prefer to have conflict without trade rather than conflict followed by trade, which implies these countries would have an incentive to commit in advance not to trade after conflict is resolved. (After conflict is resolved, incentives to trade always exist.) We will attempt to interpret these results as we derive them and in the concluding section.

Polachek (1980) has formulated the hypothesis – and found evidence in its favor – that trade reduces conflict since the higher is the trade volume between

---

[3] In 1991 James Baker, the U.S. Secretary of State, at one point tried to justify the then impending war against Iraq with the following three reasons of importance to U.S. citizens: "Jobs, jobs, jobs." Although the world is more complex than that – and the Secretary of State implicitly acknowledged that by offering different rationales (some of them with higher moral content) at other junctures – still the "jobs" rationale exemplifies the close connection even today between economic well-being and warfare, in ways however that are difficult to make sense in a traditional economic model that ignores warfare.

two countries, the costlier it is for them to engage in conflict. Although our primary motivation for this paper is to show the possibility of trade and conflict coexisting, our results are consistent with Polachek's finding since in our framework countries that find conflict without trade preferable would be likely not to trade at all, whereas those countries that do find trade preferable would devote comparatively fewer resources to conflict (or, according to a second interpretation of our model, they would actually never engage in conflict even though they would arm).

Our paper builds on Skaperdas and Syropoulos (1994) which, instead of examining conflict followed by trade, considers the possibility of negotiations and division of the resource under the threat of conflict followed by trade; that paper also contains a more general formulation of the problem we examine here. Grossman (1991, 1994) has developed another model that admits the presence of arming and competitive trading but that does not have actual conflict taking place. Other recent models in which agents make choices between production and appropriative activities (e.g., Hirshleifer, 1988; Garfinkel, 1990; Skaperdas, 1992) can be interpreted to involve bilateral trading, but the resulting welfare usually equals expected welfare under conflict and the implied allocations are anyway different from those that would emerge under competitive conditions.

In the next section we develop a basic model and derive analytical results that help develop our intuition about our framework. In Section 3 we generalize the model in several different directions and show how the simultaneous presence of many countries and a small fraction of a contested resource make conflict without trade preferable by all countries. In Section 4 we examine the effects of asymmetries in primary endowments, warrior effectiveness, and resource security. Section 5 concludes the paper.

2   The basic setting

We start with a minimal model, which we will expand in later sections. Consider two "countries," labeled 1 and 2. Each country i (=1,2) has an endowment L_i of a resource, which for our purposes we can identify with units of primary labor. Other interpretations are also possible and we will touch on them later. To produce the sole final good consumed in both countries, say "corn," labor must be combined with land. The total available quantity of land T is possessed by neither country.[4] Both countries actively contest this land by arming some of their potential workers and turning them into warriors. In particular, in each country some of the primary labor is converted into warrior labor (w_i) and the rest (l_i) is left to be combined with land:

---

[4] Again, the case in which each country clearly possesses some land is pursued later.

$$L_i = l_i + w_i \tag{5-1}$$

We suppose the settling of claims on land is determined by the actual use of force, with the relative strengths of the participants determining the winner of T in an all-out conflict. The outcome of conflict is uncertain and for a given choice of warriors, (w_1, w_2), the winning probability of country 1 is denoted by $p(w_1, w_2)$, with $1 - p(w_1, w_2)$ representing agent 2's winning probability. We assume that, when both countries have the same number of warriors, they have equal winning probabilities, and that the winning probability of each country increases as the number of its warriors increases and decreases as the warriors of its opponent country increase. Formally, we maintain the following properties for the function $p(\cdot, \cdot)$, usually called contest success function (CSF):

$$0 < p(w_1, w_2) < 1; \quad p(w_1, w_2) = 1 - p(w_2, w_1) \quad \forall\, (w_1, w_2); \quad \text{and} \quad p(\cdot, \cdot)$$

is differentiable with $p_1 \equiv \partial p_1 / \partial w_1 > 0$ and $\partial p_2 \equiv \partial p / \equiv w_2 < 0$. $\tag{5-2}$

For simplicity we assume that a constant-returns to scale Cobb-Douglas function governs production of the final good, with $\alpha\ [\in (0,1)]$ denoting the coefficient of land and thus with $1 - \alpha$ denoting the coefficient of labor.

Conflict without trade

We first consider the benchmark case in which there is winner-take-all conflict but no trade takes place after the winner is determined. The winner receives the whole land territory T and uses its labor l_i to produce corn, whereas the loser, having no land, produces nothing and possibly vanishes. We can think of this case as one in which T represents a contested territory inhabited by two peoples and, after one of them wins and takes control, the losers are expelled or massacred – unfortunately, not uncommon events in history. With the properties we have assumed, the expected payoffs of the two countries are

$$U^1 \equiv p(w_1, w_2)\, [T^{\alpha} l_1^{1-\alpha}] \tag{5-3a}$$

$$U^2 \equiv [1 - p(w_1, w_2)]\, [T^{\alpha} l_2^{1-\alpha}] \tag{5-3b}$$

Given the constraint in Eq. (5-1), the tradeoff each country faces is between the number of warriors (w_i) and productive labor (l_i) it chooses. More warriors increase the probability of winning the contested land but decrease the quantity of the final good consumed in the event of a win since there will be less labor available to be combined with land. Conversely, more productive labor decreases the probability of winning but increases the quantity of the final good that can be consumed in the event of a win. In a (Nash) equilibrium the marginal benefits and marginal costs of these two activities are equalized.[5] We should emphasize that the warriors play purely a distributional role in this model; in the event of a win they do not add anything to the production of corn.

To get a sense of the forces operating in this and the other cases we examine, we will derive analytical results with the following CSF:[6]

$$p(w_1,w_2) = w_1^m/(w_1^m + w_2^m) \quad \text{where} \quad m>0 \tag{5-4}$$

The parameter m measures the ease with which a country can increase its winning probability by an infinitesimal change in its number of warriors. We will refer to this measure as the *effectiveness* of conflict.[7]

Supposing $L_1=L_2=L$, there is a symmetric equilibrium yielding for each country the following equilibrium number of warriors (w_c) and number of laborers (l_c):

$$w_c = \frac{(m/2)L}{(1-\alpha) + m/2} \tag{5-5a}$$

$$l_c = \frac{(1-\alpha)L}{(1-\alpha) + m/2} \tag{5-5b}$$

Each country's number of warriors in equilibrium is a constant fraction of its total manpower L. A higher effectiveness of conflict (m) or a higher importance attached to land as a factor of production (α) implies higher numbers of warriors, lower numbers of laborers, and thus lower production of corn by the

---

[5] A Nash equilibrium exists when, in addition to Eq. (5-2), the CSF $p(\cdot,\cdot)$ satisfies the following property (the subscripts 1 and 2 refer to derivatives with respect to the first and second arguments, respectively):

$$p_{11}p \le p_1^2 \quad \text{(and, by symmetry, } -p_{22}(1-p) \le p_2^2)$$

Note that this property is always satisfied when the CSF is concave in each country's number of warriors (i.e., when p_{11} and $-p_{22}$ are nonpositive). This existence result follows from part a of Theorem 1 in Skaperdas and Syropoulos (1994).

[6] This functional form is not defined at $(w_1,w_2) = (0,0)$ and consequently it does not always satisfy the strict inequalities in Eq. (5-2). This can be easily remedied [by, for example, adding appropriate constant terms to the numerator and denominator of Eq. (5-4)], but since we only examine interior equilibria we have opted for this simpler specification. For an axiomatic derivation of Eq. (5-4) as well as other CSFs, see Skaperdas (1995).

[7] For the importance of such parameters in other contexts see Hirshleifer (1988, 1991) and Skaperdas (1992). Hirshleifer uses the term "decisiveness" of conflict to refer to this measure, but we would prefer to reserve this term for a CSF that allows for an impasse of conflict, with a greater probability of impasse implying greater decisiveness.

winner. Since the loser's payoff is always zero, such changes also lower the expected payoffs of the two countries.

Conflict and trade

The fate of the losers does not have to be as grim as we have just seen. Even slavery could be preferable, something amply exploited by the Romans and other conquerors through history. But there is a third alternative beyond elimination and slavery: The losers can simply be employed as wage laborers by the winners who take possession of all the land.[8] This appears to have been the practice of at least some of the colonial powers like the British and the Dutch, and to some extent earlier on by the Venetians. Thus we suppose that once conflict is resolved and land is taken by one of the two countries, the possessors of land and the laborers of both countries participate in perfectly competitive factor markets with the compensation rate of each factor being equal to its marginal product. Constant returns to scale ensure that the total output of corn exactly equals the compensation of the two factors.

Continuing to think of the two countries as the players in this expanded game, their ex ante expected payoffs are then as follows [where $p \equiv p(w_1, w_2)$]:

$$V^1 \equiv p \: \{l_1[(1-\alpha)T^{\alpha}(l_1+l_2)^{-\alpha}] + T[\alpha T^{\alpha-1}(l_1+l_2)^{1-\alpha}]\} + \\ (1-p) \: \{l_1[(1-\alpha)T^{\alpha}(l_1+l_2)^{-\alpha}]\} \qquad (5\text{-}6a)$$

$$V^2 \equiv (1-p) \: \{l_2[(1-\alpha)T^{\alpha}(l_1+l_2)^{-\alpha}] + T[\alpha T^{\alpha-1}(l_1+l_2)^{1-\alpha}]\} + \\ p \: \{l_2[(1-\alpha)T^{\alpha}(l_1+l_2)^{-\alpha}]\} \qquad (5\text{-}6b)$$

The first line of Eq. (5-6) is country 1's probability of winning times the total competitive compensation of its factors in that state. The second line is the country's probability of losing times the total compensation of its laborers (remember that the losers do not have any land). The third and fourth lines have similar interpretations for country 2. For any given choice of warriors and laborers satisfying the constraint in Eq. (5-1) and after the winner of land is determined, both the loser and the winner prefer to trade than not to trade.[9] We can gain additional insight by straightforwardly simplifying the expected payoffs in Eq. (5-6) as follows:

$$V^1 = [\alpha p + (1-\alpha)l_1/(l_1+l_2)]T^{\alpha}(l_1+l_2)^{1-\alpha} \qquad (5\text{-}7a)$$

[8] For simplicity we can assume the warriors on the losing side have fallen in battle or are incapable of productive work and that they are supported by their laboring brethren.

[9] Since we treat the two countries as single actors we abstract from collective action problems here. One obvious source of opposition within the winner country against hiring the laborers of the country that lost could come from its own laborers (if they do not receive any of the spoils of victory).

$$V^2 = [\alpha(1-p) + (1-\alpha)l_2/(l_1+l_2)]T^{\alpha}(l_1+l_2)^{1-\alpha} \tag{5-7b}$$

Note that $T^{\alpha}(l_1+l_2)^{1-\alpha}$ is the total output of corn, regardless of who the winner eventually is. By comparison, output under conflict, depending on the winner, is either $T^{\alpha}l_1^{1-\alpha}$ or $T^{\alpha}l_2^{1-\alpha}$. The expected payoffs as expressed in Eq. (5-7) then reveal that each country's payoff is in expectation a fraction of the total output of corn, where each fraction is a convex combination of the country's probability of winning and of the country's fraction of total labor. The weights in this convex combination are, respectively, the coefficients of land and labor in the Cobb-Douglas function.

Comparing the payoff functions under conflict in Eq. (5-3) with those under conflict and trade in Eq. (5-7), we can identify two important differences that determine the equilibrium choice of warriors and laborers by each country. First, as indicated already the total output of corn – the total pie available for division – is higher under conflict and trade. This difference has the effect, other things equal, of increasing the optimal number of warriors when the countries expect to engage in trade after conflict than when they do not. The other difference concerns the expected fraction of output received in each case. Under conflict it is solely determined by the CSF p, whereas under conflict and trade it is a convex combination of the CSF and of the fraction of total laborers. In the latter case an increase in the number of warriors of a country, although it increases its probability of winning, does not have to increase its expected fraction of total output since it is partly negated by the decrease in its fraction of laborers. To put it differently in analogy to a term we have already used, the expected fraction of a country under trade and conflict is less effective than the expected fraction under conflict. Consequently, this lower effectiveness under conflict and trade reduces the incentive for allocating manpower to warriors relative to the case without trade. Then, which arrangement will induce a higher equilibrium number of warriors, conflict without trade or conflict with trade? Since the two effects we just reviewed work in opposite directions – the bigger pie calls for more warriors and the lower effectiveness calls for less – there is no a priori clear answer. There is a clear answer, though, for the symmetric case ($L_1=L_2=L$) under the CSF in Eq. (5-4).

$$w_t = \frac{\alpha m L/2}{(1-a) + \alpha m/2} \tag{5-8a}$$

$$l_t = \frac{(1-\alpha)L}{(1-a) + \alpha m/2} \tag{5-8b}$$

where w_t and l_t refer to the number of warriors and laborers chosen by each country in equilibrium.[10] Since $\alpha<1$, a comparison with the quantities in Eq. (5-4) reveals that $w_t<w_c$ and $l_t>l_c$. Thus, the intensity of conflict, as measured by the numbers of warriors chosen by the two countries, is lower when the countries expect to engage in trade after conflict than when they do not; this also means that more manpower is allocated to labor. Consequently, in this *symmetric* case, higher production of corn when trade is expected comes from two distinct sources: (1) the fact that, for any given allocation of manpower, the laborers of both countries, instead of just those of the winner, are employed in the production of corn; and (2) additional manpower is freed for labor since conflict becomes less intense.

We shall see, however, that some of these results do not generally follow through. For now, we should note the values in Eq. (5-8) share the same qualitative properties as those in Eq. (5-5): The number of warriors w_t increases as the effectiveness of conflict m increases and as the importance of land as a factor of production α increases. The opposite properties hold for the number of warriors l_t.

Other interpretations

The interpretation we have given to the model thus far is one with conflict taking place over land with labor as a second production input. This may seem unnecessarily narrow, especially given our introductory remarks about conflict and trade in general. The formal model, however, affords other production as well as consumption interpretations. For production interpretations, the contested resource could be another natural resource or capital while the l_i's could stand for another intermediate input.

Probably more fertile for additional insights are consumption interpretations of the model. The contested resource T could be thought of as a final consumption good (say, "bread"), whereas the l_i could be another final good (say, "wine"). (More credibly, T could be thought of as producing by itself bread, and labor could be thought of producing wine, both with linear production functions.) Then the Cobb-Douglas function we have used could be thought of as a utility function. The expected payoffs in Eq. (5-6) would represent the expected utility of each country, given competitive markets in bread and wine (with, as earlier, trading taking place after conflict has occurred and one country has captured the contested resource). The winners would thus exchange some of their bread for some of the wine produced by the losers.

---

[10] For the payoff functions in Eq. (5-7) an equilibrium exists in general for a CSF satisfying Eq. (5-2) and the condition in footnote 5. To show this result we will need to apply Theorem 3 in Skaperdas and Syropoulos (1994).

This last interpretation of the model is partly inspired by the practice of the Venetians in many of their island possessions in the Eastern Mediterranean, especially from the fourteenth to the sixteenth centuries. They had control of all the supply of grain and imposed monoculture (e.g., vines, olives) on each island (see Braudel, 1972, pp. 155–7). As a result the usual exchange pattern was that of grain for the local monocultural variety produced by the subject population.[11]

3   When there are many countries and some land is secure

We now extend the basic model to examine additional factors that influence the incentives of countries to invest in armies and how that decision in turn affects their payoffs under pure conflict and conflict with trade. Thus far, our analysis was based on the assumption that land was contested in its entirety. Because of geography, artificial barriers, or international norms of conduct, countries may possess some land or other resource that is impossible for their enemies to reach and conquer. That is, some land may be secure and only a fraction of it may be contestable. Not surprisingly, we find the intensity of conflict is reduced when the fraction of contestable land decreases and therefore land becomes more secure.

More surprisingly, however, we find that when land is sufficiently secure and there are more than two identical countries, conflict without trade is ex ante Pareto superior to conflict with trade. Consequently, all countries would like to commit in advance not to trade (because otherwise they would always want to trade ex post, once conflict has been resolved). Suppose there are $N \geq 2$ countries with each country $i \in N \equiv \{1,2,\ldots,N\}$ possessing T_i units of secure land. With T denoting the total world supply of land, let T_0 denote the quantity that countries contest. The fraction $\tau_0 \equiv T_0/T$ represents the proportion of contested land and thus provides a measure of worldwide security. We let $\tau_i \equiv T_i/T$ ($i \equiv N$) denote country i's fraction of land that is secure. As before, every country possesses L_i units of manpower and has access to the same Cobb-Douglas production function for corn. Country i's probability of winning a global conflict is

$$p_i = w_i^m/(\textstyle\sum_{j \in N} w_j^m) \text{ for every } i \in N \tag{5-4'}$$

Every country i can transform its primary labor L_i into warriors and laborers who (along with land) produce corn, according to

$$L_i \equiv l_i + w_i/\omega_i \tag{5-9}$$

---

[11] Although our model fits this pattern, the practice of the Venetians suggests several modifications that could be pursued later on. For example, the winner can modify the supply behavior of the producers who lost the war by choosing for them the product he finds more favorable, while the market for that product as well as others is subject to the usual laws of the market.

The technological coefficient ω_i describes how many workers and warriors can be generated from one unit of initial manpower. Unilateral improvements in a country's technology of warfare or quality of warriors would translate into increase in the country's ω_i. We will study the effect of asymmetries of this parameter across countries in the next section.

Conflict without trade

As we did earlier, we first examine the case of conflict without trade. The pay-off U^i to country i that emerges as the winner in pure conflict over the contested land is given by

$$U^i \equiv p_i T^\alpha [(\tau_i + \tau_0)^\alpha l_i^{1-\alpha}] + (1-p_i) T^\alpha [\tau_i^\alpha l_i^{1-\alpha}] = \phi_i [T^\alpha l_i^{1-\alpha}] \qquad (5\text{-}10)$$

where

$$\phi_i \equiv p_i (\tau_i + \tau_0)^\alpha + (1-p_i)\tau_i^\alpha \qquad (5\text{-}11)$$

The first term in Eq. (5-10) is the output of corn country i would receive if it emerged as the winner in global conflict, an event that occurs with probability p_i. The second term in Eq. (5-10) is the output of corn country i expects to produce and consume if it were to lose the contest but retained its secure land. Depending on how much secure land a country possesses, its expected share ϕ_i can be greater or less than p_i.[12]

Suppose now that all countries are identical in every respect, i.e., $\omega_i = \omega$, $T_i = t$, $\tau_i = \tau (\Rightarrow \tau_0 = 1 - N\tau)$ and $L_i = L$ for all $i \in N$. Country i's first-order condition for welfare maximization (in the symmetric interior equilibrium) is

$$\frac{\partial U^i}{\partial w_i} = \frac{U}{w} \left[B_c - \frac{(1-\alpha)w}{\omega L - w} \right] = 0 \qquad (5\text{-}12)$$

where $U = U^i$ and $w = w_i$ for all $i \in N$ because of symmetry and

$$B_c \equiv \frac{m(N-1)\,[(\tau_0 + \tau)^\alpha - \tau^\alpha]}{N[(\tau_0 + \tau)^\alpha + (N-1)\tau^\alpha]} = \frac{m(N-1)\,[(T_0 + t)^\alpha - t^\alpha]}{N[(T_0 + t)^\alpha + (N-1)t^\alpha]} \qquad (5\text{-}13)$$

Country-related symbols in the right-hand side (RHS) of Eq. (5-12) have been dropped for simplicity. B_c is the marginal benefit (in percentages) from a 1 percent increase in a representative country's warriors. The ratio inside the bracket in Eq. (5-12) is the opportunity cost (also in percentage terms) of having additional warriors and thus forgoing some production of corn. The mar-

---

[12] Consider the two limiting cases of a country without any secure land and of a country monopolizing all the secure land that exists. In the former case we clearly have $\phi_i < p_i$, whereas in the latter we have $\phi_i > p_i$.

ginal benefit B_c depends only on exogenous parameters and each country's incentives for the allocation of its manpower between warriors and laborers depend crucially on those parameters. Using the fact that $\tau_0 = 1 - N\tau$, we can show that an increase in every country's proportion of secure land τ (and therefore a reduction in the fraction of contested land τ_0) reduces the marginal benefit to investing in warrior labor (i.e., $\partial B_c / \partial \tau < 0$). A change in the absolute size of secure land has a similar effect (i.e., $\partial B_c / \partial t < 0$).

The effect of the number of countries is more ambiguous but clean enough to understand. Specifically, we have $\partial B_c / \partial N > 0$ if and only if $\frac{1}{(N-1)^2} > \left(\frac{t}{T_0 + t} \right)^\alpha$. This inequality is always satisfied when t equals zero or is close enough to zero. Thus, in the presence of no or little secure property, the marginal benefit of allocating manpower to war increases as the number of countries increases. When land is more secure, though, the marginal benefit first increases and then decreases as N increases. In such a case there is an N for which the marginal benefit of an extra warrior is maximal; for high enough land security, this maximal benefit occurs when there are just two countries.

The representative country's equilibrium number of warriors under pure conflict is, as follows, increasing in B_c:

$$w_c = \frac{B_c \omega L}{(1-\alpha) + B_c} \tag{5-14}$$

Consequently, we can infer that conflict becomes less intense (w_c is lower) when land security is higher (t is higher or τ is higher) and the fraction of contested land τ_0 is lower. Conflict is not necessarily more intense when the world consists either of few or a large number of countries. Although when land security is low, adding an extra country intensifies conflict; when land security is high, there is a number of countries for which conflict is most intense. For high enough land security, conflict is most intense when there are just two countries and would become less intense if more countries were to be added.

A representative country's payoff in the symmetric equilibrium is given by

$$U_c = \left[\frac{1}{N} \cdot (\tau + \tau_0)^\alpha + \frac{N-1}{N} \cdot \tau^\alpha \right] \left[T^\alpha l_c^{1-\alpha} \right] =$$

$$\left[\frac{1}{N} \cdot (\tau + \tau_0)^\alpha + \frac{N-1}{N} \cdot \tau^\alpha \right] \left[T^\alpha \left(\frac{(1-\alpha)L}{1-\alpha + B_c} \right)^{1-\alpha} \right] \tag{5-15}$$

For any given number of countries N, an increase in the fraction of secure land that each country possesses raises every country's equilibrium payoff for two reasons: (1) Holding the number of workers l_c constant, an increase in the proportion of secure land τ is directly welfare-improving because the increase in expected corn production in the event of loss more than offsets the expected decrease in the acquisition of corn under a win. (2) As land becomes more secure, the optimal number of productive workers l_c is increased at the expense of warriors.

Conflict with trade

We consider now the regime in which conflict is followed by competitive trade. Country i's payoff function in this case is:

$$V_i \equiv p_i\{l_i[(1-\alpha)T^\alpha(\textstyle\sum_{j\in N}l_j)^{-\alpha}] + (T_0+T_i)\,[\alpha T^{\alpha-1}(\textstyle\sum_{j\in N}l_j)^{1-\alpha}]\} +$$
$$(1-p_i)\{l_i[(1-\alpha)T^\alpha(\textstyle\sum_{j\in N}l_j)^{-\alpha}] + T_i[\alpha T^{\alpha-1}(\textstyle\sum_{j\in N}l_j)^{1-\alpha}]\} \qquad (5\text{-}16)$$

The expressions inside the brackets are the competitive rewards delivered to productive inputs in the two possible states of the world: the first when country i wins (and thus appropriates the contestable land T_0); the second when country i is defeated (and thus is only rewarded for the services of its workers and its secure land). The payoff in Eq. (5-16) can be rewritten more compactly as

$$V^i \equiv [\alpha(\tau_i+p_i\tau_0) + (1-\alpha)l_i/(\textstyle\sum_{j\in N}l_j)]T^\alpha(\textstyle\sum_{j\in N}l_j)^{1-\alpha} \qquad (5\text{-}16')$$

In the interior symmetric equilibrium with $\tau_0=1-N\tau$, the first-order condition for welfare maximization of a representative country i is:

$$\frac{\partial V^i}{\partial w_i} = \frac{w}{V}\left[B_t - \frac{(1-\alpha)w}{\omega L-w}\right] = 0 \qquad (5\text{-}17)$$

where $V=V^i$ and $w=w_i$ for all $i\in N$ because of symmetry and

$$B_t \equiv \frac{N-1}{N}\,\alpha m\tau_0 = \frac{N-1}{N}\,\alpha m(1-N\tau) \qquad (5\text{-}18)$$

B_t is comparable to B_c and represents the marginal benefit (in percentages) from a 1 percent increase in a country's number of warriors. As with B_c, more secure land (higher t or τ and lower τ_0) leads to a lower B_t. We can also obtain $\partial B_t/\partial N > 0$ if and only if $\frac{1}{N(N-2)} > \frac{t}{T_0}$, which represents a qualitatively similar effect to that on B_c: Low levels of secure property always imply a marginal benefit increasing in the number of countries; higher levels of secure property imply a maximal level of the benefit at a certain number of countries (but not at $N=2$).

The solution to Eq. (5-17), w_t, constitutes the symmetric equilibrium and is given by

$$w_t = \frac{B_t\omega L}{(1-\alpha) + B_t} \qquad (5\text{-}19)$$

Given the effects on B_t, the equilibrium number of warriors under competitive trade with conflict are easy to characterize in terms of the basic parameters. In addition, a comparison of w_t in Eq. (5-19) to w_c in Eq. (5-14) is straightforward since the potential cause of divergence between equilibrium quantities in the two regimes can be attributed only to differences in the marginal benefit of having extra warriors. In the more basic model we examined earlier, the equilibrium number of warriors were always lowest under conflict with trade [compare Eqs. (5-8a) and (5-5a)]. This result, however, no longer holds here in this more general setting; it is now possible to have $w_t > w_c$ and therefore $l_t < l_c$. By comparing then B_t to B_c, we can then show $w_t > w_c$ if and only if the following condition is satisfied:

$$N > (1-\alpha T_0)[(T_0+t)^{\alpha} - t^{\alpha}]/t^{\alpha} \tag{5-20}$$

The expression on the right-hand side becomes smaller as secure property t becomes larger; as we have seen in the previous section, in the limiting case with complete absence of secure property this inequality cannot hold. As property becomes more secure, the number of countries for which we can have $w_t > w_c$ becomes progressively smaller. Conversely, and as long as there is some secure property ($t > 0$), there is some sufficiently large number of countries such that there is a greater equilibrium number of warriors when trade is expected to take place ($w_t > w_c$).

Utilizing Eq. (5-16') we can obtain the following payoff under trade and conflict in a symmetric equilibrium:

$$V_t \equiv \frac{1}{N} \left[T^{\alpha}(Nl_t)^{1-\alpha} \right] = \frac{1}{N} \left[T^{\alpha} \left(N \cdot \frac{(1-\alpha)L}{1-\alpha + B_t} \right)^{1-\alpha} \right] \tag{5-21}$$

Since now more warriors, and fewer laborers, can be chosen when trade is present than when it is not, the question arises as to which of the two regimes – conflict without trade or conflict with trade – is ex ante superior (i.e., whether V_t in Eq. (5-21) or U_c in Eq. (5-15) is larger). To be sure, once manpower is allocated between warriors and laborers and conflict is resolved, there is always an incentive to trade. Nevertheless, if conflict without trade were to induce higher ex ante welfare, then the countries would have an incentive to adopt commitment devices to make sure they do not trade when they are tempted to do so after conflict is resolved. For countries, the simplest commitment device is the legal restriction of trading, a historically very common practice.

U_c can exceed V_t only if the number of warriors under pure conflict is sufficiently smaller than under conflict with trade. Figure 5-1 reports typical simulation results with $N=10$ countries, $L_i=\lambda_i=\omega_i=1$, $\alpha=.1$, and for different level of conflict effectiveness m. The top panel plots the ratio w_c/w_t against the secure fraction of land owned by each country τ. (Since there are ten countries, $\tau=.1$ implies perfect land security.) Note that this ratio is lowest for

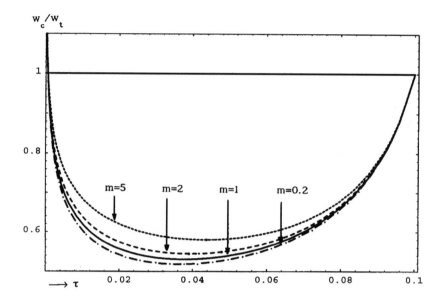

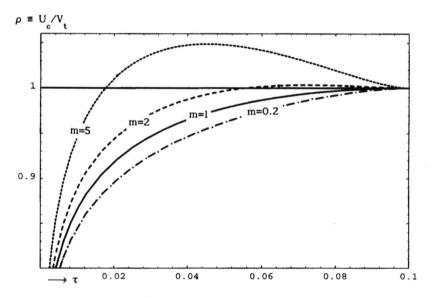

Figure 5-1.

intermediate levels of land security. The bottom panel clearly shows that the ratio $\rho \equiv U_c/V_t$ is higher than 1, and therefore conflict without trade is ex ante preferable by all countries, when land is sufficiently secure and the CSF is sufficiently effective (m is high). In fact, there is a neighborhood around $\tau=0.1=1/N$ (which is not clearly visible in the picture when m is low) for which $\rho > 1$.

To establish this last property more generally, first note that when all land is secure ($\tau=1/N$) there is obviously no point in allocating any manpower for war, and consequently in such a case we have $l_c=l_t=L$. But, since all countries are identical and there is no land to be contested under $\tau=1/N$, there is no scope for trade and therefore we have $U_c=V_t$ with $\rho=1$. It can also be shown that $\lim_{\tau\to1/N}\rho=1$. Next, differentiating ρ with respect to τ and taking limits leads to

$$\lim_{\tau\to1/N}\left(\frac{\partial\rho}{\partial\tau}\right)=-\frac{(1-\alpha)\,(N-2)N}{2}$$

(5-22)

Since ρ approaches unity as τ converges to $1/N$, it is now clear from Eq. (5-22) that pure conflict will dominate competitive trade and conflict in the neighborhood of near perfect land security if the number of countries N is larger than 2. Of course, as Figure 5-1 indicates, especially in the case of high effectiveness of the CSF, that neighborhood can be really large including ranges with low overall levels of land security.

The fact that we need at least three countries to generate this welfare superiority of pure conflict under symmetry is also helpful in understanding its occurrence. As it appears from Eq. (5-20) and its discussion, the marginal benefit of an extra warrior is more likely to be higher for the case of trade with conflict when N is high enough and land is more secure. Possessing some secure land means that a country's payoff in the event of a loss under pure conflict will not be zero; that is, in the case of a loss there will still be some land to combine with labor in order to produce corn. The more land is secure, the smaller is the difference between the payoffs in the event of a loss and in the event of a win. Also, still under pure conflict (and thus in the absence of trade), the more countries there are, the more difficult it becomes to win. Overall, under pure conflict more land security and a greater number of countries severely reduce the equilibrium number of warriors. Under conflict with trade, however, there is an opposite effect from a greater number of countries: The winner of the contested land will receive all the competitive returns from that land and the greater N is, the greater those returns will be. In other words, the payoff in the event of a win is higher under conflict with trade than under pure conflict, whereas the payoff in the event of a loss is the same. And the greater is the number of countries, the greater is the difference between these two payoffs. Hence, the equilibrium number of warriors under conflict with trade can be so much higher than that under pure conflict so as to outweigh, in terms of overall welfare, the gains from trade.

4   When countries differ

Thus far we have confined our analysis to ex ante identical countries. Asymmetries and the scope for trade emerged only after conflict had been resolved with the winner possessing more land than the losers. We now study the role of three types of asymmetries that may exist between countries: (1) differences in the productivity of warriors; (2) asymmetric distributions of secure land; and (3) differential endowments of primary labor. In addition to more predictable effects, we find how the last two types of asymmetries can lead one country to prefer pure conflict to conflict with trade and thus create paths – other than the one we found in the previous section – for trade restrictions. Because no new insights can be gained from continuing to consider many countries, hereafter we only consider interactions between two countries.

Differences in warrior productivities

Two well-armed British ships were enough to dispose of the Chinese fleet during the Opium War (1841–42), and earlier in the eighteenth century a band of British traders effectively dissolved the formerly great Mogul Empire of India. And from the Macedonians under Alexander the Great, to the Zulu under Shaka at the beginning of the previous century, to the more recent war in the Persian Gulf, technological superiority in fighting capabilities appears to have been a fundamental determinant of outcomes under conflict.

We capture technological superiority or higher warrior productivity with the parameters ω_i in Eq. (5-9), reproduced below for convenience

$$L_i \equiv l_i + w_i/\omega_i \qquad (5\text{-}9)$$

From each unit of primary labor L_i, a higher ω_i delivers a larger number of effective warrior units w_i. (That is, the actual number of warriors is w_i/ω_i.)

Figure 5-2 depicts a typical outcome of simulations where ω_1 varies in value (the other parameters take the following values: $m=L_i=\omega_2=1$, $\tau_i=.1$, and $\alpha=\frac{1}{2}$). The top panel shows the equilibrium number of effective warriors for the two countries. As expected, the country with better warriors has a greater number of effective warriors and thus a higher probability of winning. A key observation is that when there are large differences in warrior productivities, the number of effective warriors of each country and therefore the total number of effective warriors are lower than when warrior productivities are similar in the two countries. It appears when differences are large, the country with

Effective
Warriors

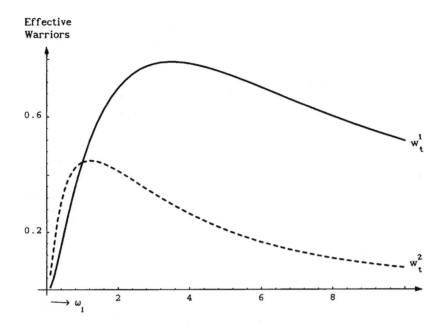

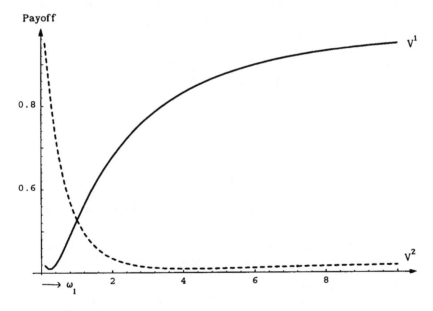

Figure 5-2.

the much less effective warriors sees that the contest for land is lopsided and decides to conserve more of its manpower for labor that, with high probability, will be employed by their opponent after conflict is resolved. The country with the more effective warriors can also relax and need fewer effective warriors and still maintain a high probability of winning. In fact, for $\omega_1>1$ country 1 also has a smaller absolute number of warriors than its opponent and therefore a larger number of productive laborers. (This last property is not shown but can inferred from the figure.)

The bottom panel of Figure 5-2 depicts the equilibrium payoffs. At very low values of ω_1, technological breakthroughs that raise ω_1 can reduce country 1's welfare, a clear instance of "immiserizing" growth as both countries devote more manpower to warriors.[13] As country 1's technological advantage continues to improve relative to that of country 2, however, its payoff increases at a declining rate. The technological laggard (i.e., country 2) initially observes a decline in its payoff but eventually, as both countries allocate more of their initial labor into useful production, its payoff increases as well.

Asymmetries in the security of land and manpower

We shall examine these last two asymmetries by letting the effectiveness of conflict parameter m and the efficiency coefficients ω_i equal unity. Then it is tedious but straightforward to derive the following equilibrium number of warriors under trade with conflict:

$$w_t^i = \frac{\alpha\tau_0\{\alpha[2(1-\alpha) + \alpha\tau_0]L_i + 2(1-\alpha)\,(1-\alpha\tau_i)\,[L_1+L_2]\}}{[2(1-\alpha) + \alpha\tau_0]\,[4(1-\alpha) + (2-\alpha)\alpha\tau_0]} \qquad i = 1,2 \qquad (5\text{-}23)$$

Utilizing Eq. (5-23), we also find

$$w_t^1 + w_t^2 = \frac{\alpha(L_1+L_2)\tau_0}{2(1-\alpha) + \alpha\tau_0} \qquad\qquad (5\text{-}24)$$

which suggests that the aggregate number of warriors observed in equilibrium is positively related to the worldwide quantity of primary labor L_1+L_2, the degree of insecurity in land ownership τ_0, and the elasticity of corn production

---

[13] Kennedy (1989, Chapter 2), apparently agreeing with other historians, attributes the intensification of warfare in Europe during the sixteenth and seventeenth centuries to the continuous technological improvements in warfare that were taking place at the time. The ever increasing war expenditures drove many of the contenders to repeated bankruptcies (Spain, France, German principalities) and led Spain to relative, if not absolute, economic decline. It should be noted that the immiserizing growth effect does not appear in our model without asymmetries, at least under the functional form in Eq. (5-4). Therefore, the intensification of warfare due to technological change noted by Kennedy is reproduced for limited parameter values (for $\omega_1<1$), and thus it does not have to be a universal phenomenon.

with respect to land α. Partial differentiation of Eq. (5-23) indicates that these conclusions also apply to each country's equilibrium number of warriors. Furthermore, an increase in a country's proportion of secure land reduces the number of warriors chosen by the country because it raises the marginal productivity of labor in corn production, which causes the opportunity cost of a warrior to increase. Finally, increases in a country's endowment of primary labor L_i raise the country's marginal benefit from building up its army more than it raises its opportunity cost, which in turn boosts its incentive to have additional warriors. Equations (5-23) and (5-24) also imply that

(1)　　If $L_1 = L_2$, then $w_t^1 > w_t^2$ iff $\tau_1 < \tau_2$

(2)　　If $\tau_1 = \tau_2$, then $w_t^1 > w_t^2$ iff $L_1 > L_2$

In equilibrium, world output of corn is given by

$$V_t^1 + V_t^2 = T^\alpha \, (l_t^1 + l_t^2)^{1-\alpha} = T^\alpha \left[\frac{2(1-\alpha) \, (L_1 + L_2)}{2(1-\alpha) + \alpha \tau_0} \right]^{1-\alpha} \tag{5-25}$$

which, as expected from Eq. (5-24), does not depend either on the distribution of primary labor or on the distribution of secure land across countries. Of course, the division of corn between countries *does* depend on the worldwide allocation of primary labor and secure land. Keeping $L_1 + L_2$ and τ_0 constant, straightforward algebra establishes that

(1)　　$\partial V_t^i / \partial \tau_i = - \partial V_t^j / \partial \tau_i > 0$ 　　for $i \neq j = 1,2$

(2)　　$\partial V_t^i / \partial L_i = - \partial V_t^j / \partial L_i > 0$ 　　for $i \neq j = 1,2$

Though we do not investigate how equilibrium quantities depend on endowments of primary labor and secure land in the case of pure conflict, the relationships are qualitatively similar to those we have established under trade with conflict for similar parameter values.

We do examine next, however, whether the presence of asymmetries can render pure conflict more desirable for at least one of the countries. First suppose that countries are identical in their endowments of primary labor (i.e., $L_1 = L_2$) and consider possible differences in the fractions of secure land they possess (α is set equal to $\frac{1}{2}$). Figure 5-3 shows how the degree of insecurity τ_0 and the distribution of secure land between the two countries determine their preferences over pure conflict and trade with conflict.

The fraction of contested land is reduced as we consider (τ_1, τ_2) pairs in the northeastern direction. For example, any distribution of (τ_1, τ_2) pairs along the straight line going through points (1,0) and (0,1) in Figure 5-3 is consistent with perfect security of land. Since each country's incentive to have additional warriors falls with increases in the degree of security of land, the equilibri-

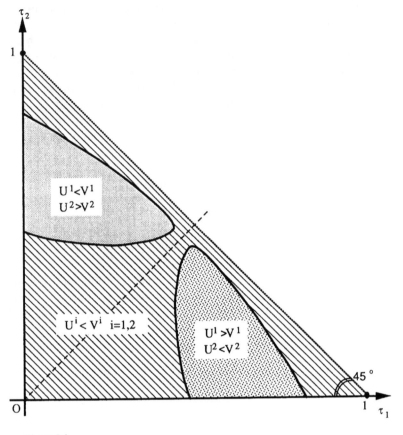

Figure 5-3.

um numbers of warriors decreases under either regime as we move down the direction of the 45° line.

There are roughly three configurations that make trade with conflict ex ante preferable by both countries: (1) when all land is nearly secure; (2) when all land is nearly insecure; or (3) when the distribution of secure land is nearly symmetric. But when the distribution of secure land is asymmetric and the degree of security is in an intermediate range, one country will ex ante prefer pure conflict to conflict with trade. The country with such preference is the one with the greater proportion of secure land; because of its relatively large holdings of land and the implied greater ability to be self-sufficient, that coun-

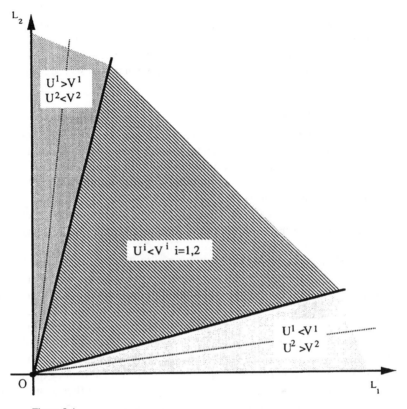

Figure 5-4.

try apparently finds the benefits of trade outweighed by the costs that the expectation of trade brings.

Figure 5-4 illustrates how payoff outcomes compare when countries differ in their primary labor endowments, under the assumption that $\tau_1=\tau_2=.1$ and $\alpha=\frac{1}{2}$. The areas between the dotted straight lines and the closest axis in the figure, identify pairs of L_1 and L_2 endowments that would induce the smallest of the two countries to allocate all its primary labor towards its army under trade with conflict. No country specializes completely in the production of warriors under pure conflict [this is, however, a consequence of the fact that the winning probability is assumed to satisfy Eq. (5-4)]. Principally because the relatively smaller country allocates larger quantities of its manpower into building arms when the possibility of trade exists than when it does not, a country will prefer pure conflict over competitive trade with conflict only when it is sufficiently larger than its rival. The existence of benefits from trade allow the smaller country to shift more manpower into warriors, a situation that is not as desirable when the country must rely on its own production of corn when trade is absent. Alternatively, with trade, the smaller country tends to specialize more in that activity that protects its (relatively abundant) secure land.

5   Concluding comments

Motivated by the historical link between trade and conflict, we examined a model which, contrary to traditional trade models, can accommodate the presence of arming, conflict, and trading. Arming, despite its resource cost, is undertaken to improve each country's likelihood of winning a disputed territory through conflict. Once conflict is resolved and the winner takes control of the disputed territory, however, all countries can engage in ordinary competitive trade. Whether the countries expect to engage in trade can have significant effects on welfare.

Initially, our own expectation was that the prospects for trade would reduce the incentives to arm, an expectation temporarily confirmed in the benchmark symmetric two-country model. But with more than two countries and some secure land, we found that arming could be higher when trade is expected than when it is not. In such a case, the prospects for trade make the reward to the winner of conflict much higher than that without trade, so that it outweighs the lower effectiveness of expected shares under trade. And arming when trade is expected can be so much higher than arming when trade is not expected that ex ante at least one country can prefer the regime of conflict without trade. Since once conflict is resolved there is always an incentive to trade, the only way such a preference can be realized is through a commitment not to trade, which is moreover clearly and convincingly communicated to all other countries (so that there can be no doubt about what will occur in the future).

One clear way of committing not to trade is simply to have enforceable legal restrictions on trade. Such restrictions, prevalent today and even more prevalent in the past, are usually attributed to strategic trade policies or to the pressures of import-competing groups. Our results suggest another channel for the imposition of trade restrictions that could be present when ownership of one or more resources is in dispute. In turn, disputed resources are more common in an anarchic international system or, if we interpret our model to apply within a single country, in countries with little or no legality and absolutist, authoritarian traditions.

References

Braudel, Fernand, *The Mediterranean and the Mediterranean World in the Age of Phillip II,* Vols. I and II, 1972, New York: Harper & Row.

Chaudhuri, K. N., *Trade and Civilisation in the Indian Ocean: An Economic History from the Rise of Islam to 1750,* 1985, New York: Cambridge University Press.

Garfinkel, Michelle R., "Arming as a Strategic Investment in a Cooperative Equilibrium," *American Economic Review,* March 1990, 80, 50–68.

Grossman, Herschel, "A General Equilibrium Model of Insurrections," *American Economic Review,* September 1991, 81, 912–21.

Grossman, Herschel, "Production, Appropriation, and Land Reform," *American Economic Review,* June 1994, 84, 705–12.

Hirshleifer, Jack, "The Analytics of Continuing Conflict," *Synthese,* August 1988, 76, 201–33.

Hirshleifer, Jack, "The Paradox of Power," *Economics and Politics,* November 1991, 3, 177–200.

Kennedy, Paul, *The Rise and Fall of the Great Powers: Economic Change and Military Conflict from 1500 to 2000,* 1989, New York: Vintage Books.

Obolensky, Dimitri, *The Byzantine Commonwealth,* 1971, New York: Praeger Publishers.

Polachek, Solomon W., "Conflict and Trade," *Journal of Conflict Resolution,* March 1980, 24, 55–78.

Skaperdas, Stergios, "Cooperation, Conflict, and Power in the Absence of Property Rights," *American Economic Review,* September 1992, 82, 720–39.

Skaperdas, Stergios, "Contest Success Functions," 1995, forthcoming in *Economic Theory.*

Skaperdas, Stergios and Constantinos Syropoulos, "Competing for Claims to Property," mimeo, February 1994.

CHAPTER 6

Increasing returns to politics in developing countries with endogenous protection in a fixed-factor model

Nakgyoon Choi
Korea Institute for Economics and Trade
Stephen P. Magee
The University of Texas at Austin

1   Introduction

This paper examines the perennial political conflict between landowners and manufacturers in developing countries. Our theory predicts that only one of them wins in the long run. The Magee and Young (1983) theorem states that rates of return to any factor of production increase with a country's endowment of that factor in a Heckscher-Ohlin-Samuelson model of endogenous protection. Magee, Brock, and Young (1989)[1] showed the conditions under which the result holds for both Leontief and Cobb-Douglas production in long-run models for advanced countries.

This paper extends Choi (1991) to explore whether increasing returns occur in a very different model, the Findlay-Wellisz fixed-factor model of endogenous protection for developing countries. The interesting economic issue is whether a politically induced price effect from more capital in an economy more than offsets the diminishing returns from more capital. The issue is analytically difficult, so simulations are required.

Consider a developing country with manufacturing imports and agricultural exports with Leontief production and logit probability of election functions. If the increasing returns result holds in developing countries, it should work as follows. If the capital endowment of the country increases, the capital lobby will channel more capital to the procapital party. This increases both the probability of election of the procapital party and the vote-maximizing tariff level that it supports on manufactured imports. The sum of these two effects raises the expected domestic price of the importable good. This politically induced price effect more than offsets the diminishing returns caused by more capital in the economy, yielding increasing returns to country factor endowments.

---

[1] The result was first advanced in Magee and Young (1983); it was proved with Cobb-Douglas production and logit probability of election functions in Young and Magee (1986); and it was elaborated and extended in Magee, Brock, and Young (1989).

Rate of Return

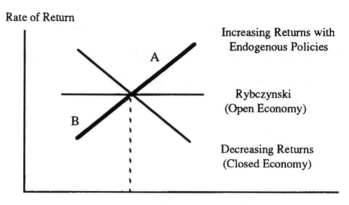

Increasing Returns with
Endogenous Policies

A

Rybczynski
(Open Economy)

B

Decreasing Returns
(Closed Economy)

Country Endowment of Capital to Land

Figure 6-1.

Figure 6-1 shows how the increasing returns result contrasts with the two usual economic cases. First, in a closed economy, exogenous additions of more capital per acre of land cause the rate of return to capital to fall because of diminishing returns. Second, the Rybczynski theorem predicts that in a small open country with no factor flows, factor returns will be independent of factor endowment ratios because of factor price equalization.

The increasing returns result is consistent with several puzzles in the economic development literature, and may help explain one or more of them. First, the implied instability of country factor endowments is consistent with the old literature on big bang theories of economic development, such as Rostow's (1960) "take-off" theory. That is, endogenous politics will induce countries that pass a certain critical level of capital accumulation to attract even more. And countries with little capital grow slowly. Rogowski (1988) suggests that labor-intensive manufacturing will be attracted to countries that already have an abundance of well educated labor. In a labor-land economy, that would correspond to a region such as A in Figure 6-1. There, labor lobbies the political system for public education, research and development, manufacturing production subsidies, etc. so that the more human capital a country has, the more it will accumulate.

Second, Mankiw, Romer, and Weil (1992) chronicle the difficulty researchers have experienced in demonstrating that developing countries are "converging" on the advanced countries. The increasing returns result predicts that convergence should not occur. This contrasts with the predictions of a neo-classical Solow (1956) growth model, in which the growth rates should be higher for low-income countries. In contrast, increasing returns suggests that poor countries with little capital will have their political systems dominated by land owners (Latin America) or labor (India). The resulting anticapital policies will hinder the growth of manufacturing and hamper economic development.

Third, Mankiw, Romer, and Weil (1992) report that observed differentials in real interest rates across countries appear smaller than the predicted differences. Again, increasing returns to politics is consistent with this anomaly. Increasing returns predicts that rates of return in poor countries should be lower than expected and the reverse in rich countries.

Fourth, Magee and Magee (1994) point out that the absence of a middle class of countries in the world is consistent with the unstable endowments prediction of increasing returns. The elaborate legal protection of intellectual property, legal protection of physical property, and government subsidies to education illustrate how countries with greater endowments of human capital reap increasing public protection for human capital investments. In fact, the increasing returns result is a potential explanation of economic development itself. It implies that developing countries with higher-than-world-average endowments of capital will experience rapid industrialization and above-average growth. In contrast, developing countries with higher-than-world-average endowments of land will experience slower industrialization and below-average growth.

Fifth, Rauch (1989) reports an interesting effect that parallels ours in the economic development literature. He shows that per-capita consumption growth should be lower in countries with higher endowments of land per capita using a Lucas-Uzawa model. The result suggests that any attempt to quantify the effects of initial country factor endowments on growth require careful separation of the economic and the political components.

Despite these anomalies that increasing returns might explain, it is not obvious that increasing returns will arise in the Findlay-Wellisz (1982) model to explain international trade in developing countries. First, Findlay-Wellisz is very different from the Heckscher-Ohlin-Samuelson model. It implies that lobbying for short-run protection will occur along industry lines (manufacturing versus agriculture), while Magee, Brock, and Young find that lobbying for long-run protection will occur along factor lines (capital versus labor), following Stolper-Samuelson.[2] Second, in the Findlay-Wellisz model, political party and voter behavior are not explicitly modeled. Rather, Findlay-Wellisz assume a reduced-form equation specifying that any increase in lobbying resources by a lobby will cause the political system to increase the policy favored by that lobby.

---

[2] There is anecdotal evidence in the United States that such short-run protection is done by industry. Magee (1980) showed that there was also industry-specific lobbying over these trade bills in Congress. But it is true that more encompassing organizations also lobbied for those bills along factor lines. Large business groups such as the National Association of Manufactures were for freer trade while the largest labor unions were generally protectionist. Finally, cross-national estimates of endogenous protection, capturing essentially long-run effects, find evidence of Stolper-Samuelson-type lobbying along factor lines.

The goal of this paper is to explore whether increasing returns can occur in the Findlay-Wellisz fixed-factor model of endogenous protection for developing countries. The results indicate an empirically plausible case in which the increasing returns result does hold. Young (1982) finds that the equilibrium of the Findlay-Wellisz model depends on the choice of the numeraire. He provides calculations showing that the lobbying equilibrium need not be unique. A second question that this paper explores is whether the lobbying equilibrium is unique.

In what follows, we set up the model in Section 2. We solve the model in Section 3 using specific values for the key parameters and develop the results in Section 4.

2   The model

Although the solutions are difficult, the basic idea in this paper is simple. We attempt to perform comparative statics on the Ricardo-Viner model of Findlay and Wellisz (1982). We follow the assumptions that a small country produces two goods (manufactures and food) and that it has two fixed factors of production (capital and land) and one mobile factor (labor). We assume that the production functions are Cobb-Douglas with constant returns to scale:

$$M = K^\alpha L_M^{1-\alpha} \tag{6-1}$$

$$F = T^\beta L_F^{1-\beta} \tag{6-2}$$

where M, T are the outputs of manufactures and food. K, L, and T are fixed supplies of capital, labor, and land. L_M and L_F are labors allocated to manufactures and food.

With a suitable choice of units, the unit cost functions of the two industries can be written in Cobb-Douglas form:

$$C_M(r,w) = r^\alpha w^{1-\alpha} \tag{6-3}$$

$$C_F(z,w) = z^\beta w^{1-\beta} \tag{6-4}$$

where r, w, z represent rental rate on K, the real wage of L, and rental per unit of land T, respectively. The numeraire is the manufactured good. If the domestic price of food in terms of manufactures is q, then the wage and rental rates are determined by the conditions for equilibrium in the two industries:

$$1 = r^\alpha w^{1-\alpha} = b^1(\omega) \tag{6-5}$$

$$q = z^\beta w^{1-\beta} = b^2(\omega) \tag{6-6}$$

where ω represents the vector of factor prices, such as r, w, z; $b^i(\omega)$, represents the unit cost function.

The system of equations is comprised of two equations with three unknowns. The system is underdetermined and cannot be solved without additional information, namely, the factor market equilibrium conditions.[3] The factor market equilibrium requires:

$$a_{11}(\omega)\, M + a_{21}(\omega)\, F = K$$

$$a_{12}(\omega)\, M + a_{22}(\omega)\, F = L_a$$

$$a_{13}(\omega)\, M + a_{23}(\omega)\, F = T$$

where $a_{ij}(\omega)$ represents the factor intensity such that $\partial b^i(\omega)\,/\,\partial \omega_j = a_{ij}$; L_a is the total available labor allocated to the production of manufactures and food. If the factor K is specific to the production of manufactures and factor T is specific to the production of food, then the Ricardo-Viner assumptions require that $a_{21} = 0$ and $a_{13} = 0$. So we note the factor market equilibrium conditions as follows:

$$\alpha\, r^{\alpha-1} w^{1-\alpha}\, M = K \tag{6-7}$$

$$(1-\alpha)\, r^{\alpha} w^{-\alpha}\, M + (1-\beta)\, z^{\beta} w^{-\beta}\, F = L_a \tag{6-8}$$

$$\beta\, z^{\beta-1} w^{1-\beta}\, F = T \tag{6-9}$$

We use the system of Eqs. (6-5), (6-6), (6-7), (6-8), and (6-9) to solve for the factor prices and production of the two goods. Then there are five unknown variables (r, w, z, M, and F) and five equations.

In the case of an equation for r, we transform the equations as follows:

From Eq. (6-5)

$$r^{\alpha} = w^{-(1-\alpha)}$$

$$r = w^{-(1-\alpha)/\alpha} \tag{6-10}$$

From Eq. (6-6)

$$z^{\beta} = q w^{-(1-\beta)}$$

$$z = q^{1/\beta} w^{-(1-\beta)/\beta} \tag{6-11}$$

Inserting Eq. (6-10) into Eq. (6-7), we will get

$$M = \frac{K}{\alpha}\, r^{1-\alpha} w^{-(1-\alpha)} = \frac{K}{\alpha}\, w^{-(1-\alpha)^2/\alpha} w^{-(1-\alpha)} = \frac{K}{\alpha}\, w^{-(1-\alpha)/\alpha} \tag{6-12}$$

Inserting Eq. (6-10) into Eq. (6-9), we will get

---

[3] Young (1988).

$$F = \frac{T}{\beta} w^{-(1-\beta)} z^{(1-\beta)} = \frac{T}{\beta} w^{-(1-\beta)} q^{(1-\beta)/\beta} w^{-(1-\beta)^2/\beta} = \frac{T}{\beta} q^{(1-\beta)/\beta} w^{-(1-\beta)/\beta}$$

(6-13)

Inserting Eqs. (6-10), (6-11), (6-12), and (6-13) into Eq. (6-9), we will get

$$(1-\alpha) w^{-(1-\alpha)} w - \alpha \frac{K}{\alpha} w^{-(1-\alpha)/\alpha} + (1-\beta) qw^{-(1-\beta)} w^{-\beta} \frac{T}{\beta} q^{(1-\beta)/\beta} w^{-(1-\beta)\beta} - L_a = 0$$

(6-14)

Collecting terms, we get

$$H (w; K, T, L_a, q) = \frac{K(1-\alpha)}{\alpha} w^{-1/\alpha} + \frac{T(1-\beta)}{\beta} q^{1/\beta} w^{-1/\beta} - L_a = 0$$

(6-15)

We note that the factor prices depend on the relative goods price q and the factor endowments K, T, and L. We express the preceding nonlinear functions in the following functions:

$$r = r (K, T, L_a, q)$$
$$z = z (K, T, L_a, q)$$
$$w = w (K, T, L_a, q)$$

We assume that the tariff rate is determined as a function of the lobbying funds by the two interest groups, manufacturing industry and food industry. We assume for convenience that labor is the only lobbying input by both industries. Then

$$t = t (L_{PM}, L_{PF})$$

(6-16)

Since the tariff raises the domestic price of food, more labor lobbying for the food industry L_{PF} will increase the tariff rate, while the reverse is true for labor lobbying for manufacturing L_{PM}.

The domestic relative price of food q is expressed in the international terms of trade as follows:

$$q = p (1 + t)$$

(6-17)

where p is the international terms of trade, and t is the tariff rate on food imports determined by the political process as influenced by the interest groups. We may express the domestic relative price by the relative lobbying funds as follows:

$$q = p \left[\frac{L_{PF}}{L_{PM}} \right]^\varepsilon$$

(6-18)

As this equation shows, the domestic price is an increasing function of the lobbying funds by the food industry and a decreasing function of the lobbying funds by the manufacturing industry.

The labor market clearing condition is

$$L = L_M + L_F + L_{PM} + L_{PF} = L_a + L_p \tag{6-19}$$

where L_a represents the labor available in the economy for the production; in short, we call it production labor. L_p represents the labor available for the lobbying activities called political labor. We assume that labor is mobile between the production sectors; that is, we assume that the labor available for production L_a is not a specific factor, but a mobile factor. We implicitly assume, however, that the production labor does not move into the political sector in our short-run model, as we will explain later.

Even if we specify the special functional form of Cobb-Douglas, it would be almost impossible to get closed form solutions. Findlay and Wellisz (1982) consider how lobbying affects the rents on land and capital. For example, the farmers act collectively in taking into account the effect of their lobbying on the price of land. Both factors set up and maximize functions for the net benefits from engaging in the political process.[4] This approach leads to rather complicated first-order conditions for a Cournot-Nash equilibrium of lobbying. Simpler conditions can be obtained if we assume that each faction maximizes revenue net of wages.[5] This objective function is identical to that of Findlay and Wellisz when there are constant returns to scale in production. Let $R^F(q,\omega)$ and $R^M(\omega)$ be the net revenue from production of farmers and manufacturers when ω is the vector of the factor prices. Then

$$R^F(q,\omega) = qF(q,\omega) - wL_F(q,\omega),$$

$$R^M(\omega) = M(\omega) - wL_M(\omega)$$

where $L_F(q,\omega)$ and $L_M(\omega)$ are the derived demand functions for farm and manufacturing labor.

$$\frac{\partial R^F}{\partial L_F} = \frac{\partial}{\partial L_F}[qF - wL_F] = \frac{\partial}{\partial L_F}[qT^\beta L_F^{1-\beta} - wL_F] = (1-\beta)\,qT^\beta L_F^{-\beta} - w = 0$$

Then

$$L_F = (1-\beta)^{1/\beta}\,Tq^{1/\beta}\,w^{-1/\beta} \tag{6-20}$$

Inserting this into the food production function, we will get the following unconditional production function.

---

[4] Findlay and Wellisz (1982, p. 228).
[5] Young (1982, p. 239).

$$F = (1-\beta)^{(1-\beta)/\beta} \, Tq^{(1-\beta)/\beta} \, w^{-(1-\beta)/\beta}. \tag{6-21}$$

We may check the following Hotelling's lemma:

$$\frac{\partial R^F}{\partial w} = \frac{\partial}{\partial w}\,[qF - wL_F] = \frac{\partial}{\partial w}\,[q(1-\beta)^{(1-\beta)/\beta}Tq^{(1-\beta)/\beta}\,w^{-(1-\beta)/\beta} - wL_F]$$

$$= (1-\beta)^{(1-\beta)/\beta}\,Tq^{1/\beta}\,w^{-1/\beta} - (1-\beta)^{1/\beta}\,Tq^{1/\beta}w^{-1/\beta} - L_F\,(q,\omega)$$

$$= -\,L_F\,(q,\omega)$$

In the same way, we may check the following properties:

$$\frac{\partial R^M}{\partial w} = -L_M\,(q,\omega), \quad \frac{\partial R^F}{\partial q} = F\,(q,\omega)$$

We also get the following

$$L_M = (1-\alpha)^{1/\alpha}\,Kw^{-1/\alpha}$$

Farmers take as given the lobbying level L_{PM} of manufacturers and choose lobbying L_{PF} to maximize production profits net of lobbyists' wages:

$$\text{Max } R^F\,(q,\omega) - w\,L_{PF}$$

The first-order condition is

$$\frac{\partial R^F}{\partial q}\,\frac{\partial q}{\partial L_{PF}} + \left[\frac{\partial R^F}{\partial w} - L_{PF}\right]\left[\frac{\partial w}{\partial L_{PF}} + \frac{\partial w}{\partial q}\,\frac{\partial q}{\partial L_{PF}}\right] - w = 0$$

Using the dual relations,[6] this reduces to

$$F\,\frac{\partial q}{\partial L_{PF}} - w - [L_F + L_{PF}]\left[\frac{\partial w}{\partial L_{PF}} + \frac{\partial w}{\partial q}\,\frac{\partial q}{\partial L_{PF}}\right] = 0 \tag{6-22}$$

Or

$$F\,\frac{\partial q}{\partial L_{PF}} = w + [L_F + L_{PF}]\left[\frac{\partial w}{\partial L_{PF}} + \frac{\partial w}{\partial q}\,\frac{\partial q}{\partial L_{PF}}\right]$$

The left hand side gives the effect on the revenue from food sales of the marginal change in domestic price from additional lobbying. The right-hand side gives the marginal rise in wage costs from additional lobbying. This equals the wage of the marginal lobbyist plus the effect on the total wage bill of the wage increase resulting from lobbying. This wage increase is the result of (1) the increased demand for lobbyists and (2) the increased demand for farm labor as a result of the induced rise in food prices.[7]

[6] Young (1982) showed two dual relations, Eqs. (6-22) and (6-26).
[7] Young (1982, p. 240).

The explicit form of $\partial w/\partial L_{PF}$ can be obtained using the nonlinear implicit functions $H(w;)$ because $\partial w/\partial L_{PF}$ can be solved using the implicit function theorem. Then

$$\frac{\partial w}{\partial L_{PF}} = -\frac{\partial H/\partial L_{PF}}{\partial H/\partial w}$$

$$= -\frac{1}{\dfrac{K(1-\alpha)}{\alpha^2}w^{-(\alpha+1)/\alpha} + \dfrac{T(1-\beta)}{\beta^2}q^{1/\beta}w^{-(\beta+1)/\beta}} \tag{6-23}$$

And

$$\frac{\partial w}{\partial q} = -\frac{\partial H/\partial q}{\partial H/\partial w}$$

$$= -\frac{\dfrac{T(1-\beta)}{\beta^2}w^{-1/\beta}q^{(1-\beta)/\beta}}{\dfrac{K(1-\alpha)}{\alpha^2}w^{-(\alpha+1)/\alpha} + \dfrac{T(1-\beta)}{\beta^2}q^{1/\beta}w^{-(\beta+1)/\beta}} \tag{6-24}$$

Then the first-order condition, Eq. (6-22) will be

$$(1-\beta)^{(1-\beta)/\beta}Tq^{(1-\beta)/\beta}w^{-(1-\beta)/\beta}\varepsilon p\frac{1}{L_{PM}}\left[\frac{L_{PF}}{L_{PM}}\right]^{\varepsilon-1} - w - [L_{PF} + (1-\beta)^{1/\beta}Tq^{1/\beta}w^{-1/\beta}]$$

$$\cdot\left[\frac{-1 + \varepsilon p\dfrac{1}{L_{PM}}\left[\dfrac{L_{PF}}{L_{PM}}\right]^{\varepsilon-1}\dfrac{T(1-\beta)}{\beta^2}q^{(1-\beta)/\beta}w^{-1/\beta}}{\dfrac{K(1-\alpha)}{\alpha^2}w^{-(\alpha+1)/\alpha} + \dfrac{T(1-\beta)}{\beta^2}q^{1/\beta}w^{-(\beta+1)/\beta}}\right] = 0 \tag{6-25}$$

Manufacturers take as given the lobbying L_{PF} of food industry and choose lobbying L_{PM} to maximize production profits net of lobbyists' wages:

$$\text{Max } R^M(\omega) - wL_{PM}$$

which yields the first-order condition

$$- w - [L_M + L_{PM}]\left[\frac{\partial w}{\partial L_{PM}} + \frac{\partial w}{\partial q}\frac{\partial q}{\partial L_{PM}}\right] = 0 \tag{6-26}$$

The interpretation of Eq. (6-26) is similar to that of (6-22). When we use Eqs. (6-23) and (6-24) we get

$$- w - [L_{PM} + (1-\alpha)^{1/\alpha} K w^{-1/\alpha}]$$

$$\cdot \left[\frac{-1 - \varepsilon p \dfrac{L_{PF}}{L_{PM}^2} \left[\dfrac{L_{PF}}{L_{PM}} \right]^{\varepsilon-1} \dfrac{T(1-\beta)}{\beta^2} q^{(1-\beta)/\beta} w^{-1/\beta}}{\dfrac{K(1-\alpha)}{\alpha^2} w^{-(\alpha+1)/\alpha} + \dfrac{T(1-\beta)}{\beta^2} q^{1/\beta} w^{-(\beta+1)/\beta}} \right] = 0 \tag{6-27}$$

Consider the signs of the first derivatives. Let

$$\psi(q, w, \varepsilon, L_{PF}, L_{PM}) = \left[\frac{-1 + \varepsilon p \dfrac{1}{L_{PM}} \left[\dfrac{L_{PF}}{L_{PM}} \right]^{\varepsilon-1} \dfrac{T(1-\beta)}{\beta^2} q^{(1-\beta)/\beta} w^{-1/\beta}}{\dfrac{K(1-\alpha)}{\alpha^2} w^{-(\alpha+1)/\alpha} + \dfrac{T(1-\beta)}{\beta^2} q^{1/\beta} w^{-(\beta+1)/\beta}} \right]$$

$$\equiv \frac{-1+C}{A+B}$$

where

$$A = \frac{K(1-\alpha)}{\alpha^2} w^{-(\alpha+1)/\alpha}, \quad B = \frac{T(1-\beta)}{\beta^2} q^{1/\beta} w^{-(\beta+1)/\beta}$$

$$C = \varepsilon p \frac{1}{L_{PM}} \left[\frac{L_{PF}}{L_{PM}} \right]^{\varepsilon-1} \frac{T(1-\beta)}{\beta^2} q^{(1-\beta)/\beta} w^{-1/\beta}$$

We may assume the following:

$$\frac{\partial \psi}{\partial q} = \frac{C'(A+B) - (-1+C)B'}{(A+B)^2} > 0$$

which is positive when $B'(C-1) < C'(A+B)$.

3   Solutions

Generally, we cannot obtain the analytical solutions for the system of nonlinear equations. We cannot get the effects of comparative static changes on the actions of the individual players and on the equilibrium of the game using the first-order conditions derived in the last section. So we obtain our results for some plausible values of the parameters. Consider $\alpha = \beta = \varepsilon = .5$ and $p = 1$ (we generalize these results in a subsequent draft). We are being conservative here in testing for increasing returns because a value of $\varepsilon = .5$ is low for the elasticity of domestic prices with respect to relative lobbying resources. A low value for the elasticity of product prices with respect to relative lobbying resources biases the results against increasing returns. Recall that Young and Magee (1986) found that increasing returns holds no matter how low the value of this elasticity. From Eq. (6-15), we can write

$$Kw^{-2} + T \left[\frac{L_{PF}}{L_{PM}} \right] w^{-2} - L_a = 0$$

yielding

$$w = L_a^{-1/2} \left[K + T \left[\frac{L_{PF}}{L_{PM}} \right] \right]^{1/2}$$

The problem is further simplified by assuming that

$$\frac{\partial L_a}{\partial L_{PF}} = \frac{\partial L_a}{\partial L_{PM}} = 0$$

This means that labor for political lobbying does not move into the production sector in the short run. Namely, labor for political lobbying has no opportunity cost in terms of production labor. This assumption means that lobbying activities will not affect each industry's determination of labor employment directly, but they will affect the tariff rate, and thus the domestic relative goods' price and factor returns, and each industry's determination of labor employment indirectly. In a sense, this assumption is plausible in that it makes the political side of the Ricardo-Viner model short run like the economic side. Each industry first decides how they employ the inputs to maximize their profit, while assuming that the other industry's lobbying activities are given.

Then

$$\frac{\partial w}{\partial L_{PF}} = \frac{1}{2} T[L - L_{PM} - L_{PF}]^{-1/2} \left[\frac{1}{L_{PM}} \right] \left[\frac{KL_{PM} + TL_{PF}}{L_{PM}} \right]^{-1/2}$$

$$\frac{\partial w}{\partial q} = T[L - L_{PM} - L_{PF}]^{-1/2} \left[\frac{L_{PF}}{L_{PM}} \right]^{1/2} \left[\frac{KL_{PM} + TL_{PF}}{L_{PM}} \right]^{-1/2}$$

$$\frac{\partial q}{\partial L_{PF}} = \frac{1}{2} \frac{1}{L_{PM}} \left[\frac{L_{PF}}{L_{PM}} \right]^{-1/2}$$

$$\frac{\partial w}{\partial L_{PM}} = -\frac{1}{2} T[L - L_{PM} - L_{PF}]^{-1/2} \left[\frac{L_{PF}}{L_{PM}^2} \right] \left[\frac{KL_{PM} + TL_{PF}}{L_{PM}} \right]^{-1/2}$$

$$\frac{\partial q}{\partial L_{PM}} = -\frac{1}{2} \frac{L_{PF}}{L_{PM}^2} \left[\frac{L_{PF}}{L_{PM}} \right]^{-1/2}$$

Substituting these into Eq. (6-22), we will get

$$(1/4)\, T \left[\frac{L_{PF}}{L_{PM}}\right]^{1/2} [L - L_{PM} - L_{PF}]^{1/2} \left[K + T\left[\frac{L_{PF}}{L_{PM}}\right]\right]^{-1/2} \frac{1}{L_{PM}} \left[\frac{L_{PF}}{L_{PM}}\right]^{-1/2}$$

$$- [L - L_{PM} - L_{PF}]^{-1/2} \left[K + T\left[\frac{L_{PF}}{L_{PM}}\right]\right]^{1/2}$$

$$- \left[(1/4)T[L - L_{PM} - L_{PF}]\frac{L_{PF}}{L_{PM}}\left[K + T\left[\frac{L_{PF}}{L_{PM}}\right]\right]^{-1} + L_{PF}\right]$$

$$\cdot \left[\frac{1}{2}\, T[L - L_{PM} - L_{PF}]^{-1/2} \left[\frac{1}{L_{PM}}\right]\left[\frac{KL_{PM} + TL_{PF}}{L_{PM}}\right]^{-1/2}\right.$$

$$+ T[L - L_{PM} - L_{PF}]^{-1/2} \left[\frac{L_{PF}}{L_{PM}}\right]^{1/2} \left[\frac{KL_{PM} + TL_{PF}}{L_{PM}}\right]^{-1/2} \frac{1}{2}\frac{1}{L_{PM}}\left[\frac{L_{PF}}{L_{PM}}\right]^{-1/2}\right]$$

$$= 0$$

Collecting terms, we get

$$(1/4)\, T[L - L_{PM} - L_{PF}]\frac{1}{L_{PM}}$$

$$- \left[K + T\left[\frac{L_{PF}}{L_{PM}}\right]\right] - \left[(1/4)T[L - L_{PM} - L_{PF}]\frac{L_{PF}}{L_{PM}}\left[K + T\left[\frac{L_{PF}}{L_{PM}}\right]\right]^{-1} + L_{PF}\right]$$

$$\cdot \left[\frac{1}{2}\, T\left[\frac{1}{L_{PM}}\right] + \frac{1}{2}\, T\,\frac{1}{L_{PM}}\right] = 0$$

For convenience, let $L_{PM} = m$, $L_{PF} = f$. Then

$$T(L - m - f)(Km + Tf) - 4(Km + Tf)(Km + Tf) - [T^2 f(L - m - f) + 4Tf(Km + Tf)] = 0$$

Equivalently

$$(L - m - f)(KTm + T^2 f - T^2 f) - 4(Km + Tf)(Km + 2Tf) = 0$$

Finally we get

$$- 8T^2 f^2 - 13KTmf + LKTm - (KT + 4K^2)m^2 = 0 \qquad (6\text{-}28)$$

Again substituting these into Eq. (6-26), we will get

$$- [L - L_{PM} - L_{PF}]^{-1/2} \left[K + T \left[\frac{L_{PF}}{L_{PM}} \right] \right]^{1/2}$$

$$- \left[0.25K [L - L_{PM} - L_{PF}] \left[K + T \left[\frac{L_{PF}}{L_{PM}} \right] \right]^{-1} + L_{PM} \right]$$

$$\cdot \left[- \frac{1}{2} TL^{-1/2} \left[\frac{L_{PF}}{L_{PM}^2} \right] \left[\frac{KL_{PM} + TL_{PF}}{L_{PM}} \right]^{-1/2} \right]$$

$$- \frac{1}{2} TL^{-1/2} \left[\frac{L_{PF}}{L_{PM}} \right]^{1/2} \left[\frac{KL_{PM} + TL_{PF}}{L_{PM}} \right]^{-1/2} \frac{L_{PF}}{L_{PM}^2} \left[\frac{L_{PF}}{L_{PM}} \right]^{-1/2} \right] = 0$$

Collecting terms, we get

$$- \left[K + T \left[\frac{L_{PF}}{L_{PM}} \right] \right]^2 - \left[0.25K(L - L_{PM} - L_{PF}) + L_{PM} \left[K + T \left[\frac{L_{PF}}{L_{PM}} \right] \right] \right]$$

$$\cdot \left[- \frac{1}{2} T \left[\frac{L_{PF}}{L_{PM}^2} \right] - \frac{1}{2} T \frac{L_{PF}}{L_{PM}^2} \right] = 0$$

For convenience, let $L_{PM} = m$, $L_{PF} = f$. Then

$$- 4(Km+Tf)^2 + Tf(KL-Km-Kf+4Km+4Tf) = 0$$

or

$$- 4K^2m^2 - 8TKfm - 4T^2f^2 + TKLf - TKfm - TKf^2 + 4TKfm + 4T^2f^2 = 0$$

Equivalently

$$- 4K^2m^2 - 5TKfm + TKLf - TKf^2 = 0 \tag{6-29}$$

We end up with the following system of two equations with two unknown variables, f and m.[8]

$$- 8T^2f^2 - 13KTmf + LKTm - (KT+4K^2)m^2 = 0 \tag{6-28}$$

$$- 4K^2m^2 - 5TKfm + TKLf - TKf^2 = 0 \tag{6-29}$$

---

[8] When we solve the more general case where p is not set to be one, the two equations, (6-28) and (6-29), will be as follows:

$$f^2(-5T^2p^4-3T^2p^2) + mf(-5TKp^2-T^2p^4+T^2p^2-4TKp^2-4TK) + f(T^2Lp^4-T^2Lp^2)$$
$$+LKTp^2m - (KTp^2+4K^2)m^2 = 0$$
$$- 4K^2m^2 - 5TKp^2fm + TKLp^2f + Tp^2(4Tp^2-4T-K)f^2 = 0$$

We cannot obtain the analytical solutions for this system of two equations.

We can solve this system of equations. When we solve Eq. (6-28), we get

$$f = \frac{13Km \pm \sqrt{(41K^2 - 32KT)m^2 + 32LKTm}}{-16T}$$

We define that f should be positive. Then f has one solution, as follows:

$$f = \frac{-13Km + \sqrt{(41K^2 - 32KT)m^2 + 32LKTm}}{16T} \qquad (6\text{-}30)$$

Plug this into Eq. (6-29), and we get

$$-4K^2m^2 + (-5TKm + TKL)\frac{-13Km + \sqrt{(41K^2 - 32KT)m^2 + 32LKTm}}{16T}$$

$$-K\frac{210K^2m^2 - 32KTm^2 + 32LKTm - 26Km\sqrt{(41K^2 - 32KT)m^2 + 32LKTm}}{16T}$$

$$= 0$$

Collecting terms, we get

$$(33KT - 210K^2)m^2 - 19KTLm =$$
$$(5Tm - 26Km + LT)\sqrt{(41K^2 - 32KT)m^2 + 32LKTm}$$

Squaring both sides of the above equation, we get

$$(33KT - 210K^2)^2m^3 + 361K^2T^2L^2m - 38KTL(33KT - 210K^2)m^2$$
$$= (5Tm - 26Km + LT)^2[(41K^2 - 32KT)m + 32LKT]$$

Then we get

$$am^3 + bm^2 + cm + d = 0$$

Where

$$a = -16384K^3 - 18432K^2T - 800T^3 + 8256T^2K$$
$$b = TL[480T^2 - 4997TK + 11546K^2]$$
$$c = T^2L^2[288T - 1262K]$$
$$d = 32T^3L^3$$

We can easily find out that a is always negative in case of positive T and K; b is positive when $T > 6.95K$ or $T < 3.46K$; c is positive when $T > 4.38K$. Through the appropriate choice of units, we can get positive values for b, c when $T > 6.95K$; d is naturally positive because T and L are positive. We determine the curve of this cubic equation by checking the first derivative.

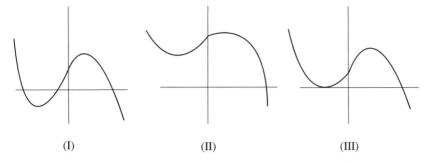

(I)   (II)   (III)

Figure 6-2.

Let $am^3 + bm^2 + cm + d = f(m)$. Then $f'(m) = 3am^2 + 2bm + c$. $f'(m)$ has two solutions, as follows:

$$m = \frac{1}{3a}[-b \pm \sqrt{b^2 - 3ac}]$$

We know that the vertical intercept d is positive, and that ac is negative, and

$$\sqrt{b^2 - 3ac} > b$$

So

$$\frac{1}{3a}[-b + \sqrt{b^2 - 3ac}] < 0, \quad \frac{1}{3a}[-b - \sqrt{b^2 - 3ac}] > 0$$

This means that one curvature point is positive, and another curvature point is negative. In other words, there is one and only one unique positive solution for the lobbying activity. Young (1982) shows that the lobbying equilibrium in the Ricardo-Viner model of endogenous tariff theory may not be unique. There could be two equilibria, one of which involves lower tariffs and lower welfare because resources have been diverted into nonproductive lobbying. He proposes that nonuniqueness of the Nash equilibrium implies that the data of the political and economic system need not determine the outcome of that system.

When we solve the preceding cubic equation, we get the three possible solutions: (1) one positive solution and two negative solutions [Figure 6-2, (I)]; (2) one positive solution and two imaginary solutions [Figure 6-2, (II)]; (3) one positive solution and one negative solution [Figure 6-2, (III)]. The point is that, in any case, we get only one positive solution for L_{PM}. We show this using Figure 6-2.

To find out which one is correct, we insert the negative solution of $f'(m)$ into $f(m)$. Then

$$\frac{1}{27a^2}\left[-b + \sqrt{b^2 - 3ac}\right]^3 + \frac{b}{9a^2}\left[-b + \sqrt{b^2 - 3ac}\right]^2 + \frac{c}{3a}\left[-b + \sqrt{b^2 - 3ac}\right] + d$$

$$= \frac{1}{27a^2}\left[-b^3 + 3b^2\sqrt{b^2 - 3ac} - 3b^3 + 9abc + (b^2 - 3ac)\sqrt{b^2 - 3ac}\right]$$

$$+ \frac{b}{9a^2}\left[2b^2 - 3ac - 2b\sqrt{b^2 - 3ac}\right] + \frac{c}{3a}\left[-b + \sqrt{b^2 - 3ac}\right] + d$$

$$= \frac{3b^3}{27a^2} - \frac{bc}{3a} - \frac{2b^2\sqrt{b^2 - 3ac}}{27a^2} + \frac{2c}{9a}\sqrt{b^2 - 3ac} + d$$

If this expression is positive, then the smaller curvature point is above the horizontal axis, which means that graph II is correct. Then we may use the formula solving the cubic equation for the case in which there is one real root and two conjugate imaginary roots. We get the following result:

Result 1: Let

$$a = -16384K^3 - 18432K^2T - 800T^3 + 8256T^2K$$
$$b = TL[480T^2 - 4997TK + 11546K^2]$$
$$c = T^2L^2[288T - 1262K]$$
$$d = 32T^3L^3$$

The equilibrium lobbying activity of manufacturing industry has the following unique solution:

$$L_{PM} = \left[-\frac{\vartheta}{2} + \sqrt{\frac{\vartheta^2}{4} + \frac{\zeta^3}{27}}\right]^{1/3} + \left[-\frac{\vartheta}{2} - \sqrt{\frac{\vartheta^2}{4} + \frac{\zeta^3}{27}}\right]^{1/3} - \frac{b}{3a} \qquad (6\text{-}31)$$

where

$$\vartheta = \frac{c}{a} - \frac{b^2}{3a^2}, \quad \zeta = \frac{1}{27}\left[\frac{2b^3}{a^3} - \frac{9bc}{a^2} + 27\frac{d}{a}\right]$$

When we insert Eq. (6-31) into Eq. (6-30), we can get a unique solution of L_{PF}.

As we find in result 1, the lobbying equilibrium is unique. Thus the varying tariff levels can arise only from variations in parameters of the model such as endowments.

4   Increasing returns in the Ricardo-Viner model

We now derive the specific factors model version of Magee-Young theorem. It states that with endogenous politics, there are increasing returns to factor endowments. That is, the more capital an economy has, the higher will be the returns to capital. In the Heckscher-Ohlin-Samuelson model setting, factor endowments play a key role in determining the pattern of trade (the Heckscher-Ohlin theorem) but do not influence factor returns because of the factor price equalization theorem.[9]

In Young and Magee (1986), relative endowments determine not only a country's trade pattern but also its structure of trade protection: A high relative endowment of capital leads the political system to supply policies that are more favorable to capital owners. The Magee-Young theorem contrasts with the Rybczynski result that capital returns will be independent of factor endowments for an open trading economy, and with the diminishing returns result that capital returns will decline with more capital in a closed economy.[10]

Result 2: If the endowment ratio of land to capital increases, the labor-intensive industry will contribute lobbying funds relatively more than the capital-intensive industry when

$$\min [A,B] < \frac{L_{PF}}{L_{PM}} < \max [A,B]$$

where

$$A = \sqrt{\frac{9K^2 + 16KT}{64T^2}} - \frac{3K}{8T} \ , \quad B = \sqrt{\frac{5K^2 + KT}{6T^2}} - \frac{K}{T}$$

Proof: Dividing Eqs. (6-28) and (6-29) by K^2m^2, we get

$$-8\left[\frac{T}{K}\right]^2 \left[\frac{f}{m}\right]^2 - 13 \left[\frac{T}{K}\right]\left[\frac{f}{m}\right] + L \left[\frac{T}{K}\right]\frac{1}{m} - \frac{T}{K} - 4 = 0 \tag{6-32}$$

$$-4 - 5\left[\frac{T}{K}\right]\left[\frac{f}{m}\right] + L \left[\frac{T}{K}\right]\left[\frac{f}{m}\right]\frac{1}{m} - \left[\frac{T}{K}\right]\left[\frac{f}{m}\right]^2 = 0 \tag{6-33}$$

Multiplying Eq. (6-32) by f/m, then we subtract Eq. (6-33) from Eq. (6-32) to get

$$g\left(\frac{f}{m},\frac{T}{K}\right) = -2 \left[\frac{T}{K}\right]^2 \left[\frac{f}{m}\right]^3 - 3 \left[\frac{T}{K}\right]\left[\frac{f}{m}\right]^2 + \left[\frac{T}{K}\right]\left[\frac{f}{m}\right] - \left[\frac{f}{m}\right] + 1 = 0 \tag{6-34}$$

According to the implicit function theorem,

---

[9] Magee, Brock, and Young (1989, Chapter 12).
[10] Magee, Brock, and Young (1989, p. 166).

$$\frac{\partial\left[\dfrac{f}{m}\right]}{\partial\left[\dfrac{T}{K}\right]} = -\frac{\partial g / \partial\left[\dfrac{T}{K}\right]}{\partial g / \partial\left[\dfrac{f}{m}\right]} = \frac{\dfrac{f}{m}\left[-4\left[\dfrac{T}{K}\right]\left[\dfrac{f}{m}\right]^2 - 3\left[\dfrac{f}{m}\right] + 1\right]}{6\left[\dfrac{T}{K}\right]^2\left[\dfrac{f}{m}\right]^2 + 6\left[\dfrac{T}{K}\right]\left[\dfrac{f}{m}\right] - \left[\dfrac{T}{K}\right] + 1}$$

Let $b(f/m) = -4\left[\dfrac{T}{K}\right]\left[\dfrac{f}{m}\right]^2 - 3\left[\dfrac{f}{m}\right] + 1,$

$$v(f/m) = 6\left[\dfrac{T}{K}\right]^2\left[\dfrac{f}{m}\right]^2 + 6\left[\dfrac{T}{K}\right]\left[\dfrac{f}{m}\right] - \left[\dfrac{T}{K}\right] + 1$$

We can easily find that there are three possible cases. We show $b(f/m)$ and $v(f/m)$ in Figure 6-3. We find that case I is not acceptable because we assume that T is greater than K. In the region between the two horizontal intercepts in cases II and III, the derivative is positive. The condition is

$$\min [A,B] < \frac{L_{PM}}{L_{PF}} < \max [A,B]$$

where

$$A = \sqrt{\frac{9K^2 + 16KT}{64T^2}} - \frac{3K}{8T}, \quad B = \sqrt{\frac{5K^2 + KT}{6T^2}} - \frac{K}{T}$$

Q.E.D.

The relative specific factor returns (r/z) are not affected by the change in the labor available in the economy in the short run case in the Ricardo-Viner model.

Result 3: The change in the labor available for economic production does not affect the relative specific factor returns. That is, $\partial (r/z) / \partial L_a = 0$.
    Proof:

$$\frac{\partial\left[\dfrac{r}{z}\right]}{\partial L_a} = \frac{\partial}{\partial L_a}\left[\frac{w^{-(1-\alpha)/\alpha}}{q^{1/\beta}w^{-(1-\beta)/\beta}}\right] = \frac{\partial\left[q^{-1/\beta}\right]}{\partial L_a} = -\frac{1}{\beta}q^{-(1+\beta)/\beta}\frac{\partial\left[\dfrac{L_{PF}}{L_{PM}}\right]}{\partial L_a} = 0$$

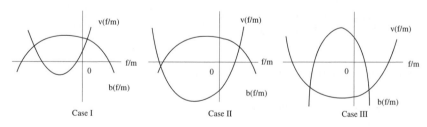

Case I   Case II   Case III

Figure 6-3.

Because

$$\frac{\partial L_a}{\partial L_{PM}} = \frac{\partial L_a}{\partial L_{PF}} = 0, \text{ by assumption.}$$

Q.E.D.

Once we obtain the effect of the endowment ratio change on the relative lobbying activities, we can determine the effect of endowment ratio change on the relative factor returns. Result 3 means that the Magee-Young theorem holds in the Ricardo-Viner model.

Result 4: In the two-good, one-mobile-factor, two-specific-factors model, there are increasing returns to either specific factor. For example, if the country's endowment ratio of capital to land increases, then the relative factor return to capital increases. The more capital an economy has, the higher will be the returns to capital.

Proof: When we differentiate the relative factor returns with respect to the ratio of endowment ratio, we get

$$\frac{\partial\left[\dfrac{r}{z}\right]}{\partial\left[\dfrac{K}{T}\right]} = \frac{\partial}{\partial\left[\dfrac{K}{T}\right]}\left[\frac{w^{-(1-\alpha)/\alpha}}{q^{1/b}w^{-(1-\beta)/\beta}}\right] = \frac{\partial}{\partial\left[\dfrac{K}{T}\right]}\left[q^{-1/\beta}w^{(1-\beta)/\beta - (1-\alpha)/\alpha}\right]$$

This derivative ends up with

$$\frac{\partial\left[\dfrac{r}{z}\right]}{\partial\left[\dfrac{K}{T}\right]} = \frac{\partial q^{-2}}{\partial\left[\dfrac{K}{T}\right]} = -2q^{-3}\frac{\partial\left[\dfrac{L_{PF}}{L_{PM}}\right]}{\partial\left[\dfrac{K}{T}\right]}$$

This expression should be positive because $\partial\left[\frac{L_{PF}}{L_{PM}}\right] / \partial\left[\frac{K}{T}\right] < 0$ from Result 2. As we note in the beginning of this section, this version of Magee-Young theorem holds when the boundary condition is satisfied. Q.E.D.

5   Summary and implications

We find in this paper conditions under which there are increasing returns to factor endowments in Findlay and Wellisz's (1982) Ricardo-Viner model of endogenous protection. It had been shown earlier to hold in the Heckscher-Ohlin-Samuelson model. Here, we derive analytical solutions for the Findlay and Wellisz model using Cobb-Douglas production and specific parameter values. The Findlay-Wellisz model has two goods, two specific factors, and one mobile factor of production. Findlay and Wellisz's paper was based on a short-run Ricardo-Viner model. Magee, Brock, and Young's model of endogenous protection was based on the long-run Heckscher-Ohlin-Samuelson model. This paper follows Findlay and Wellisz in using a reduced-form general equilibrium model, which assumes that party and voter behavior are exogenous. If the more general result holds in all Findlay-Wellisz cases, there are important implications for developing countries, because the Findlay-Wellisz model has been applied there extensively.

As a second result, we establish that a unique solution holds for each of the two factors' levels of lobbying. Findlay and Wellisz (1982) assumed that the lobbying equilibrium is unique, but they did not show that the welfare loss is a monotonically increasing function of the tariff level. While Young's (1982) possibility of multiple tariff equilibria in Findlay and Wellisz might be a pervasive problem, we found a unique equilibrium here.

References

Balisacan, Arsenio M. and James A. Roumasset, "Public Choice of Economic Policy: The Growth of Agricultural Protection," *Weltwirtschaftliches Archiv Review of World Economics*, 1987, 123, 232–48.

Baldwin, Robert E., *The Political Economy of U.S. Import Policy,* 1986, Cambridge: MIT Press.

Becker, Gary S., "A Theory of Competition Among Pressure Groups for Political Influence," *Quarterly Journal of Economics,* 1983, 98, 371–400.

Bhagwati, Jagdish N., "Directly Unproductive, Profit-Seeking DUP Activities," *Journal of Political Economy,* 1982, 90, 988–1002.

Brander, James A. and Barbara J. Spencer, "Export Subsidies and International Market Share Rivalry," *Journal of International Economics,* 1985, 18, 83–100.

Brock, William A. and Stephen P. Magee, "The Economics of Special-Interest Politics: The Case of the Tariff," *American Economic Review,* 1978, 68, 246–50.

Brock, William A. and Stephen P. Magee, "Tariff Formation in a Democracy," in John Black and Brian Hindley (eds.), *Current Issues in Commercial Policy and Diplomacy,* 1980, New York: St, Martins Press.

Buchanan, James M., Robert D. Tollison, and Gordon Tullock, *Toward a Theory of the Rent-Seeking Society,* 1980, College Station, Texas A & M University Press.

Choi, Nakgyoon, *Essays in International Trade: Endogenous Tariff Theory,* 1991, PhD Dissertation in Economics, University of Texas at Texas at Austin.

Findlay, Ronald J. and Stanislaw Wellisz, "Endogenous Tariffs, the Political Economy of Trade Restrictions and Welfare," in Jagdish N. Bhagwati (ed.), *Import Competition and Response,* 1982, Chicago: University of Chicago Press, 223–38.

Hillman, Arye, *The Political Economy of Protection,* 1989, New York: Harwood Academic Press.

Krueger, Anne O., "The Political Economy of the Rent-Seeking Society," *American Economic Review,* 1974, 64, 291–303.

Lindbeck, Assar, "Redistribution Policy and Expansion of the Public Sector," *Journal of Public Economics,* 1985, 28, 309–28.

Magee, Stephen P., "Endogenous Protection: A Survey," forthcoming in D. C. Mueller (ed.), *Handbook of Public Choice,* 1995, New York: Cambridge University Press.

Magee, Stephen P. and Christopher S. Magee, "Economic Development with Increasing Returns to Politics," 1994, mimeo, University of Texas at Austin.

Magee, Stephen P. and Leslie Young, "Multinationals, Tariffs and Capital Flows with Endogenous Politicians," in C. P. Kindelberger and D. Audretsch (eds.), *The Multinational Corporation in the 1980s*, 1983, Cambridge: MIT Press.

Magee, Stephen P., William A. Brock, and Leslie Young, *Black Hole Tariffs and Endogenous Policy Theory: Political Economy in General Equilibrium*, 1989, New York: Cambridge University Press.

Mankiw, N. G., David Romer, and David Weil, "A Contribution to the Empirics of Economic Growth," *Quarterly Journal of Economics*, 1992, 407–37.

Mayer, Wolfgang, "Endogenous Tariff Formation," *American Economic Review*, 1984, 74, 970–85.

Michaely, Michael, Demetris Papageorgiou, and Armeane M. Choksi (eds.), *Liberalizing Foreign Trade: Vol. 7, Lessons of Experience in the Developing World*, 1991, Cambridge, Mass.: Basil Blackwell.

Olson, Mancur, *The Logic of Collective Action: Public Goods and the Theory of Groups*, 1965, Cambridge: Harvard University Press.

Rauch, James E., "The Question of International Convergence of Per Capita Consumption," 1989, presented at the 1989 NBER Summer Institute Workshop on International Trade.

Rogowski, Ronald, *Commerce and Coalitions*, 1988, Princeton: Princeton University Press.

Rostow, Walt Whitman, *The Stages of Economic Growth*, 1960, London: Cambridge University Press.

Solow, Robert M., "A Contribution to the Theory of Economic Growth," *Quarterly Journal of Economics*, 1956, 70, 65–94.

Stolper, Wolfgang and Paul A. Samuelson, "Protection and Real Wages," *Review of Economic Studies*, 1941, 9, 58–73.

Tollison, Robert D., "Rent Seeking: A Survey," in D. C. Mueller (ed.), *Handbook of Public Choice*, 1994, Cambridge, Mass.: Basil Blackwell.

Tulloch, Gordon, "The Welfare Cost of Tariffs, Monopolies and Theft," *Western Economic Journal*, 1967, 5, 224–32

Vousden, Neil, *The Economics of Trade Protection*, 1990, New York: Cambridge University Press.

Young, Leslie, "Comment on Findlay and Wellisz," in Jagdish N. Bhagwati (ed.), *Import Competition and Response*, 1982, Chicago: University of Chicago Press.

Young, Leslie, "International Trade Lecture Notes," 1988, Department of Economics, University of Texas.

Young, Leslie and Stephen P. Magee, "Endogenous Protection, Factor Returns and Resource Allocation," *Review of Economic Studies*, 1986, 53, 407–19.

CHAPTER 7

Demosclerosis, or special interests "R" us: An information rationale for political gridlock

Susanne Lohmann
University of California, Los Angeles

1   Introduction

Modern democracies are trapped in a collective dilemma. In many cases, government policies are biased in favor of special interests at the expense of the general public, and they are often inefficient in the sense that the total losses imposed on the majority exceed the total gains enjoyed by the minority. While special interests form a minority on any one policy dimension, just about every citizen is a member – whether active or not – of some special interest group on some policy dimension; indeed, many citizens are members of more than one special interest group. Each citizen prefers being favored by government policy even at the expense of inefficiencies imposed on the society at large, but relative to the status quo involving inefficient government policies on all dimensions, each citizen would be better off if government did not cater to special interests at all.

The persistence of this problem, labeled "demosclerosis" by Jonathan Rauch (1994), is puzzling.[1] Voters clamor for government to streamline and reduce the scope of its redistributive activities. But any serious attempt to implement the expressed wish of the general public requires cutting the pet programs of special interests, and any politician who would do so can count on being dead on arrival at the polls. Yet in the aggregate special interests *are* the general public. It is thus hard to avoid the conclusion that demosclerosis is due to some kind of voter illusion.

From a theoretical perspective, the persistence of such political gridlock is puzzling. After all, political competition and other constituent elements of democracy have been celebrated for their potential to lead to efficient policy outcomes (Wittman 1989). Indeed, political competition appears to allow for an easy solution to the collective dilemma just described: Surely a political

This paper is part of a research progam that is financially supported by National Science Foundation Grant SRB-9308405.

[1] Rauch popularizes and expands on ideas originally developed by Olson (1982).

entrepreneur who stood for election offering to eliminate all the perks enjoyed by special interests would be elected unanimously.

Based on ideas developed in Lohmann (1994), this article provides an informational rationale for the persistence of demosclerosis, explaining why voters and their political representatives are trapped in the collective dilemma. In particular, I argue that political competition does not allow a society to break free because the electorate cannot effectively monitor whether political candidates who promise to eliminate the policy bias toward special interests will keep their promises once elected. As a consequence, office-motivated incumbents will share the incentives of their predecessors to bias policy toward special interests.

On a positive note, my analysis suggests that, while elections are costly in the sense that they create the preelection policy bias, they also generate benefits: The voters (imperfect) monitoring ensures that competent policy makers are more likely to survive than are their incompetent counterparts.

2   The model

This section provides a simple model of the collective dilemma by extending Lohmann (1994) to a multidimensional setting. The model is stripped of many extraneous considerations that might be important in practice but would detract from the informational rationale underlying the problem of demosclerosis; but the argument is quite robust with regard to numerous extensions.

The model consists of one policy maker (whose challenger is waiting in the wings); three voters, indexed $i = 1,2,3$; and three policy dimensions, indexed $j = 1,2,3$. For each issue j, the voter with the same index, $i = j$, is defined to be the special interest; the other two voters, $i \neq j$, constitute the general public.

On policy dimension j, voter i desires the policy maker to take a favorable action $\hat{a}_{ij}$. The voter's utility decreases quadratically with the distance between the action $a_j \in R$ taken by the policy maker and the voter i's ideal point $\hat{a}_{ij}$. The action preferred by the general public is normalized to zero, whereas the ideal point of the special interest is strictly positive:

$$\hat{a}_{ij} = \begin{cases} 0 & \text{for } i \neq j \\ \hat{a} & \text{for } i = j \end{cases} \tag{7-1}$$

$\hat{a} > 0$. Thus, one of the defining characteristics of special interests is that their preferences over the policy maker's actions conflict with those of the general public. The parameter $\hat{a}$ captures the severity of the conflict of interest.

Special interests and the general public do have a common interest, namely to ensure that a policy maker of above-average total competence controls policy. Each political candidate is characterized by a vector of issue-specific competence parameters, $[c_1, c_2, c_3]$. The parameter c_j is a random variable drawn from a normal distribution with zero mean and strictly positive but finite variance σ_c^2. The voters' utility increases with the incumbent's competence on each policy dimension.

In summary, voter i's one-period utility function on policy dimension j is specified as

$$U_{ij} = -\tfrac{1}{2}\,(a_j - \hat{a}_{ij})^2 + c_j \tag{7-2}$$

Neither special interests nor the general public can directly observe the actions taken by the incumbent policy maker on any one dimension, and political candidates are privately informed about their competence parameters.

Special interest j can, however, observe the outcome of the policy process governing issue j, Π_j. The individual cannot fully disentangle the underlying forces; but she knows that the outcome is determined by the incumbent's action a_j and his competence c_j, as well as a process shock p_j:

$$\Pi_j = -\tfrac{1}{2}\,(a_j - \hat{a})^2 + c_j + p_j \tag{7-3}$$

The process shock is a random variable drawn from a normal distribution with zero mean and strictly positive but finite variance σ_p^2. In a simple way, this assumption captures the random nature of the interaction of multiple (unmodeled) actors and circumstances affecting the outcome of a complex policy process.

The general public observes the outcome of the policy process only indirectly, as mediated by market processes. A member of the general public i experiences the outcome of the policy and market processes governing issue j, Θ_{ij}. The individual cannot fully disentangle the underlying forces, but she knows that the outcome is determined by the incumbent's action a_j and his competence c_j, as well as the process shock p_j and a market shock m_{ij}:

$$\Theta_{ij} = -\tfrac{1}{2}\,a_j^2 + c_j + p_j + m_{ij} \tag{7-4}$$

The market shock is a random variable drawn from a normal distribution with zero mean and weakly positive, finite variance σ_m^2. This assumption captures the random nature of the interaction of multiple (unmodeled) actors and circumstances that determine the ultimate consequences of political decision making for voters' daily lives.

Thus, a second defining characteristic of special interests is that they are better informed than is the general public. Special interests observe the outcomes of policy processes, whereas the members of the general public experience only these outcomes as mediated by market processes. The parameter σ_m^2 captures the degree to which special interests are better informed: the informational disparity increases with this variance. The special case of $\sigma_m^2 = 0$ is obtained if special interests and the general public are equally well informed.

Political candidates care about aggregate welfare, or they derive utility from being in power. The one-period utility function of a political candidate is given by

$$V = \sum_{i=1}^{3} \sum_{j=1}^{3} U_{ij} + S$$

(7-5)

where the index variable S (survival) can take on one of two values:

$$S = \begin{cases} \overline{S} & \text{if the political candidate is in power in the period under consideration,} \\ 0 & \text{otherwise,} \end{cases}$$

(7-6)

$\overline{S} \in [0,\infty)$. The parameter $\overline{S}$ captures the degree to which political candidates are office-motivated: It is equal to zero if they are concerned only about aggregate welfare, and it goes to infinity as the (re)election goal becomes dominant.

The model has two periods.[2] Time subscripts are omitted whenever possible to avoid notational clutter. For simplicity, I assume that second-period utilities are not discounted.

The time sequence of events is as follows. In the first period, nature draws the incumbent policy maker's competence parameters as well as the process and market shocks. The policy maker then acts on each policy dimension. Special interests observe the outcomes of the policy processes governing their respective issues, and the members of the general public experience the outcomes of the policy and market processes. Each voter i subsequently chooses whether to vote for the incumbent ($v_i = 1$) or a challenger ($v_i = 0$). The incumbent remains in power if he receives a majority of the vote. Otherwise he is replaced by the challenger, in which case nature draws the challenger's competencies. The policy maker who is in power in the second period then acts on each policy dimension. Finally, the game ends, and the players' payoffs are realized.

The model is now solved by backwards induction, employing a refinement of the sequential equilibrium concept (Kreps and Wilson, 1982).[3] In the second period of the game, the incumbent policy maker takes the set of actions that maximizes his expected utility. There are no reelection incentives in the second (and last) period of the game. As a consequence, the policy maker's action on each issue maximizes aggregate welfare.

The first-order condition of his maximization problem for issue j is given by

---

[2] Extending the model to more than two periods, while maintaining the finite-horizon setting, is straightforward. The extension to an infinite-horizon setting is more complicated, but the qualitative results regarding the existence and direction of policy and selection biases are robust; see Lohmann (1994) for a more extensive discussion.

[3] Voters are restricted to use weakly undominated voting strategies; see Lohmann (1994) for a more extensive discussion.

$$(-3a_j + \hat{a}) = 0 \tag{7-7}$$

The equilibrium second-period action

$$a_{j,t=2} = \frac{1}{3}\,\hat{a} \tag{7-8}$$

is an equiweighted average of the voters' ideal points; the subscript t indexes time.

Since the second-period action maximizes aggregate welfare, it also serves as a normative benchmark. It is clearly of interest to examine whether the incumbent's first-period actions are biased in favor of special interests due to the electoral incentives he faces. Such a bias has the potential to lower first-period expected welfare to the extent that special interests gain less than the general public loses.

Expected aggregate welfare in the second period is given by

$$E \sum_{i=1}^{3}\sum_{j=1}^{3} U_{ij,\,t=2} = -\hat{a}^2 + \text{prob}(S = \overline{S})\, E\left(\sum_{j=1}^{3} c_j \mid S = \overline{S}\right) \tag{7-9}$$

where E is an expectations operator denoting ex ante expectations; $\text{prob}(S = \overline{S})$ is the probability that the first-period incumbent wins the election; and $E\left(\sum_{j=1}^{3} c_j \mid S = \overline{S}\right)$ is his total competence conditional on survival. Note that aggregate welfare decreases with the severity of the conflict of interest between the general public and special interests, as measured by the parameter $\hat{a}$.

The second term in Eq. (7-9) reflects the *selection bias* that has the potential to increase second-period aggregate welfare if competent policy makers are more likely to survive into the second period than are incompetent ones. (There is no potential for a selection bias in the first period.) The first term in Eq. (7-9), which captures second-period aggregate welfare net of the gains generated by the selection bias, serves as a normative benchmark for first-period aggregate welfare, allowing us to assess the welfare consequences of the policy bias. (There is no potential for a policy bias in the second and last period of the game.)

At the end of the first period, the voters decide whether to vote for the incumbent or the challenger. Their votes cannot affect their first-period utilities; they can influence only their second-period expected utilities. Each voter votes for the incumbent if she expects to be better off if the incumbent remained in power. Since both the incumbent and the challenger choose the same set of actions in the second (and last) period of the game, the only difference between the two candidates is given by their expected competencies. The voter has no information (other than her prior) about the challenger's competencies so that the expected competence of the challenger is zero on each policy dimension. Voters cannot directly observe the incumbent's competencies, but each voter can observe the outcome of the policy process on one dimension and the outcome of the policy and market processes on the other two dimensions. On any one dimension, outcomes are correlated with the incumbent's competence so that voters can use their observations to form an estimate of the incumbent's competence. The inferences formed by special interests are confounded by the process shocks, and those of the general public by process and market shocks.

On policy dimension j, the solution to the signal extraction problem solved by special interest j is given by

$$E_j c_j = \sigma_c^2/(\sigma_c^2 + \sigma_p^2) [\Pi_j + \tfrac{1}{2} E^* (a_j - \hat{a})^2] \tag{7-10}$$

where the expectations operator E_j denotes expectations formed based on the observation Π_j, and E^* is a rational expectations operator. The corresponding expression for a member of the general public i is given by

$$E_{ij} c_j = \sigma_c^2/(\sigma_c^2 + \sigma_p^2 + \sigma_m^2) [\Theta_{ij} + \tfrac{1}{2} E^* a_j^2] \tag{7-11}$$

where the expectations operator E_{ij} denotes expectations formed based on the observation Θ_{ij}.

Individual j's voting strategy is given by[4]

$$v_j = \begin{cases} 1 & \text{if } E_j c_j + \sum_{i \neq j} E_{ji} c_i \geq 0 \\ 0 & \text{otherwise} \end{cases} \tag{7-12}$$

From the incumbent's perspective, the probability that individual j casts her vote in his favor is given by

$$\begin{aligned} \text{prob}(v_j = 1) &= \text{prob}[-\tfrac{1}{2} (a_j - \hat{a})^2 + c_j + p_j + \tfrac{1}{2} E^* (a_j - \hat{a})^2 \\ &\quad + \alpha \sum_{i \neq j} (-\tfrac{1}{2} a_i + c_i + p_i + m_{ji} + \tfrac{1}{2} E^* a_i^2) \geq 0] \\ &= \text{prob}[p_j + \alpha \sum_{i \neq j} (p_i + m_{ji}) \geq -c_j - \alpha \sum_{i \neq j} c_i \\ &\quad + \tfrac{1}{2} (a_j - \hat{a})^2 - \tfrac{1}{2} E^* (a_j - \hat{a})^2 + \alpha \sum_{i \neq j} (\tfrac{1}{2} a_i^2 - \tfrac{1}{2} E^* a_i^2)] \\ &= 1 - F[-c_j - \alpha \sum_{i \neq j} c_i + \tfrac{1}{2} (a_j - \hat{a})^2 - \tfrac{1}{2} E^* (a_j - \hat{a})^2 \\ &\quad + \alpha \sum_{i \neq j} (\tfrac{1}{2} a_i^2 - \tfrac{1}{2} E^* a_i^2)] \end{aligned} \tag{7-13}$$

where $\alpha \equiv (\sigma_c^2 + \sigma_p^2) / (\sigma_c^2 + \sigma_p^2 + \sigma_m^2)$ and $F(.)$ is the joint distribution function of $p_j + \alpha \sum_{i \neq j} (p_i + m_{ji})$. (Note that $0 < \alpha < 1$ for $0 < \sigma_m^2 < \infty$ and $\alpha = 1$ for $\sigma_m^2 = 0$.)

---

[4] The symmetry of the model ensures that voters' strategies are not subject to the swing voter's curse (Feddersen and Pesendorfer, 1993). Extending the model to integrate the Feddersen and Pesendorfer analysis would complicate the argument enormously without qualitatively changing the results; see Lohmann (1994) for a more extensive discussion.

The policy maker wins the election for sure if two or more individuals cast their vote for the incumbent. The probability that he remains in power increases with the probability that any one individual casts her vote for the incumbent:

$$\partial \text{prob}(S = \overline{S})/\partial \text{prob}(v_j = 1) = \tfrac{1}{2} \qquad (7\text{--}14)$$

which is equal to the ex ante probability that exactly one other individual is casting her vote for the incumbent so that individual j's vote is decisive.

The probability of survival is thus a function of the action a_1 taken by the incumbent (the analysis is symmetric for actions a_2 and a_3):

$$\partial \text{prob}(S = \overline{S})/\partial a_1 = -\tfrac{1}{2} f(-c_1 - \alpha c_2 - \alpha c_3)(a_1 - \hat{a})$$
$$-\tfrac{1}{2}\,\alpha\!f(-c_2 - \alpha c_1 - \alpha c_3)\,a_1 - \tfrac{1}{2}\,\alpha\!f(-c_3 - \alpha c_1 - \alpha c_2)\,a_1 \qquad (7\text{-}15)$$

where $f(.)$ is the joint density function of $p_j + \alpha \sum_{i \neq j}(p_i + m_{ji})$; note that rational expectations on the part of the voters implies that

$$\tfrac{1}{2}(a_j - \hat{a})^2 - \tfrac{1}{2} E^*(a_j - \hat{a})^2 = \tfrac{1}{2} E^* a_i^2 = 0 \qquad (7\text{-}16)$$

The first-order condition for the policy maker's first-period maximization problem is given by

$$(-3a_1 + \hat{a}) + [\partial \text{prob}(S = \overline{S})/\partial a_1]\sum_{j=1}^{3} c_j + [\partial \text{prob}(S = \overline{S})/\partial a_1]\,\overline{S} = 0 \qquad (7\text{-}17)$$

This first-order condition can be compared with the corresponding condition for the second-period maximization problem in Eq. (7-7). The first bracketed term in Eq. (7-17), which reflects the incumbent's desire to maximize first-period aggregate welfare, is the only one that also appears in Eq. (7-7).

The equilibrium first-period action is given by

$$a_{1,t=1} = \tfrac{1}{3}\,\hat{a}\,\beta(c_1, c_2, c_3) \qquad (7\text{-}18)$$

where

$$\beta(c_1, c_2, c_3) \equiv [3 + \tfrac{1}{2}(\overline{S} + \sum_{j=1}^{3} c_j)\,3\,f(-c_1 - \alpha c_2 - \alpha c_3)]\,/$$

$$\{3 + \tfrac{1}{2}(\overline{S} + \sum_{j=1}^{3} c_j)\,\cdot$$

$$[f(-c_1 - \alpha c_2 - \alpha c_3) + \alpha\!f(-c_2 - \alpha c_1 - \alpha c_3) + \alpha\!f(-c_3 - \alpha c_1 - \alpha c_2)]\}$$

The first-period action is thus a function of the incumbent's competence. To examine the existence and direction of a *systematic* policy bias, I take the expectation of the first-period action; that is, I calculate the average action across competence types:

$$Ea_{1,t=1} = \tfrac{1}{3}\,\hat{a}\,E\beta \tag{7-19}$$

where $\phi \equiv f(0)$. A comparison of Eqs. (7-8) and (7-19) shows that on average across competence types policy is unbiased only if $E\beta = 1$ or equivalently $(1 + \tfrac{1}{2}\,\bar{S}\,\phi)\,/\,[1 + \tfrac{1}{2}\,\bar{S}\,\phi(1 + 2\alpha)/3] = 1$. This is the case if at least one of the following two conditions is satisfied: (1) $\alpha = 1$, or, equivalently, $\sigma_m^2 = 0$; or (2) $\bar{S} = 0$. In other words, the systematic policy bias is zero if there is no informational asymmetry between the special interest and the general public, or if the incumbent places zero weight on the reelection objective.

Otherwise the incumbent's action is systematically biased towards the special interest. The policy bias increases with the severity of the informational asymmetry, as measured by σ_m^2, and with the weight $\bar{S}$ the incumbent places on the reelection objective. As σ_m^2 and $\bar{S}$ go to infinity, the first-period action converges to the ideal point of the special interest.

A comparison of the first-order conditions for the first- and second-period maximization problems in Eqs. (7-17) and (7-7), as well as the first- and second-period actions in Eqs. (7-19) and (7-8), allows me to identity another preelection effect. The second term in Eq. (7-17) indicates that an incumbent of above-average total competence has a survival motive even if he places zero weight on the reelection goal per se. Since the incumbent cares about aggregate welfare in the second period, he would prefer himself to be in power in the next period rather than a challenger of average total competence. The higher is the total competence of the incumbent, the stronger are his incentives to favor special interests in order to improve his reelection chances. Conversely, incumbents with low competencies prefer not to be reelected; perversely, they bias their actions in favor of the general public to thwart their reelection chances. (Clearly, a more realistic model would allow incumbents not to stand for election.) In the first period the incumbent's desire to increase second-period aggregate welfare thus introduces some variability into policy outcomes; but the effect averages out across competence types so that there is no systematic bias.

Expected social welfare in the first period is given by

$$E \sum_{i=1}^{3} \sum_{j=1}^{3} U_{ij,\,t=1} = -\,\hat{a}^2[(E\beta)^2/2 - E\beta + 3/2] \tag{7-20}$$

Expected welfare attains its maximum $(-\hat{a}^2)$ if $E\beta = 1$ or equivalently $\sigma_m^2 = 0$ or $\bar{S} = 0$; that is, if policy bias is zero because there is no informational asymmetry between special interests and the general public, or because the incumbent places zero weight on the reelection objective. The policy bias that emerges otherwise generates a deadweight social loss: Special interests gain less than the general public loses. The preelection variability of policy that is created by the differential survival incentives of various competence types also leads to a deadweight social loss.

At this point, it is useful to examine the mechanics of the policy bias in more detail. How can a policy maker achieve a net gain in political support if he biases policy on any one dimension toward one voter at the expense of the other two voters, even though the losses imposed on the general public exceed the benefits enjoyed by the special interest? A voter may experience a favorable outcome because she is lucky, because the incumbent biased policy in her favor, or because the incumbent is exceptionally competent. Since the voter has incentives to reelect an incumbent of above-average total competence, she attempts to disentangle the forces underlying the favorable policy outcome. At the margin, *and for given expectations about the incumbent's action,* the policy maker can mimic an increase in competence vis-à-vis the special interest by biasing policy in her favor, at the expense of an apparent decrease in competence vis-à-vis the general public. Compared to the general public, the better informed special interest places a higher weight on the possibility that a favorable outcome is caused by the policy maker's competence. If the incumbent biases policy toward the special interest, the increase in the probability of survival caused by the resulting increase in the probability that the special interest votes for the policy maker dominates the decrease in the probability of survival caused by the resulting decrease in the probability that the members of the general public support the incumbent – at least up to a point. By continuity, this argument holds even if the policy bias is associated with some inefficiency.

In equilibrium, of course, the incumbent's attempt to fool the voters must be futile. Rational expectations imply that, on average across competence types, the voter's expectations about the policy maker's actions are correct in equilibrium: Rational voters are aware of the policymaker's manipulations. Ironically, the incumbent is trapped in the counterproductive policy bias precisely because the voters expect him to bias policy. If he fails to follow their expectations, he reduces his reelection chances to an unacceptable level. The voters' expectations are thus fulfilled in equilibrium.

In short, the incumbent cannot systematically improve his chances of survival: He is reelected if he is lucky, as is the case if the process and market shocks are positive, or if he is exceptionally competent. His probability of survival is strictly increasing in his total competence:

$$\partial \text{prob}(S = \bar{S} \mid \sum_{j=1}^{3} c_j) / \partial (\sum_{j=1}^{3} c_j) > 0 \tag{7-21}$$

Conditional on survival, the expected total competence of the second-period incumbent is above average:

$$E(\sum_{j=1}^{3} c_j \mid S = \overline{S}) > 0 \qquad (7\text{-}22)$$

This selection bias increases expected aggregate welfare in the second period [see Eq. (7-9)]. The more informed is each voter, the stronger is the selection bias:

$$\partial E \, (\sum_{j=1}^{3} c_j \mid S = \overline{S}) \, / \, \partial \, \sigma_p^2 < 0 \qquad (7\text{-}23)$$

$$\partial E \, (\sum_{j=1}^{3} c_j \mid S = \overline{S}) \, / \, \partial \, \sigma_m^2 < 0 \qquad (7\text{-}24)$$

While elections are costly in the sense that they create both the preelection policy bias and preelection policy variability, they also generate benefits: Competent policy makers are more likely to survive than are their incompetent counterparts.

3   Summary and conclusion

The following assumptions of my model are crucial for the results regarding the existence and direction of policy and selection biases. An office-motivated incumbent faces an electoral challenge. The voters' utility depends on the actions taken by the incumbent, as well as his competencies, neither of which they directly observe. Among the voters, special interests observe the outcomes of policy processes, while the members of the general public experience only these policy outcomes as mediated by market processes. Special interests are thus better informed than the general public in the sense that they can form a more precise estimate of the incumbent's competencies.

The analysis generates the following implications. The preelection period is subject to a systematic policy bias toward special interests, as well as policy variability, both of which reduce aggregate welfare. The policy bias increases with the severity of the informational asymmetry between special interests and the general public and with the strength of the reelection goal. Election outcomes favor incumbents of above-average competence, who are more likely to survive compared to their less competent counterparts. This selection bias increases aggregate welfare.

It is useful to compare and contrast the intuition underlying my analysis with the argument made by Olson (1965, 1982), who proposes that the policy bias toward special interests is driven by the logic of collective action: Smaller groups are better able to overcome the free rider problem of becoming organized than are large groups. My analysis suggests that political decision making may be biased towards well informed groups of voters at the expense of their ill informed counterparts, even when voters are otherwise undifferentiated.

However, the informational asymmetry between special interests and the general public that underlies my results may be driven by the Olsonian logic of collective action. Lohmann (1994) endogenizes this asymmetry as resulting from individual decisions to invest in costly information gathering efforts: Being a minority, special interests are better able to overcome the free rider problem associated with such efforts, compared with the members of the general public.

My analysis also allows for a more precise assessment of why policy makers and voters find it difficult, and perhaps impossible, to break free of the so-called collective dilemma. After all, political candidates know that they cannot systematically increase their chances of remaining in power by biasing policy towards special interests, and voters understand the inefficiencies generated by the policy bias. So all players are in unanimous agreement that they would be better off if they could break the political gridlock. However, no political candidate can credibly promise to eliminate the policy bias toward special interests: Once elected, he shares the electoral incentives of his predecessors, and the electorate cannot effectively monitor whether he kept his promises.

This raises the question whether the problem of demosclerosis can be mitigated if the political process is reformed. Jonathan Rauch (1994) notes:

> For many people, it is almost an article of faith that political reform is the key to revitalizing government and reducing the power of "special interests." The idea is that if Americans can't stop each other from forming interest groups, then at least we can reform the political process to reduce our groups' influence on our government. We would isolate government from lobbies, as the body might wall off a tumor. ... Nonetheless, expectations for process reforms are generally too high, and, indeed, tend to miss the point. *The process isn't the problem. The problem is the problem.*[5] (p. 160)

Exactly. Here, as well as in my earlier work (Lohmann 1994), I attempt to identify the nature of the problem. It exceeds the compass of this article to analyze various political reform proposals; but my analysis suggests that a proposal that does not come to grips with the informational asymmetry underlying the problem of demosclerosis is unlikely to succeed.

References

Feddersen, Timothy J., and Pesendorfer, Wolfgang, "The Swing Voter's Curse," 1993, mimeograph, Northwestern University.

Kreps, David M., and Robert Wilson, "Sequential Equilibria," *Econometrica* 1982, 50, 863–93.

---

[5] Italics added by Susanne Lohmann.

Lohmann, Susanne, "Electoral Incentives, Political Intransparency, and the Policy Bias Toward Special Interests," 1994, mimeograph, University of California at Los Angeles.

Olson, Mancur, *The Logic of Collective Action,* 1965, Cambridge: Harvard University Press.

Olson, Mancur, *The Rise and Decline of Nations: Economic Growth Stagflation. and Social Rigidities,* 1982, New Haven: Yale University Press.

Rauch, Jonathan, *Demosclerosis: The Silent Killer of American Government,* 1994, New York: Times Books.

Wittman, Donald, "Why Democracies Produce Efficient Results," *Journal of Political Economy,* 1989, 97, 1395–424.

CHAPTER 8

Deforestation, investment, and political stability

Robert T. Deacon
University of California, Santa Barbara
University Fellow, Resources for the Future

1   Introduction

When governments are volatile or predatory, the individual's incentive to invest is reduced. Instability in the laws and institutions that govern ownership subjects the future return to an investment to confiscation risk – by outright seizure of assets, failure of government to enforce laws of property, or opportunistic taxation. Rule by an elite group rather than by laws can have a similar effect, since the individual's claim to property depends on remaining in favor with the ruling group and on the group's hold on power. Weakened ownership, in turn, dampens the incentive to accumulate and conserve capital of all sorts, including forests, mineral reserves, and ordinary produced capital. In what follows the relationship between insecure ownership and the conservation of forests is examined empirically, using data from two very different sources.[1] The first is historical accounts of the extent of forest cover and patterns of forest use over the last three thousand years, primarily in the Mediterranean basin. The second is a database that allows statistical analysis of the deforestation rates, investment rates, and political attributes of over 100 countries during the 1980s.

Environmental outcomes and patterns of natural resource use vary widely across countries. A quick examination of cross-country environmental data shows that this is true for rates of deforestation, concentrations of air pollutants, availability of sanitation and safe drinking water, and participation in international environmental treaties.[2] Those who study natural resource and

This research was supported by National Science Foundation Grant SBR-9223315. Paul Murphy provided research assistance. The author benefited from conversations with William Hyde and from comments by Ken Ardon and the editors. The views expressed are solely the author's responsibility.

[1] Recent interest in the process whereby forests are converted to agriculture, pasture, and wasteland stems from a number of concerns, including global increases in atmospheric carbon, species extinction due to habitat loss, and displacement of indigenous forest dwellers.

[2] See, for example, the data reported in Chapters 16, 17, 19, 20, 23, and 24 of World Resources Institute (1994).

environmental problems have devoted little attention to this variation until recently, however, and the recent literature has focused on a single factor, income variation, as a potential cause. Relationships between income and environmental indicators, so-called environmental Kuznets curves, have now been estimated for air and water pollutants, forest cover, and solid waste generation.[3] Without denying the importance of this work, the search for reasons why environmental outcomes differ among countries is far from complete.[4]

The present paper extends this search in a different direction by studying cross-country variations in the nature of government, particularly those aspects that affect security of ownership, as a possible reason for differences in deforestation.[5] At a very general level the relationship between deforestation and ownership security seems intuitively clear. Allowing a forest to grow and provide a stream of output in future years, rather than consuming it immediately, is an act of investment. An individual will not make the necessary initial sacrifice without some assurance of receiving the future benefit.

While this intuitive generalization is appealing, a more complete understanding of the relationship requires one to consider the specific processes involved in deforestation and to examine how each is affected, if at all, by insecure ownership. Insecure ownership induces short harvest rotations on land used to grow trees for timber or biomass for shifting cultivation. Short rotations can, in turn, cause forest land to degenerate into wasteland; so a positive relationship between security and the maintenance of forest cover is expected via this process. Insecure ownership also weakens incentives to develop plantation forests and village wood lots for timber and fuel wood. The timber and fuel provided by these planted stands reduce pressure on natural forests; so secure ownership favors maintenance of natural forests by this process as well.

Secure ownership also lowers the cost of ordinary produced capital, however, and this can give rise to indirect effects that either reinforce or offset any direct effects on forest cover. The outcome depends on patterns of complementarity between forest resources and other capital. Two examples will illustrate these possibilities. Insecure ownership hinders investments in capital-intensive agriculture. Absent soil improvement, irrigation, and other such

---

[3] See Grossman and Krueger (1991) and World Bank (1992). Cropper and Griffiths (1994) present an analysis of population growth and deforestation rates.

[4] The common belief that income growth is itself endogenous, determined by deeper forces, is one important reason for continuing the search.

[5] There is a second possible connection between resource use and the form of government. The degree of popular representation a government practices presumably influences both the levels of public good environmental amenities provided and decisions involving the use of publicly owned natural resources. In a democracy these decisions respond to the preferences of the median citizen, but nondemocratic governments may reach entirely different outcomes, possibly controlling externalities only to suit the preferences of the group in power. This possibility is not explicitly examined here.

investments, yields per acre tend to be low, and farmers seeking to meet subsistence food requirements are forced to expand agriculture further into forest margins than they would otherwise. This possibility, emphasized in historical accounts presented later, reinforces the positive direct link between insecurity and deforestation. On the other hand, ownership insecurity can prevent investment in plant and equipment for milling timber into lumber and pulp. This reduces the profitability of commercial timber harvests, lowering this source of deforestation pressure.[6] Ultimately, the direction of the relationship between deforestation and insecure ownership is an empirical question, though there is at least a mild expectation that the two are positively related.[7]

The environmental effects of lax enforcement of nominal ownership rights has been examined in a few recent papers. Southgate, Sierra, and Brown (1991) showed that security of tenure, as measured by the prevalence of adjudicated land claims, is negatively related to deforestation rates in Ecuador. Alston, Libecap, and Schneider (1994) present evidence from Brazil that the existence of adjudicated land claims enhances incentives for agricultural investments.[8] This work clearly is important and it indicates that the hypothesis of primary interest here has empirical content. At another level, however, the adjudication of ownership claims is endogenous and varies from country to country. The benefit of establishing nominal title to a parcel of land depends partly on the stability and predictability of government policies. If the rule of law is not well established the individual land user may not find it worthwhile to file a claim.[9] It is therefore appropriate to examine direct measures of government stability when testing for a relationship between ownership security and forest conservation.

An extensive empirical literature has arisen on a closely related topic, the effect that insecure ownership, as indicated by measures of political instability, has on rates of investment and economic growth. Barro (1991) examined cross-country data and found certain measures of political turmoil to be negatively related to growth and investment rates, suggesting the influence of incomplete ownership in volatile political regimes. Persson and Tabellini (1994), Ozler and Rodrik (1992), Alesina et al. (1991), and others have corroborated the importance of political factors in the investment behavior of countries.[10]

---

[6] Sedjo (1983, pp. 20–1) demonstrates the importance of milling costs for commercial timber harvests.

[7] Deacon (1994) presents evidence that deforestation and political instability are positively related. Some of the results reported there are summarized in Section 3.

[8] Pearce and Bann (1993) summarize results from additional unpublished work on the determinants of deforestation.

[9] Alston et al. (1994) provide empirical evidence from Brazil that land claim adjudication is slower and less extensive in areas where there are jurisdictional disputes over which government controls land use.

[10] Romer (1989) surveys much of this literature and Levine and Renelt (1992) assess the robustness of results reported by various authors.

The remainder of this paper examines the hypothesis that political insecurity hinders incentives to invest in forest conservation in particular and in other forms of capital more generally. The following section organizes historical accounts of the use of forests during times of political turmoil and conflict. Most of the information presented is drawn from the Mediterranean region. The related questions how insecurity affects agricultural investments and the effect of capital intensive agriculture on the maintenance of forest cover are also emphasized.

2   Historical evidence from the Mediterranean basin and elsewhere

Thirgood (1981) traces the history of forests in the Mediterranean region, as far as the record can be pieced together from literary sources, historical accounts, works of art, and scientific study. He also relates this natural history to the human history of the region, to see how humans and forest have interacted over the last three millennia. Although he attributes the present unnaturally sparse forest cover and degraded soils of the region to several factors, the role of social unrest emerges as a consistent theme in his descriptions. In a summary statement, he describes the process of degradation as "… a gradual wearing away, accelerated in times of political uncertainty and anarchy. … [During] long periods, while the natural cover may have suffered, there was maintenance of site. But in times of social unrest or change … deterioration continued apace until either a new vegetation cover developed, or man again came into equilibrium."[11] Others who have studied this process cite similar social factors. The following narrative outlines the specific historical episodes and the base of evidence that underlies their assessments. The information assembled is specifically organized to focus on the hypothesis of interest, that political stability and the fate of forests are causally connected.

Forest use under the Greek and Roman civilizations

The forests of antiquity were far from being the free access wastes of some later eras. Organization and control of forest use – even the development of forest plantations – occurred at an early date. The Roman civilization provides numerous examples of the kinds of forest protection and management that can emerge under stable government with a well developed rule of law. Forest legislation on the Italian peninsula dates to the early days of the Roman republic, in the fifth century B.C. In pagan times, woods and forests were sacred and overseen by forest guardians associated with the priesthood (Anon., 1967). As the Republic grew, forests came under state ownership, and by 400 B.C. a class of custodians had arisen charged with guarding and patrolling the state's forests. This ancient "forest service":

[11] Thirgood (1981, pp. 150–1).

... was at first custodial in nature and without technical duties. In time, this administration became responsible for tending and managing the forests, with responsibility for felling and extraction, and for the protection of watersheds. There were forest guards who enforced respect for contracts, controlled exploitation and grazing, and performed many of the functions of a modern forest service. Woodlands were enclosed for state and private hunting preserves. Land leases and published decrees were issued containing restrictions on timber cutting and stipulations for replanting.[12]

Deliberate, long-term investments in forest growth also were common. Mirov (1967, pp. 4, 5, 245, 247) reports that significant tree planting was undertaken by Etruscans, Romans, and others, and that pines were introduced into many regions of the Mediterranean basin where they had not grown naturally. Romans regularly maintained coppice woods with annual cuts: Pliny, in his *Historia Naturalis,* mentions specific rotation periods between harvests of chestnut and oak (Thirgood, 1981, p. 45).

Examples of investment in forest conservation can also be found in other stable, classical cultures, In Greece, Plato's laws include special provisions for "holy" areas in forests (Thirgood, 1981, p. 43). Fines were levied on citizens who profited from illegal use, and laws were administered by local magistrates. Setting fires and removing wood and leaf fodder was forbidden. Interestingly, Fernow (1913) reports that these groves were lost when a major source of instability was introduced – the early Christian fanatics who destroyed the sacred groves as part of a campaign to obliterate pagan relics.

During the stable Ptolemaic period (332–30 B.C.) in Egypt, the felling of trees was under state control, with penalties for unauthorized use. According to Thirgood (1981, p. 92):

> The papyri describe a country-wide programme of tree planting on wasteland, private property and royal estates, and along the banks of rivers and canals. Trees were raised in state nurseries. In these plantations laws regulated felling, lopping and removal of fallen trees, and provided for exclusion of sheep and goats from young plantations.

The extent of agricultural investments under classical civilizations

There is widespread evidence that stable civilizations created conditions amenable to sophisticated agricultural investments. As argued earlier, the resulting high yields per acre may have contributed to the maintenance of for-

---

[12] Thirgood (1981, p. 44). He reports that the Romans also knew of the relationship between tree cover and water supply regulation. In the fourth century B.C. Pliny referred to the occurrence of devastating torrents after mountain forests were cut and remarked that these had previously held and absorbed the rain.

est cover by obviating the spread of agriculture into forest margins.[13] Reifenberg (1955, p. 83) reports that Hammurabi, the Amorite king who ruled during the rise of the Babylonian Empire around 1700 B.C., adopted a land code that required owners to keep irrigation canals, dykes, and river embankments in good repair, while the state built and maintained major water works. The same author describes sophisticated agriculture in Palestine during the eighth century B.C., and emphasizes the need for a strong administration to protect flourishing agricultural communities from nomadic raids (Reifenberg, 1955, p. 87). Murphey (1951, pp. 120, 122, 125) presents a remarkable array of archaeological evidence of extensive Roman investments in water delivery systems and other agricultural capital during their rule of North Africa. Significantly, these improvements lasted only as long as North Africa was ruled by stable laws and government. They were maintained by the Romans and under subsequent Byzantine rule, but were largely wrecked and abandoned following invasions by nomads in the seventh and eighth centuries A.D.

The advanced agricultural methods practiced by the classical civilizations of the Mediterranean during the first millennium B.C. included mechanical and chemical improvement of the soil, plant breeding, introduction of exotic species, and practice of soil conservation.[14] Thirgood (1981, pp. 109–10) describes Roman agricultural practice in Palestine as including

> ... soil care, seed production stations, routine use of fertilizers, ... tree planting, orchards, windbreaks, irrigation works and aqueducts. [This] period marked the high point in agricultural development. Soil conservation measures, crop rotation, organic fertilization and terracing were widely applied.

In a subsequent passage he points out that "... these conditions, with all they implied for intensive care and investment in terrace maintenance and intensive agriculture, could only persist so long as there was a stable government. ..."

The *pax romana* and the relatively stable Byzantine era that succeeded it was followed by turmoil, and several writers conclude that this led to the decay of agricultural investments and to environmental deterioration, particularly in the Middle East. Reifenberg (1951, p. 80) makes a telling observation in this regard: "... [I]t was during times of firm rule only that agriculture flourished in the Levant. With the break-down of efficient administration, the state was no longer able to protect the cultivator against the plundering nomad. We shall see again and again how the desert spread over all forms of civilization whenever there was a deterioration of political conditions." Thirgood (1981, p. 22) ascribes the contraction of settled agriculture in the Eastern Mediterranean largely to political instability and economic deteriora-

---

[13] High agricultural productivity also favors population growth which, ceteris paribus, intensifies pressure on forests. This possibility is discussed later.

[14] Thirgood (1981, pp. 28–30).

tion in the disintegrating Roman Empire and to the invasion of nomadic tribes. He notes that the landscape was transformed from agriculture to pastoralism, and failure to maintain terracing on hills hastened soil erosion. An apt summary of the connection between stability and the maintenance of agricultural investments is provided by Murphey (1951, p. 124): "No military conquest is conducive to the maintenance of civil order nor the administrative and technical organization which an intricate irrigation economy requires, especially when the conquerors are nomads."[15]

The decline of forests in times of war and social turmoil

Insecurity regarding asset ownership and the future return to investment and conservation actions reaches a peak when nations are at war. Studying how forests fare during such conflicts thus brings the hypothesis of interest into sharp focus. War can affect the extent of forests in two ways. First, the insecurity that accompanies war reduces forest conservation motives to minimal levels, and this tends to reduce forest cover. There is a potentially contrary second force, however, as war often causes the annihilation or enslaving of populations and with reduced demands for use, forests might expand. Thirgood (1981, p. 58) weighs both factors and concludes that, overall, the dominant effect of war on Mediterranean forest cover has been adverse. Some of the forest destruction caused by war is direct – the use of wood in war implements, the use of fire in battles, and so forth. Less obvious, but arguably more important, is the resulting insecurity:

> In addition to deliberate or accidental destruction and excessive exploitation, wars and invasions have had a profound effect in upsetting established use patterns. In the Mediterranean environment there is a clear relationship between the security that accompanies stable government and good husbandry of the land. Disruption of settled government has almost inevitably led to an increase in pastoralism. This has been so from the breakdown of the Roman Empire, when the nomads were no longer kept beyond the fron-

---

[15] Some attribute deforestation and land degradation in the region to climate change. Both Butzer (1961) and Murphey (1951) disagree and cite archaeological evidence to support their conclusion. Butzer (1961, p. 47) notes that "The archaeological evidence does not support a hypothesis of climatic deterioration in historical times; rather it indicates the abandonment of wide areas as a result of economic deterioration and political instability, nomadic incursions and the decline of urban activity." Others have claimed extensive deforestation during Roman rule of the Mediterranean and cited such degradation as a cause of the Empire's eventual decline. Thirgood (1981, p. 31) considers and rejects this possibility. Rather, he concludes that, despite extensive forest clearing, there was little loss of fertility during classical times "… and despite considerable inroads and with the exception of the denuding of the arid, thin-soiled areas, extensive timber forests still remained at the end of the classical period and natural regeneration was able to maintain forests in being" (1981, p. 46).

tiers, through the Moslem invasions of the early Middle Ages, and the upheavals of the Crusades, down to the disruptions of the Second World War and its aftermath.[16]

Fernow (1913, p. 10) speaks of the "widespread devastation of large forest areas" during the Jewish wars chronicled by the historian Josephus. He also notes that the Persian wars in Greece that preceded the ascendancy of Alexander the Great caused widespread forest destruction. He later notes that in Great Britain during the revolution of Cromwell, beginning in 1642 and during Cromwell's reign, "a licentious devastation of the confiscated or mortgaged noblemen's woods took place."[17] He also notes that large areas of woodland along the Scottish borderland, originally maintained by residents for domestic uses, was laid waste in Cromwell's time.

Thirgood recounts specific examples of war's effects in southern Italy, Greece, and elsewhere. In his estimation the Greek forests suffered extensive devastation in the confusion that followed the Greek War of Independence in 1821. More generally, he notes: "At this time, and during subsequent periods of national emergency, political instability resulted in the destruction and degradation of many forest areas that had previously been protected by their inaccessibility."[18]

The susceptibility of forests to destruction by fire makes them uniquely vulnerable during time of war or political unrest. Firing the forests can both be a war-making tactic and a way to deny resources to one's enemy. Thirgood (1981, p. 67) describes its use as a weapon of war in the Persian invasions of Greece, in the Peloponnesian War between Athens and Sparta, during the Arab Invasions of North Africa, in the Mamelukes defense of the Levant against the Crusaders, and by both sides in the Castilian-Moorish wars on the Iberian Peninsula, where fires were set to prevent forest cover from concealing approaches to fortresses.[19]

Several observers have described the devastation of forests throughout Europe that accompanied World War II. Teclaff (1956, pp. 307–8) describes the history of East-Central European forests during the twentieth century and notes that the most rapid losses occurred during this conflict. The rate of forest cutting in Poland during the five years of German occupation was two and

[16] Thirgood (1981, p. 58).

[17] Fernow (1913, pp. 373–4).

[18] Thirgood (1981, p. 58).

[19] Destroying forests by fire also has been used as a gesture to dispute an enemy's claim to, or physical control of, an area of land. "The Syrians set fire to the forest in the 1940s in protest against the French Regime. In Cyprus, fire was an established form of resistance to forest regulation and control, and a much exploited method of terrorist escape during the campaign prior to independence. Subsequent communal unrest and violence has been marked by outbreaks of widespread incendiarism, even extending to the use of military aircraft for this purpose" (Thirgood, 1981, p. 67).

one-half to three times as rapid as in prewar days. A United Nations forestry report on the entire continent reports that vast areas of European forest suffered heavy damage during the war, "from excessive and destructive cutting, actual war devastation, and wholly inadequate reforestation."[20] Lowenthal (1956, pp. 275–7) notes that "overcutting" occurred in France during and immediately following World War II. He also reports data showing that forest cover in France advanced monotonically between 1863 and 1953, except during the war years when it declined.

Absent war, the same sort of insecurity can arise in periods of anarchy or lax government enforcement of laws. The record from France during and after the Revolution is instructive. Lowenthal (1956, p. 275) cites the turmoil and excesses of the Revolution, "the wiping out of feudal forest privileges and widespread pillaging which followed," together with the abolishment of ecclesiastical claims to vast tracts of forest land, as sources of significant forest reduction. Fernow (1913, p. 219) elaborates on this theme, explaining that the revolutionary law of 1791 abolished existing jurisdictions and legal restraints on land use. The result was "widespread destruction and devastation of forest property against which legislative attempts of the republican government were entirely powerless."

Reifenberg (1955, p. 104) and Thirgood (1981, p. 114) describe a relevant episode from the Ottoman empire during the nineteenth century. After the traditional feudal system of land tenure was abolished, popular zeal for a more egalitarian land allocation system led to the Turkish *mesha* system of assigning land to farmers. Land was held in common by village communities and divided into parcels that were reassigned among individuals by lot every one to three years. "Nobody was interested in investing money or labor in land which changed hands from time to time. ... No terraces were maintained or constructed, no trees planted and no manure applied to the land."[21]

The observation that forests are burned and plundered, and that soils and other natural assets are poorly maintained in time of war and following the upheaval of traditional legal systems, may surprise no one. It is useful nonetheless to document the available evidence of such phenomena, because the forces of interest are most easily observed at such times. Ownership of land and assets is least certain in these circumstances; hence concern over costs and benefits that might be incurred in the distant future are least pressing. In such conditions, when the needs of the immediate present are all important, the connection between insecurity and the absence of incentives to invest and conserve resources is clearest.

---

[20] Teclaff (1956, p. 308).

[21] Reifenberg (1955, p. 104). Thirgood (1981, p. 114) points out that the attempt at egalitarian assignment of land went even further, and with additional consequences for the environment. "Individual narrow strips ran straight up the mountain sides, maintaining equity by including both valley and hill land [in each farmer's parcel]. In consequence, ploughing up and down slopes was customary," a practice that caused accelerated soil loss.

Cultural differences between nomadism and settled agriculture

Several writers have pointed out the marked difference in how the land and its forests, soil, and other resources are used by nomads versus settled agriculturalists. To the latter, the future well-being of immediate family and descendants depends on maintaining the land's productivity. Nomadic pastoralists, on the other hand, occupy the land in a transient manner; so there is little impetus to form cultural norms that would favor long-term investments in the conservation of a specific site.

Thirgood (1981, pp. 69–71) considers grazing by nomadic cultures the most obvious and probably the most significant agent in deforestation, mainly because close cropping of new buds by goats and sheep prevents forest regeneration. He is careful to point out that while Roman agriculturalists grazed animals, the form this grazing took was far different from that practiced by nomads, and that indeed the Romans placed much importance on keeping the nomad's flocks and camels beyond the bounds of cultivated lands. He also notes that intentional deforestation to increase grazing land, a common practice in less settled cultures, is never mentioned among Roman treaties on agricultural practice.

The economic differences between settled agriculture and nomadism as ways of life thus make it necessary to qualify the hypothesized connection between stable government and the conservation of land and forests. In the former culture land is owned; so an individual's wealth depends on the condition of the land and environment at a specific location. In the latter, the owned assets are mobile. While the nomad's well-being is affected by the state of the environment in general, it is not tied to the condition of any specific site. If stable government and well developed laws of ownership arise in a society of nomads, they may well lead to investments in mobile assets. Incentives to practice conservation in the use of immobile natural resources such as soils and forests will still be lacking, however. Waterer (1949), in his study of land use in Jordan, stresses this cultural distinction in his description of two types of grazing, "local" and "migratory":

> Local grazing was that practiced by the static communities over lands in the vicinity of their villages ... [and] the flocks are kept off the cultivated cereal lands during the short growing season. ... In the case of migratory grazing the flocks are mostly owned by nomadic tribesmen who have no basic villages. They ... have little interest in crops except as a potential source of fodder to be preyed on.[22]

After noting the importance of migratory grazing for his study area, he comments in passing that "In such circumstances it is easy to understand why Jordan has few trees ... ."

---

[22] This passage is from a quotation in Thirgood (1981, p. 76).

There is some evidence that nomadism, as a way of life, can arise endogenously from conditions of instability and insecurity. Thirgood (1981, p. 74) cites such an occurrence in Spain. Though traditionally a settled agricultural society, migratory grazing was for a time promoted by government as a deliberate policy. This occurred during the long period of struggle with the moors, when livestock came to be regarded as one of the few safe possessions.[23]

When the two types of society exist in proximity, conflicts seem inevitable. In such instances the economic viability of settled agriculture depends, in part, on an ability to prevent encroachment by nomads. The organization of such defenses is a collective act which, in turn, generally requires a stable government. Hence, political stability may promote forest conservation via this indirect route. Thirgood (1981, p. 70) makes this point emphatically: "Throughout the Mediterranean, vast areas legitimately belonging to crop husbandry have been taken over by pastoralists in the absence of strong central government." Reifenberg (1955, p. 80) reinforces this with reference to land use in the Levant. Commenting on the deforestation, soil erosion, sanding up of fertile land, and swamp formation that occurred there, particularly in Mameluke and Turkish times, he draws a connection between such deterioration and the ability of settled agriculturalists to repel nomadic incursions:

> It can be shown that it was in periods of firm rule only that agriculture flourished in the country. With the breakdown in efficient administration the state is no more able to protect the cultivator against the plundering nomad. We see again and again that the desert spreads over all forms of civilization whenever a deterioration of political conditions ensues.

Thirgood (1981, p. 85), expanding on the Levantine experience, points out that: "hard-won rehabilitation [of habitat], resulting from many years of dedicated effort, may be set at naught by short-term political disturbance."

Historical evidence from the twentieth century

While the preceding discussion stressed the role that insecurity plays in the use of forests, this clearly is only one of several factors. Many observers point to the forces of population growth and technological change as important factors in the decline of forests in the Mediterranean and other environments.[24]

---

[23] Religion is another cultural factor that obviously influences land use and the extent of forests. In particular, religious practices can influence rules of land ownership in ways that affect investment and conservation incentives regardless of the degree of stability and security. Reifenberg (1955, p. 104) notes that Moslem doctrine regards all uncultivated lands as commons, with rights of pasturage accorded to all herd owners, and that the same rule applies to cultivated land after harvest. He describes the resulting effect on natural vegetation as "devastating" and notes that "At the same time most of the forests could be exploited without any restraint."

[24] Thirgood (1981, pp. 26, 27, 34, 35, 62) presents evidence that both technological advance and population growth have led to the decline of forest cover.

Population and technology may, in turn, be affected by political conditions, thus complicating the overall relation between security and the extent of forests. Political stability fosters economic growth, which allows population to grow unless controlled deliberately by the culture. Eventually, uncontrolled population growth may put pressure on forests and lead to land degradation. Technical advances also affect resource use, and it is in times of political stability that economic conditions are most conducive to innovation and the use of new technologies. These arguments suggest that political stability may lead indirectly, through increases in population and technological change, to declines in forests.

Recent experience in the comparatively peaceful circumstances prevailing in North America during the last century and in Europe since World War II clearly indicates that deforestation is not the inevitable result of population growth and technical advance, however. Populations have grown steadily on both continents over these periods, and the advance in technology has been unparalleled. Yet the result has not generally been massive deforestation and land degradation. Sedjo and Lyon (1990, pp. 5–7) point out that the once denuded forests of New England and the Lake States have gradually been replaced by naturally regenerated second-growth forest over the last 130 years. Forest cover in New England, less than 50 percent at the Civil War, is over 80 percent at present and vigorous forests now cover parts of the U.S. South that were once farmed.

Between 1954 and 1984 the total forest area in Europe grew by over 15 percent, and some expansion was recorded in almost all countries.[25] Lowenthal (1956, p. 272) reports data, at approximately 10-year intervals, on the area of forest land in France during the first half of this century. In each period reported except one, the forested area increased. The sole exception is a 4 percent decline recorded during the Second World War. Between 1892 and 1953 the reported acreage in France's forests increased from 9.5 to 11.4 million hectares, or 20 percent.

Technological advance and population growth do not therefore necessarily lead to the decline of forest acreage, even when the result is a heavy demand for forest products. Sedjo and Lyon (1990, p. 28) make this point cogently by noting that the area of temperate forests of the North has increased by an estimated 2 percent since World War II, despite the fact that these forests are the dominant source of the world's supply of timber.

3   Recent evidence from a cross section of countries

While the earlier historical record is informative, it is largely anecdotal and qualitative; the available database is far too sparse to permit formal testing of

[25] Sedjo and Lyon (1990, p. 28).

the hypotheses of interest. Such tests require consistently measured data on forest cover and the other variables. Quantitative information on forest cover across countries and over time has become far more complete since World War II, however. The present section makes use of this more extensive database for statistical testing, using data drawn from a sample of countries during the 1980s. Two sorts of relationships are examined. The first is between cross-country variations in deforestation rates and the political attributes of countries. While this relationship has been emphasized in the discussion to this point, it is largely a corollary of a more general principal – that political instability depresses incentives to invest. Hence, a second, more general hypothesis is examined as well, that investment rates vary systematically with political conditions. These tests require data on deforestation rates, investment rates, and measures of political security.

Data on forest cover in a sample of countries were taken from United Nations Food and Agriculture Organization (Food and Agricultural Organization, 1988).[26] Forest cover is reported for 1980 and 1985, including acreage in both a closed and an open forest.[27] From these data a deforestation rate was computed for each country. Deforestation is defined as the proportionate change in forest cover between 1980 and 1985, measured as a positive number if forest cover was reduced.[28] Data on gross domestic product and investment, by country and year, were taken from Summers and Heston (1991) and used to form an investment rate variable, the fraction of national income invested. Relevant political attributes, described shortly, were obtained from Banks (1990).

The sample used for statistical testing includes 120 countries, 20 of which are defined as high income by the World Bank. Table 8-1 lists these countries and partitions them into three deforestation groups, depending on the fraction of 1980 forest cover lost during 1980–85. High deforestation countries are

---

[26] FAO periodically reported data on forest cover by country as early as 1948, but this practice was discontinued in 1961 due partly to questions over the accuracy of published figures. Growing concern with deforestation during the 1970s led FAO to collect and publish forest cover data for 1980 and 1985, with emphasis on greater accuracy. These assessments covered 129 countries in 1980 and 84 countries in 1985. Data from an auxiliary source were used to extend the 1985 figures to the remaining countries, as explained in Deacon (1994). A forest assessment was also completed for 1990, but the country-specific forest cover numbers are projections based on population growth and are inappropriate for the present purpose. See Cropper and Griffiths (1994).

[27] Closed forest includes broad-leaved, coniferous, and bamboo forests, with tree crown cover exceeding 20 percent of the land. An open forest consists of mixed forest and grasslands with at least 10 percent tree cover.

[28] Basing empirical analysis on a deforestation rate implicitly involves first-differencing data on forest cover. This is advantageous because first-differencing eliminates the effect on forest cover of factors that are constant in a given country over time, e.g., climatic conditions and geophysical attributes.

Table 8-1. *Countries in sample*

Low- and middle-income countries				
High defor.	Low defor.			Afforestation
Afghanistan	Angola	German D.R.	Papua New G.	Albania
Costa Rica	Argentina	Ghana	Paraguay	Hungary
Cote d'Ivoire	Bangladesh	Greece	Peru	
Ecuador	Benin	Guatemala	Philippines	
El Salvador	Bhutan	Guinea	Poland	
Gambia	Bolivia	Guyana	Portugal	
Guinea-Bissau	Botswana	India	Romania	
Haiti	Brazil	Indonesia	Rwanda	
Iraq	Bulgaria	Iran	Senegal	
Jamaica	Burkina Faso	Kenya	Sierra Leone	
Lebanon	Burundi	Korea, North	Somalia	
Liberia	Cambodia	Korea, South	Sudan	
Malawi	Cameroon	Lao P.D.R.	Swaziland	
Nepal	Cent. Afr. Rep.	Madagascar	Tanzania	
Nicaragua	Chad	Malaysia	Togo	
Niger	Chile	Mauritius	Trin. & Tob.	
Nigeria	China	Mali	Tunisia	
South Africa	Colombia	Mexico	Turkey	
Sri Lanka	Congo	Mongolia	Uganda	
Syria	Cuba	Morocco	Uruguay	
Thailand	Czechoslov.	Mozambique	Venezuela	
	Domin. Rep.	Myanmar	Vietnam	
	Ethiopia	Namibia	Yugoslavia	
	Fiji	Pakistan	Zaire	
	Gabon	Panama	Zambia	
			Zimbabwe	

High-income countries				
High defor.	Low defor.			Afforestation
Israel	Australia	F.R. Germany	Norway	Canada
	Austria	Ireland	Spain	U. K.
	Cyprus	Italy	Sweden	
	Denmark	Japan	Switzerland	
	Finland	Netherlands	United States	
	France	New Zealand		

Excludes countries with fewer than 500,000 population of less than one percent forest cover in 1980. See text for definitions.

those that lost more than 10 percent. Low deforestation countries lost 0 to 10 percent, and "afforestation" countries gained forest cover. Although Brazil, Indonesia, and the Philippines are often prominently noted in discussions of deforestation, they appear here as low deforestation countries. While the annual loss of forest acreage is large in these countries, their percentage deforestation rates are low because initial forest acreage is so great. In percentage terms their deforestation rates range from 0.5–0.9 percent per year. By comparison, deforestation rates in Afghanistan, Cote d'Ivoire, and Haiti averaged 3.7–5.0 percent per year during the same time span.

The political attributes of high versus low deforestation countries

Two kinds of political factors are examined. The first are measures of instability and general lawlessness – indicators that government lacks the power, stability, and popular support to enforce laws of property. Specific indicators include the occurrence of guerrilla warfare, armed revolt, and the frequency of major constitutional changes. The complete set is listed and defined in Table 8-2 under "measures of government instability or precursors to change." Absent reliable enforcement by government and predictable legal interpretations of property claims, a private individual's incentive to invest, either in forest conservation or other projects, is weak. A similar argument can be made for assets nominally owned by government as well. When government lacks the ability to enforce controls on how government forests are used, they tend to be treated as free access resources, a phenomenon evident in the colonization of national parks and government forest reserves by squatters in Latin America. Also, government presumably acts as a conduit for action by those segments of society who control it, whether a popular majority or privileged elite. If government's grip on power is tenuous, the incentive for those presently in control to take future-oriented government actions is weak as a consequence.

Political measures in the second group indicate whether a country is ruled by individuals and dominant elites rather than by laws and anonymous institutions. The variables used include dummies to indicate whether the head of government is a military dictator, whether a legislature exists, and so forth, as well as variables that measure the frequency of political purges and changes in chief executive, The complete set is defined in Table 8-2 as "indicators of non representation or repression."[29] By hypothesis, the average citizen's ownership claim is weaker and less predictable when it depends on the favor of a

---

[29] The chief executive of government is a premier only if chosen by elected representatives indicating, jointly, that the selection process is democratic and that the legislative branch exercises substantial power. Representation is thus relatively strong if the executive is a premier and weaker if not.

Talbe 8-2. *Political variables examined*

Measures of government instability or precursors to change:

Political assassination: Any politically motivated murder or attempted murder of a high government official or politician.

General strike: A strike of 1,000 or more workers aimed at national government policies or authority.

Riot: Any violent demonstration of more than 100 citizens involving the use of physical force.

Antigovernment demonstration: A peaceful gathering of at least 100 people for the primary purpose of displaying opposition to government policies or authority.

Guerilla warfare: The presence of any armed activity, sabotage, or bombings carried on by independent bands of citizens or irregular forces and aimed at the overthrow of the present regime.

Revolution: An attempted illegal or forced change in top government elite, or armed rebellion intended to gain independence from the central government.

Major government crisis: A rapidly developing situation that threatens to bring the downfall of the present regime—excluding revolt aimed at such overthrow.

Coup d'etat: A successful extraconstitutional or forced change in the top government elite and/or its effective control of the nation's power structure, including successful revolutions.

Major constitutional changes: The number of basic alterations is a state's constitutional structure, e.g., altering the roles of different branches of government, but excluding minor constitutional amendments.

Government regime change: A change in the type of regime, e.g., civilian, military, protectorate, in charge of government.

Indicators of nonrepresentation or repression:

Government executive is military: The individual who exercises primary influence in shaping the country's major internal and external decisions is in the armed services.

Government executive not elected: Individual who exercises primary influence in shaping the country's internal and external policies is not chosen by direct or indirect election.

Executive is not a premier: The executive is not drawn from the legislature of a parliamentary democracy.

No legislature exists: Self explanatory.

Legislature is elected: Legislature exists and legislators are chosen by direct or indirect popular election.

Political Purges: Frequency of systematic eliminations, by jailing or execution, of political opposition within the ranks of the regime or the opposition.

Changes in executive: Number of times per year that control of the executive changes to a new individual independent of the predecessor.

Source: Banks (1991)

specific individual or clique rather than the persistence of established political and legal institutions. The clique's allies may lose property if it is deposed. Those not in favor with the ruling elite may find that government enforces laws selectively and redistributes assets toward its friends, whether by direct confiscation or by taxation and regulation. Accumulating capital in such circumstances may simply invite redistribution.

The general hypotheses of interest are that political instability and repression are positively associated with deforestation and negatively associated with investment. Recall that the hypothesized relationship between political factors and deforestation is unclear on theoretical grounds. The *direct* effect of ownership insecurity is to reduce incentives for investments of all sorts, including conservation of forest capital. These direct effects include reduced incentives to maintain private wood lots and to create forest plantations, shortened rotations for forests used for timber harvests and shifting cultivation and, more generally, less care taken to maintain long-term uses of forests. *Indirect* effects, stemming from possible complementarities between produced capital and forest cover, can either reinforce or offset the direct effects, however. The examples given in the Introduction cited the indirect effects of political security on the capital intensity of agriculture, a reinforcing effect, and on the cost of capital used in processing timber for pulp and lumber, an offsetting effect. Whether the net direction of the relationship is positive or negative is necessarily an empirical question.

Table 8-3 compares mean political attributes of high versus low deforestation countries for the period 1980–85.[30] High-income countries were excluded from these computations to deflect the potential criticism that these nations are somehow "special" and therefore not comparable to developing countries. The "measures of government instability" are defined in such a way that figures in the first column will exceed those in the second if the hypothesis is correct. This expectation is confirmed for nine of the ten measures and the differences are significant at 10 percent for three, frequencies of revolutions, guerrilla warfare, and major constitutional changes.[31] Tests for association with measures of "nonrepresentation" are generally as expected as well. The first five comparisons indicate that deforestation is high where the degree of representation is

---

[30] This rather crude test for association was chosen to overcome data limitations. Given the nature of the data, there is a high proportion of zeros among indicators of political instability and dummy variables to indicate regime type are often zero or one. Correlations involving these variables tend to be low as a consequence. Further, the political attributes of interest are inherently hard to measure and the variables examined here are at best imperfect. The extent of forest cover also is measured with error. Comparing means across countries reduces the influence of such factors by averaging.

[31] Unexpectedly, coups d'état are slightly more frequent in low deforestation countries, but not significantly so.

Table 8-3. *Deforestation and political attributes (mean political attributes, 1980–85)*

	High deforestation countries, μ_H	Low deforestation countries, μ_L	t-statistic* H_O: $\mu_L < \mu_H$	$Pr > t$
Measures of government instability or precursors to change				
Political assassinations**	.0822	.0264	0.94 (24)	.18
General strikes**	.0245	.0142	0.88 (34)	.19
Riots**	.0468	.0284	1.04 (28)	.15
Antigovernment demonstrations**	.0645	.0482	0.82 (49)	.21
Guerilla warfare	.3333	.2051	1.31 (31)	.10
Revolutions	.3258	.1859	1.63 (29)	.06
Major government crises	.1439	.0684	1.08 (25)	.14
Coups d'état	.0303	.0384	0.39 (31)	.36
Major constitutional changes	.1136	.0705	1.41 (31)	.08
Government regime changes	.0727	.0436	1.08 (30)	.14
Indicators of nonrepresentation or repression				
Government executive is military	.2424	.0940	1.80 (27)	.04
Nonelected executive	.4394	.3184	1.11 (33)	.14
Executive is not a premier	.6136	.4124	1.79 (36)	.04
No legislature exists	.1742	.1410	0.49 (36)	.31
Legislature is elected*	.7879	.8419	0.72 (35)	.24
Political purges	.0909	.0620	0.74 (30)	.23
Changes in executive*	.1136	.1624	1.16 (50)	.13
Number of countries	22	78	—	—

Note: Excludes 20 "high income" countries.
* t-statistics are for the one tailed test H_O: $\mu_H \leq \mu_L$ versus H_a: $\mu_H > \mu_L$, except in tests involving *Legislature is elected* and *Changes in executive* where the inequalities are reversed.
** Annual rates per million population.

low, e.g., where the country's chief executive is a military dictator, where no legislature exists, and so forth. Frequent political purges indicate that competition for political power is not tolerated; so the finding that deforestation is high where purges are common is not unexpected. Changes in executive include legal, constitutionally mandated changes, and hence might indicate competition in the executive branch. If so, such changes should be more common in low deforestation countries. Alternatively, more frequent executive change might signal greater instability in government policy and hence greater deforestation. The comparison in Table 8-3 weakly supports the former interpretation.

To summarize, all but one of the 17 comparisons are consistent with expectations. Only five of the differences are significant at 10 percent, however. When the sample is expanded to include high-income countries, the differences become much sharper. The t-statistics rise for all comparisons except coups d'état, which falls to near zero, and 10 of the 17 differences become significant at 10 percent.[32]

Similar comparisons of mean political attributes were performed for countries with high versus low investment rates, where "high investment" indicates that a country spent at least 10 percent of gross domestic product on investment during 1980–85. In summary, 14 of the 17 comparisons went in the expected direction – with lower investment rates in countries with unstable or repressive political systems – and 12 of the differences were significant. Only one of the significant differences, for "government crises," was contrary to expectations, and all the differences found significant in deforestation comparisons were significant in investment comparisons.

This indicates that low investment and rapid deforestation are, in general, associated with the same set of political attributes. This finding receives further support from simple correlations between political factors and, alternately, investment rates and deforestation rates. Average investment rates, by country, for the period 1980–85 are most strongly correlated with the following five political factors: guerrilla warfare ($\rho = -.27$), revolutions ($\rho = -.42$), constitutional changes ($\rho = -.19$), military executives ($\rho = -.25$), and "executive is not a premier" ($\rho = -.30$). The same five political factors are among the six political variables most closely correlated with deforestation rates, though the correlations are generally weaker.[33]

Principal components analysis

It is unlikely that the attributes examined really contain 17 distinct dimensions of a country's political make-up, but theory alone provides little guidance

---

[32] To test the joint association between deforestation and the full set of political variables, a logit regression was estimated using a categorical variable denoting high versus low deforestation countries as the dependent variable and the political measures as regressors. When all 17 measures are included and the sample includes all 120 countries, the regression is significant at a probability level of .02. All but four of the political measures have signs that accord with the differences in means reported earlier, and none of the four with perverse signs approach significance. When high-income countries are excluded, the probability of no relationship rises to .15. If variables with z-statistics below .5 are excluded, however, the probability level falls to .02 and the number of perverse signs falls to one.

[33] Despite this close agreement, the correlation between investment rates and deforestation is relatively weak, $-.22$.

regarding which measures are redundant. Additionally, the limited observations available for deforestation rates makes it desirable to reduce the number of political factors included in empirical analysis. These considerations suggest using the method of principal components to compress the available political variables to a data set of more manageable dimension.

Principal components analysis is a descriptive device for representing the variation of several covarying variables in one or a few indexes. Loosely speaking, it forms new variables as linear combinations of an original data set, and the new terms are computed in a way that preserves as much of the variation in the original data as possible. More precisely, the first principal component is the linear combination of original variables that has maximal variance subject to the constraint that it be of unit length. The second principal component is the linear combination of maximum variance, subject to the unit length requirement and to the constraint that it be orthogonal to the first principal component. Additional principal components can be computed in like fashion and some subset used in place of the original data.[34]

The first six principal components account for 75 percent of the variance in the original set of political variables, and Table 8-4 shows the weights used to form them.[35] For reasons that become apparent shortly, attention is confined to the first, third, and sixth principal components, denoted PC1, PC3, and PC6. Regarding PC1, relatively large positive weights are attached to the frequency of revolutions, coups, constitutional changes, and regime changes – all measures of political change. The presence of a military executive, a nonelected executive, and no legislature enter with positive weight, and an elected legislature receives negative weight; collectively, these factors indicate an absence of popular representation. In effect, then, PC1 combines frequent government change and rule by cliques or individuals. PC3 assigns positive weights to frequent political assassinations, guerrilla warfare, revolutionary activity, and purges, as well as negative weight to frequent changes in executive. Though the last item is ambiguous, the first four can be characterized as measures of politically motivated violence. PC6 strongly emphasizes "executive is not a

---

[34] Alternatively, one can interpret the first principal component as the constructed $n \times 1$ vector $\mathbf{p}$ that minimizes the sum of squares of $\mathbf{X}-\mathbf{a'p}$, where $\mathbf{X}$ is the $n \times k$ matrix of original data, $\mathbf{a}$ is a $k \times 1$ vector of constants, and $\mathbf{p}$ is constrained to have unit length. The second principal component is computed similarly, substituting residuals from the first principal component in place of $\mathbf{X}$. See Theil (1971, pp. 46–55). This technique is subject to two well known shortcomings. First, the principal components are sensitive to the scaling of the original variables, e.g., to whether distance is measured in inches or miles. Second, the constructed variables may have no ready interpretation, i.e., the weights that form the principal components may show no clear pattern. The first consideration was assessed by experimenting with different scalings, and the second can be judged later when the composition of the principal components is reported.

[35] These principal components result from scaling all political variables to have zero mean and unit variance.

Table 8-4. *Principal components: 1980–85 political indicators*
(all countries, N=120)

Variable:	Variable weights for principal components					
	1	2	3	4	5	6
Political assassinations	0.1632	0.2406	0.3159	0.2081	−0.3801	0.1845
General strikes	0.0943	0.4695	−0.0705	0.0921	0.2691	0.2660
Riots	0.0154	0.4379	0.1642	−0.3884	−0.1981	−0.1759
Antigovernment demonstrations	0.0736	0.4587	0.0630	−0.4222	−0.0839	−0.0218
Guerrilla warfare	0.1547	−0.0117	0.5543	0.2985	0.0221	0.0821
Revolutions	0.2884	−0.0656	0.3831	0.2353	0.1934	0.0252
Major government crises	0.1297	0.3158	−0.1665	0.2541	0.4709	−0.1210
Coups d'état	0.3085	−0.0909	−0.2289	0.1810	−0.1953	−0.2480
Major constitutional changes	0.3141	0.0464	0.0736	0.0828	−0.3662	−0.1761
Government regime changes	0.3529	0.0019	−0.1801	0.0780	−0.2924	−0.0072
Government executive is military	0.3457	−0.0983	−0.1326	−0.1704	−0.0011	0.0622
Nonelected executive	0.2446	−0.2564	−0.0691	−0.1299	0.1873	−0.0449
No legislature exists	0.3692	−0.0941	−0.0809	−0.2340	0.1296	−0.1028
Executive is not a premier	−0.1882	0.0537	0.0394	0.2019	−0.0407	0.7918
Political purges	0.0868	0.0222	0.3808	−0.1951	0.3647	−0.3109
Legislature is elected	−0.3589	0.1272	0.0723	0.2488	−0.1567	0.0894
Changes in executive	0.1693	0.3177	−0.3339	0.3503	0.0900	−0.0307

premier," with negative weight, while the other factors follow no clear pattern. These interpretations, though admittedly somewhat arbitrary, are used to characterize these principal components in what follows.

When PC1–PC6 were regressed on deforestation rates and on average investment rates over the 1980–85 period, the results shown in Table 8-5 were obtained. The reason for focusing attention on PC1, PC3, and PC6 is now clear: These three variables are significant or near significant in both regressions.[36] This corroborates an earlier result: The political variables associated

[36] To test the sensitivity of results to the scaling of variables, principal components were computed for unscaled variables. (Recall that the principal components reported in Table 8-4 were computed after scaling all political variables to have zero mean and unit variance.) Briefly, the principal components obtained showed different loading factors and thus did not have the inter-

Table 8-5. *Political determinants of deforestation and investment (all countries, 1980–85)*

	Deforestation regressions		Investment regressions	
	Coefficient	t-statistic	Coefficient	t-statistic
PC1 (Change & repression)	.0070	2.760	−1.5006	−4.796
PC2	.0044	1.241	.5043	1.113
PC3 (Political violence)	.0097	2.282	−1.4356	−2.614
PC4	−.0045	−1.005	−.2370	−0.425
PC5	−.0010	−0.189	−.0748	−0.109
PC6 (Exec. not a premier)	.0109	1.847	−1.8483	−2.496
Constant	.0553	9.818	18.3560	25.712
R^2	.14	—	.25	—
N	120	—	117	—
Prob > F	.0070	—	*	—

* less than .00005

with rapid deforestation are also associated with low rates of investment. In addition, the relative magnitudes of coefficients for PC1, PC3, and PC6 are very similar in the two regressions, indicating that the pattern of associations with political factors is quantitatively consistent.

4   Conclusions

The evidence presented here indicates that political insecurity and social upheaval generally are associated with the degradation of forests and other natural assets. This relationship is evident in the history of Western Civilization and the evolution of forest cover over the last three thousand years. It also shows up in correlations between measurable indicators of political unrest and loss of forest cover during a very recent period. The economic argument offered to explain this correlation stresses the effect of political turmoil and social unrest on the individual's incentive to invest, i.e., to take present actions that will pay off only in the distant future. Laws, legal contracts, and the force of reputation normally provide the assurances the individual needs to warrant taking such future-oriented actions. When legal and political institutions are volatile or predatory, the investor's claim to future returns is less certain and incentives to take such

pretations given in the text. In general, however, it was again found that the same principal components tended to be significant in both regressions and with opposite sign. The analysis in the text also was repeated with high-income countries excluded from the data set. The results obtained were not markedly different from those reported.

actions are commensurately diminished. This interpretation of the empirical relationship is supported by the association shown between ordinary investment and the same measures of political insecurity. It should be stressed, of course, that this is just a general tendency and that it may be nullified or reversed in specific circumstances. On balance, however, the evidence suggests that a loss of security in the rewards from resource conservation, often caused by political turmoil and a breakdown of legal institutions, is destructive.

The statistical tests indicate that both ordinary investment in produced capital and the conservation of forest cover are relatively high in countries with stable, representative political institutions. Further, the differences in political characteristics tend to be large quantitatively across these groups. This suggests an interesting possibility for patterns of economic growth and use of the environment. Two groups of countries might be identified, one with stable institutions and a favorable climate for resource conservation and ordinary investment, and the other in opposite circumstances. In the first group, arguably "the best of all worlds," individuals are secure, economic growth proceeds, and the environment is afforded a degree of protection. Those in the worst of all worlds experience political repression, economic stagnation, and environmental deterioration. Policy advice is a tricky matter in such circumstances. Simply advising those stuck in the worst of all worlds to mimic the investment and resource conservation practices of their better-off brethren will have no beneficial effect. Indeed, those in the bad state are acting sensibly, given their circumstances. Rather, the appropriate direction for policy in this case is to search for actions that will foster the development of stable political institutions and rule by law rather than individuals.

Identifying specific policies to accomplish this is not at all straightforward, however. While stress has been placed on the empirical and historical relationship between unstable politics and the low investment levels and resource degradation experienced in many countries, political insecurity is itself endogenous and results from forces that are only poorly understood. Political unrest, along with the insecurity and repression it can bring, may result from wealth inequality, from rapid population growth and the consequent dilution of a country's land and other natural resources, or from cultural and religious factors. Understanding these factors, as well as the chain of causation that connects them to political unrest and ultimately to investment and resource conservation incentives, is centrally important to any policy that seeks to affect the way forests and other natural resources are used.

References

Alesina, Alberto, Sule Ozler, Nouriel Roubini, and Philip Swagel, "Political Instability and Economic Growth," Working Paper No. 4173, 1992, Cambridge, Mass.: National Bureau of Economic Research.

Alston, Lee J., Gary D. Libecap, and Robert Schneider, "An Analysis of Property Rights, Land Value, and Agricultural Investment on Two Frontiers in Brazil," 1994, mimeo, Urbana: University of Illinois.

Anon, "Ancient Roots, New Growth," *Unasylva,* 1967, 21, 1, 84, p. 1.

Banks, A. S., "Cross-National Time-Series Data Archive," 1990, Center for Social Analysis, Binghamton: State University of New York, September 1979 (updated to 1990).

Barro, Robert, "Economic Growth in a Cross Section of Countries," *Quarterly Journal of Economics,* 1991, 61 (May), 407–44.

Butzer, K. W., "Climatic Change in Arid Regions Since the Pliocene," 1961, in L. Dudley Stamp (ed.), *A History of Land Use in Arid Regions,* Paris: UNESCO.

Cropper, Maureen and Charles Griffiths, "The Interaction of Population Growth and Environmental Quality," *American Economic Review,* 1994, 84, 2 (May), 250–4.

Deacon, Robert T., "Deforestation and the Rule of Law in a Cross Section of Countries," *Land Economics,* 1994, 70, 4 (November), 414–30.

Fernow, B. E., *A Brief History of Forestry: in Europe, the United States, and Other Countries,* 1913, Washington D.C.: University Press.

Food and Agriculture Organization, *An Interim Report on the State of the Forest Resources in the Developing Countries,* 1988, Rome: United Nations.

Grossman, Gene M. and Alan B. Krueger, "Environmental Impacts of a North American Free Trade Agreement," Working Paper No. 3914, 1991, Cambridge, Mass.: National Bureau of Economic Research.

Levine, D. and Ross Renelt, "A Sensitivity Analysis of Cross-Country Growth Regressions," *American Economic Review,* 1992, 82, 4 (September), 942–64.

Lowdermilk, W. C., "Introduction," in A. Reifenberg, *The Struggle Between the Desert and the Sown: The Rise and Fall of Agriculture in the Levant,* 1955, Jerusalem: The Government Press.

Lowenthal, David, "Western Europe," in S. Haden-Guest, J. K. Wright, and E. M. Teclaff (eds.), *A World Geography of Forest Resources,* 1956, New York: The Ronald Press.

Mirov, N. T., *The Genus Pinus,* 1967, New York: Ronald Press.

Murphey, Rhoads, "The Decline of North Africa Since the Roman Occupation: Climatic or Human?" *Annals of the Association of American Geographers,* 1951, XLI, 3 (September), 116–32.

Ozler, Sule and Dani Rodrik, "External Shocks, Politics, and Private Investment: Some Theory and Empirical Evidence," Working Paper No. 3960, 1992, Cambridge, Mass.: National Bureau of Economic Research.

Pearce, David and Camille Bann, "North-South Transfers and the Capture of Global Environmental Value," 1993, mimeo, Center for Social and Economic Research on the Global Environment, London: University College.

Persson, Torsten and Guido Tabellini, "Is Inequality Harmful for Growth?" *American Economic Review,* 1994, 84, 3 (June), 600–22.

Reifenberg, A., *The Struggle Between the Desert and the Sown: The Rise and Fall of Agriculture in the Levant,* 1955, Jerusalem: The Government Press.

Romer, Paul, "Capital Accumulation in the Theory of Long-Run Growth," in R. Barro (ed.), *Modern Business Cycle Theory,* 1989, Cambridge: Harvard University Press.

Sedjo, Roger A. and Kenneth S. Lyon, *The Long-Term Adequacy of World Timber Supply,* 1990, Washington: Resources for the Future, Inc.

Sedjo, Roger A., *The Comparative Economics of Plantation Forestry,* 1983, Washington: Resources for the Future.

Southgate, Douglas, Rodrigo Sierra, and Lawrence Brown, "The Causes of Tropical Deforestation in Ecuador: A Statistical Analysis," *World Development,* 1991, 19, 9, 1145–51.

Summers, Robert and Alan Heston, "The Penn World Table Mark V," *Quarterly Journal of Economics,* 1991, 61 (May), 225–39.

Teclaff, Eileen M., "East Central Europe," in S. Haden-Guest, J. K. Wright, and E. M. Teclaff (eds.), *A World Geography of Forest Resources,* 1956, New York: The Ronald Press.

Theil, Henri, *Principles of Econometrics,* 1971, New York: John Wiley & Sons.

Thirgood, J. V., *Man and the Mediterranean Forest: A History of Resource Depletion,* 1981, London: Academic Press.

Tsoumis, G., *Forestry in Greece,* 1964, Yale Forest School News, 52.3L35-37, as cited in Thirgood (1981, p. 62).

Waterer, R. R., "Some Observations on the Forest and Land Use in General in Jordan," typescript, 1949, as cited in Thirgood (1981, p. 75).

World Resources Institute, *World Resources, 1993–94,* 1994, New York: Oxford University Press.

World Bank, *World Development Report 1992: Development and the Environment,* 1992, Oxford: Oxford University Press.

CHAPTER 9

Violence and the assignment of property rights on two Brazilian frontiers

Lee J. Alston
University of Colorado and University of Illinois
Gary D. Libecap
University of Arizona and NBER
Robert Schneider
World Bank

1   Introduction

Frontiers are often associated with violent conflict over property rights to land. Battles between claim jumpers and miners and between cattle raisers and sheep herders are part of the mythology of the nineteenth-century American West.[1] Similarly, popular accounts of settlement in the Brazilian Amazon point to widespread violence over land.[2] Yet conflict in the assignment of property rights is not inevitable. Indeed, if tenure institutions are supplied smoothly as land values rise, then settlement of the frontier can be routine with few disputes over property rights. In contrast, where clearly defined tenure is not supplied in a timely manner as potential land values increase, then violent conflict is a possible outcome. Tenure services are supplied through the political process, and a variety of problems can arise to complicate delivery. These include overlapping government jurisdictions with competing land agencies assigning tenure to the same land; multiple land agencies within the same government with different constituents who are granted title to the same land; government subsidies and other infrastructure programs that unexpectedly and sharply raise land values, attracting new claimants; and insufficient agency budgets and staffs to process and police titles.

This chapter examines the development of property rights to land in two Brazilian frontiers: in the southern state of Paraná during the coffee agricul-

We thank James Dalen, Jr., Jeffrey Fuller, Ricardo Tarifa, and especially Bernardo Mueller for their research assistance, Linda Cohen for her comments at the conference on "Political Economy of Rent Seeking and Conflict" (UC Irvine, May 1994), and the World Bank and NSF (grant SES 92113603) for financial support.

[1] For general discussion, see Anderson and Hill (1975, 1991), Libecap (1978, 1979, 1989), Hallagan (1978), and Umbeck (1981).

[2] See Rone (1991).

tural between 1940 and 1970 and in the Amazon state of Pará during the period of rapid migration to the region after 1970. Examination of frontier conditions allows us to observe both the demand for property rights and the supply of tenure institutions by government. The empirical analysis employs Brazilian agricultural census data from 1940 through 1985, with observations at the county (*município*) level. We can identify those areas where jurisdictional conflicts existed and where violent conflict among claimants occurred.

2   The titling process

Before describing the data and the analytical framework used in the analysis, it is important to summarize the process by which individuals can claim and receive title to land in Brazil. In Brazil, government land (*terra devoluta*) is open for private occupation and claiming, much as it was in North America in the nineteenth century. Generally, as with the U.S. Homestead Act of 1862, the land claim is to be occupied by the claimant and improved for agricultural use for a prescribed amount of time – a year for claims on government land or five years for claims to private land based on adverse possession. Once surveyed, land claims are filed with government land agencies that monitor compliance with the land laws, process title applications, and ultimately issue title.

To initiate the titling process, claimants generally must organize collectively, travel to a local agency office, and formally request surveys and documentation of their land claims. Group organization is necessary because land agencies usually wait until a threshold number of requests are made before traveling to the site. When they respond, agency officials take a census of settlers in the area, survey and mark claims, and grant claimants an authorization to occupy or *authorização do ocupação* or a *licensa de ocupação*. The authorizations are forwarded to the state or federal government, depending on the government unit involved, for final recording. Normally, title applications can be processed within two to five years, but if the initial claimant moves to a different site and sells the claim, the title application must be reprocessed, extending the titling time.[3]

Within Paraná, the state government had jurisdiction over land settlement, except in the western *municípios,* where there was dispute over jurisdiction between the federal and state governments (Foweraker, 1981, pp. 88–92). This dispute may have delayed the assignment of clear property rights to land and encouraged conflict among settlers over claims (Westphalen, Machado, and Balhana, 1968). We examine this issue in the following empirical analysis.

---

[3] If the settler improves and occupies the land, agency officials will return and grant a provisional title, while final title is being processed in Brasília or Belém. If, when the agency returns to the colony, the claimant has moved on or "sold" the squatter claim, the process of titling begins again. The agency tends to acknowledge the new claimant who holds the authorization or provisional title as long as the individual is a genuine settler and not a large land speculator.

In some cases, particularly in Paraná, private land companies obtained large tracts of land from the state government, recruited settlers, and issued titles. For example, the Companhia de Terras do Norte do Paraná obtained 12,463 square kilometers of land in the north, and sold urban and rural lots to settlers and extended railways and roads. The *municípios* included in the company's holdings accounted for over 12 percent of the size of Paraná in 1960.[4] Because the company gained clear legal title to its land before attracting colonists and was a residual claimant in the titling process, it may have transferred title more quickly and completely than did the state government (Foweraker, 1981, p. 130; Nicholls and Paiva, 1969, pp. 27–30).

In Pará, government policy on the frontier has been different in a number of ways from that in Paraná. First, both the federal and state governments have been involved in titling. In *municípios* with largely federal land, the federal land agency, INCRA (National Institute for Colonization and Agrarian Reform), processed land claims, whereas in *municípios* with state lands, the state land agency, ITERPA, administered private claims. A second difference between the land claiming processes in Paraná and Pará is that in Paraná private migration decisions as land values rose drove claiming activities, while in Pará migration was stimulated by directed (subsidized) colonization programs of the federal government. Government infrastructure investment and subsidized colonies brought settlers to the Amazon before land values had risen to a level that otherwise would have attracted migrants. Further, in Pará declining budgets for land agencies limited their ability to process title applications. Budget problems especially affected INCRA, whose budget peaked in 1976, leading to a lag in the assignment of title (Yokota, 1981, p. 33).

A third difference between settlement and titling in the two states is violent conflict among competing claimants. Although there was confusion over property rights to land in the western *municípios* in Paraná where the federal and state governments competed for jurisdiction, in Pará there has been violence between small holders and ranchers, particularly in southeastern Pará along the Belém-Brasília highway in the *município* of Conceição do Araguaia and others near Marabá. Ranchers have been subsidized by the Superintendency for the Development of Amazonia (SUDAM), a federal agency that administered a series of credit benefits and fiscal incentives (Schneider, 1994, pp. 2–6), whereas settlement by small holders has been encouraged by INCRA. With the census data we can examine the effects on the titling process of conflicting government jurisdiction in Paraná and violent conflict over land in Pará.

---

[4] This percentage was calculated using the map in Nicholls and Paiva (1969, p. 28) and the area of the *municípios* within the company's jurisdiction from IBGE, *Anuario Estatístico do Brazil* (1965, pp. 42–3).

3   Characteristics of the census data

The analysis of the conflict and violence in the assignment of property rights to land employs data from the Brazilian Agricultural Censuses from 1940 through 1970 for Paraná and from 1970 through 1985 for Pará and one from surveys of small farmers in Pará. The census data are by *município* (county). There are 79 *municípios* in Pará in the four census periods, whereas in Paraná the number of *municípios* grows from 49 in 1940 to 288 by 1970 through subdivision of existing *municípios*.[5] In general, the data are averages for each *município,* and they include average land value per hectare, distance from the *município* capital to the state capital (Curitiba and Belém) as a measure of remoteness from the market and administrative center, the proportion of *município* farmers with title, average farm size in the *município,* average soil quality for the *município,* population density, and average investment per hectare in the *município.*[6]

4   Analytical framework

The role of property rights in entry and resource use decisions is discussed by Libecap (1989), North (1990), and Feder and Feeny (1991). In general, exclusive rights to land provide the collateral necessary for farmers to access capital markets; promote land-specific investment by providing long-term security of ownership; reduce the private costs of defending claims; and increase the exchange value of land by widening the market. When inherent land values are low and not changing rapidly on the frontier, informal tenure arrangements are appropriate, and violence is unlikely. Such arrangements are of minimal cost and serve to demarcate individual claims and to arbitrate local disputes. Low land values and small expected increases in value limit competition over claims and provide for relatively homogeneous claimants, who can reach agreement on property rights.[7] Moving away from the frontier toward market centers, locational land rents rise with expectations for further increases, and competition for control intensifies. Informal arrangements no longer will be sufficient to allow claimants to appropriate potential land rents. With greater competition, private enforcement costs will increase, uncertainty of control

---

[5] For 1970 for Pará, we have only 78 *municípios* because of problems with the census measure of investment in one *município*.

[6] As we describe in Alston, Libecap, and Schneider (1995a), some of the variables, such as investment, are constructed using census data. In all cases where prices are involved it is necessary to deflate. All values for Paraná are in 1970 cruzeiros and all values for Pará are in 1985 cruzeiros. The index used to deflate prices was the general price index calculated by Fundação Getúlio Vargas. For the period 1940–44, the price index for São Paulo found in IBGE, *Estatísticas Históricas do Brasil* (1990, pp. 226–36, 285–86) was used.

[7] For an analysis of the impact of low resource values and homogeneity of claimants on property rights institutions, see Libecap (1978).

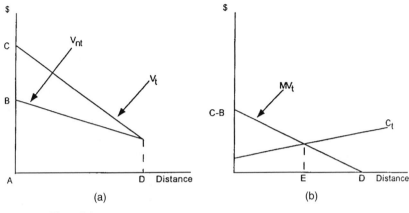

Figure 9-1.

will rise, and violent conflict becomes more likely. The other rent-enhancing advantages of formal tenure, such as collateral or gains from more extensive trade, will be limited. Hence, individual claimants will have incentives to form lobby groups to push for government provision of tenure services.

Successful lobby efforts involve the organization and delivery of votes and/or campaign funds to politicians. Politicians, in turn, have incentives to provide titling services in response to lobby pressure, but the costs of titling will affect the timing and extent of formal property rights provided by government. Politicians respond to multiple constituent group demands in allocating a limited budget. More remote sites on the frontier involve greater administrative costs, and hence from a cost perspective should receive fewer titling services. Closer sites, however, can be titled at lower average cost.

Figure 9-1 organizes the analytical framework for the empirical analysis. In frontier areas, distance to market is a primary determinant of land value. Transportation costs grow with distance from the market center, reducing the net profitability of economic activities. At some distance, transportation costs are high enough to make economic activity unfeasible, since the returns do not cover the opportunity costs of the marginal laborer. Hence, the land is not occupied and remains in forest. This land is beyond the economic frontier. This discussion suggests that those who settle the frontier will have relatively lower opportunity costs, with limited education and experience, all else constant.

In Figure 9-1(a), assuming homogeneous land, the horizontal axis represents distance from the market/administrative center, and the vertical axis reflects the market value of a hectare of land. Value is determined by the production possibilities from the land, which are negatively related to distance and positively related to inherent quality, land-specific investments, and market exchange. Title also adds value to land. Formal, state-enforced title represents the most secure form of property rights to land. Title signals government endorsement of an individual's land claim; that is, with title, ownership is enforced by the courts and the police power of the state. Under these circumstances, title provides claimants with the long-term security of ownership and collateral necessary to access formal capital markets for land-specific investments. Formal, enforced title also reduces the private costs of defending claims, such as private marking and patroling of claims, because the state assumes many of those responsibilities. Finally, by signaling government recognition of current land ownership, a title increases the exchange value of land by widening the market. Those buyers from more distant areas, who may have higher-valued uses for the land and access to capital markets, have the assurance that land exchange contracts will be recognized by the courts and enforced by the state. Absent title, land exchange occurs in more narrow markets among local buyers and sellers who are familiar with informal local property rights arrangements. These regional practices typically are not enforced by the courts or understood by potential buyers from more distant areas.[8]

In the figure, lines V_t and V_{nt} illustrate the net present value of land with or without title, less private enforcement costs. At the market center (point A in the figure), titled and untitled land will have different net present values (BC in the figure) because of differences in productivity-enhancing investments, exchange possibilities, and private enforcement costs. Indeed, at point A, where transportation costs are the lowest, the contribution of title to land value is the greatest. Potentially high-valued, but untitled land at the market center will be subject to more intense competition, raising private enforcement costs, and increasing uncertainty of control. These conditions reduce investment, exchange, and production possibilities, lowering potential land values. By contrast with title, the state assumes most of the enforcement costs, guarantees ownership, and thereby promotes investment, exchange, and production. These activities raise values to point C in the figure.

Moving from the market center at point A toward the frontier, the contribution of title declines. With higher transportation costs, land values are lower and competition for ownership is reduced, requiring less state enforcement of title. Potentials for exchange and production decline. Hence, line V_t has a negative slope with respect to distance, and the slope is greater than that for line V_{nt}. At some remote distance, D, the two value lines converge. Similarly, the costs of not having title decline with distance from point A toward the frontier. With higher transportation costs and lower land values, competition is less and

---

[8] On the nineteenth-century U.S. mining frontier, the need to obtain formal judicial recognition of mineral claims was a major reason for the establishment of government institutions. See Libecap (1978).

private enforcement costs are reduced. As a result, the slope of line V_{nt} declines less with distance.

Figure 9-1(b) outlines demand and supply conditions for title. The vertical axis reflects the marginal value of title, which is the distance between lines V_t and V_{nt}, and the private costs of obtaining title. The line MV_t, which is the marginal value of title, has a negative slope, reflecting the declining contribution of title to land value with movement from the market center toward the frontier. Individuals with more education, farming experience, and wealth likely will have higher marginal values of title than will those with less human and physical capital because the former may be able to take better advantage of the opportunities made possible by title.

Line C_t, which describes the marginal private costs of obtaining title, has a positive slope. As distance from the market center increases, the private costs of obtaining title rise. Individuals must mark their claim boundaries, have them surveyed, and record them to obtain title. Further, claimants may have to organize and lobby government land agencies to provide titling services. Travel to the administrative center to record land claims and to file for title, as well as to lobby for titling services, will rise with distance. In most frontier areas, the market and administrative center are the same. The human and physical capital assets of claimants may also lower the private costs of obtaining title. Those claimants with more education, wealth, and experience are more apt to know how to use the bureaucracy to their advantage and to be able to lobby politicians to provide and police land titles.

In the case at hand, claimants would not seek to have title to the right of point E, where the marginal value and marginal private costs of title intersect. The private returns to having title do not compensate for the private costs of obtaining it. In the most remote regions, individuals will rely on local, informal property rights arrangements and hold their claims as squatters. To the left of point E, however, individuals are motivated to obtain title. Indeed, the greatest marginal returns to having title, in terms of changes in land value, occur at the market center.

Government policy will affect the private costs of obtaining title and the position of line C_t. The social costs of providing title include the private costs to the individual claimant and the costs borne by the government in assigning, administering, and enforcing title. The government costs also rise with distance from the administrative center, and hence one would expect government to provide fewer titling services at more remote locations toward the frontier. Politics affect the private benefits and costs of title. Government policy determines who receives title (through the allocation formula), when it is assigned (through marking and survey policies, pricing, and other settlement requirements), whether it is secure (through enforcement practices), and how conflicts are adjudicated (through the police and courts). Each of these will be determined through the political process. Government may lower the private costs of obtaining title and hence shift line C_t to the right by subsidizing titles. For example, politicians may travel to the site and exchange titles with farmers for promises of electoral support. In either case, government policy may lead to a shifting of point E to the right, towards the frontier with a process of possible "premature" titling.[9] Such grants, if large and remote, would be difficult to police, and hence may be subject to invasion by squatters and violent conflict. Alternatively, the existence of multiple land agencies, confused jurisdictions over government land, violent conflict, and fluctuating agency budgets may serve to delay the provision of tenure services and to raise the private costs to individual claimants. These conditions may shift line C_t to the left and move point E toward the market center, delaying the assignment of title. Any delay in the assignment of recognized and enforced title would contribute to the likelihood of violent conflict over land.

In Brazil, state and federal agencies have jurisdiction in different areas, different constituents, and varying budget environments. State agencies, in response to local constituent demands, may be more likely to subsidize the private costs of obtaining title, whereas federal land agencies may be less responsive to local demand and more vulnerable to changing national budget priorities. Even in the absence of subsidies, it seems likely that it would be more costly for local squatter organizations to effectively lobby politicians in remote Brasília, which is the nation's capital and headquarters for INCRA, than in comparatively nearby Belém, the state capital for Pará and headquarters for the state land agency, ITERPA. Hence, the private costs of obtaining title from state government land agencies may be less than those for obtaining title from federal agencies.

As long as land values rise smoothly and expectedly and government responds in a timely manner to demands for title, violent conflict over property rights is unlikely. But politics can affect both the expected rental stream and the response of government to demands for title, and make violence an outcome of the settlement process. New (and largely unanticipated) government programs to develop highways and other infrastructure can dramatically raise expected land rents from settlement and attract competing claimants. Additionally, the promise of government infrastructure investment will attract speculative settlement of lands that otherwise would not justify occupation at that time. Governments also may subsidize settlement directly by bringing claimants to the frontier. Direct settlement, however, will induce more migra-

---

[9] The notion of premature titling suggests that title is provided at a point where the social costs exceed the social marginal returns to title. We do not have data on the social costs of providing title.

tion to the frontier as others seek to benefit from the expected rise in land rents. These induced migratory flows may greatly exceed the capacity of titling agencies to process claims and lead to uncertainty over property rights and potential conflict for control.[10]

As land becomes more valuable from these policies, competing political coalitions of claimants will form to lobby government agencies for title. Influential wealthy constituents may demand that the government provide them with grants and title to large blocks of land. These grants will be controversial on distributional grounds, and their boundaries will be difficult to police. Infringement by other claimants will lead to subsequent conflict, raising enforcement costs, lowering land values, and increasing the likelihood of violence. Alternatively, grants of government land to the poor may be demanded as part of income redistribution schemes. These conflicting demands will be more serious if agency jurisdictions are unclear or if government jurisdictions overlap (for example, state versus federal). Under these circumstances, competing settlement and titling policies may emerge, with obvious potentials for violence. Even when jurisdictions are not disputed, sufficient budgets for processing land claims may not be forthcoming, so that titles are delayed, inviting conflict. The time horizons of politicians involved in land distribution are short, but consistent tenure policies require long-term commitments. Budgets are limited, face competing political demands, and expenditure mandates fluctuate. Changing macroeconomic conditions or new demands on government budgets can divert resources from the assignment and enforcement of land titles on the frontier as land rents rise. Hence, insufficient appropriations may restrict the ability of land agencies to provide title to settlers who migrated to the frontier with the expectation of ultimately receiving formal tenure.

Governments can transfer some of the costs of titling by selling land in large blocks to private land companies that in turn will subdivide and title the land for agricultural development, as long as government will recognize and enforce the titles. Since private companies are residual claimants from land sales, they may have more incentive than government officials to assign titles quickly and at low cost to settlers.

We use this simple framework to analyze government policies, the assignment of property rights, and violence in two frontier Brazilian states, Paraná and Pará.[11]

---

[10] For a description of governmentally induced migration in the Brazilian Amazon state of Rondonia, see Mueller (1980).

[11] For discussion of the moving frontier in Brazil, see Sawyer (1984), Santos (1984), and Moran (1989a, 1989b).

5   **Empirical analysis of the assignment of property rights and violence in two frontier Brazilian states: Paraná and Pará**

Property rights and violence on the frontier in Paraná and Pará

There was rapid settlement of Paraná after 1940 due to high coffee prices and declining yields in the neighboring state of São Paulo. The population of the state rose from 1,236,274 in 1940 to 6,929,868 by 1970.[12] Between 1940 and 1960, the amount of agricultural land almost doubled and the number of farms increased more than fourfold. On the western and northern frontiers, cropland increased by over seven times.[13] Average per-hectare farm land values in constant 1970 cruzeiros rose from Cr$ 98 in 1940 to Cr$ 674 in 1970.[14] Similarly, through directed colonization projects and other subsidies, initiated by the federal government in the late 1960s, the population of Pará grew from 2,167,018 in 1970 to 4,318,400 in 1985.[15] The land in farms doubled in the 1960s and again in the 1970s, and the number of farms rose sharply. Vast tracts of new lands were opened through construction of regional road systems, and these additions, as well as the isolation of the region from the rest of Brazil, kept land values comparatively low. In 1980, only 5 percent of the land in Pará had been cleared of forest and placed into agriculture, whereas in Paraná, 65 percent of the land was cleared and in agriculture.[16] Census data indicate that per-hectare farm land values in constant 1970 cruzeiros grew from Cr$ 41 in 1970 to Cr$ 153 in 1980 in Pará.[17] Even so, Pará real land values in 1970 were less than half those in Paraná in 1940 (in constant 1970 prices), and 1980 Pará land prices remained less than half of Paraná land prices in 1950.[18]

With the exception of western *municípios,* land distribution policies appear to have been relatively straightforward in Paraná. Squatting – the occupation

---

[12] IBGE, *Anuário Estatístico do Brasil* (1990, p. 183).

[13] Nicholls and Paiva (1969, p. 8).

[14] IBGE, *Censo Agropecuário, Paraná* (1940, p. 244; 1970, p. 77). The index used to deflate prices was the general price index calculated by Fundação Getúlio Vargas. For the period 1940–44, the price index for São Paulo found in IBGE, *Estatísticas Históricas do Brasil* (1990, pp. 226–36, 285–6), was used. The values reported in the text are the total value of farm land in Paraná divided by total farm area.

[15] IBGE, *Anuário Estatístico do Brasil* (1991, pp. 180, 183).

[16] The cleared area, as reported in the census includes land in permanent crops, temporary crops, planted pasture, natural pasture, planted forest, and unused but useable land. It is divided by the area of each state.

[17] IBGE, *Censo Agropecuário,* Pará (1970, p. 178; 1980, p. 282). The index used for deflating was the general price index provided by Fundação Getúlio Vargas. The values reported in the text are the total value of farm land in the state divided by total farm area.

[18] Paraná land values in 1940 were Cr$ 98 per hectare in 1970 prices, while those in Pará in 1970 were Cr$ 41 per hectare. In 1950, Paraná land prices were Cr$ 312, while in 1980, Pará land prices were Cr$ 153. These data are from the IBGE, *Censo Agropecuário,* Paraná (1940, p. 244; 1950, p. 184); Pará (1980, p. 282). The following factors were used to convert nominal prices to 1970 prices: 1940–70, 885.133; 1950–70, 230.552; 1970–80, 29.616.

of land without title – was limited at the aggregate state level. Census data for the state level show that the proportion of farm land held by squatters peaked at 9.3 percent in the late 1950s and the proportion of farms operated by squatters peaked at 13.5 percent somewhat earlier, in the late 1940s.[19] Within Paraná, the state government had sole jurisdiction over land settlement, except in the western *municípios,* where there was dispute over jurisdiction between the federal and state governments, and these were the areas where violence among claimants occurred.[20] The intergovernment dispute likely delayed the assignment of clear property rights to land and encouraged conflict among settlers over claims.[21]

The effect of confused jurisdiction between the governments is reflected in squatting data. In 1950, the average percentage of land operated by squatters in the nine western *municípios* was 21 percent, but in the northern frontier where there was no jurisdiction conflict, the level of squatting was low. In those 26 *municípios,* only an average of 2 percent of the land was occupied by squatters. In 1950, the western region accounted for 66 percent of Paraná's squatters and 84 percent of all squatted land, while the northern region had 16 percent of total squatters and 8 percent of squatted land.[22] By the 1970 census, there was much less variation in squatting across the state, and overall only 5.1 percent of the farm land was occupied by squatters, and 9.0 percent of the farms were operated by squatters. Those proportions continued to decline through 1985.[23]

In the northern region, where titles were provided more routinely and there was less violent conflict, the state government had sold much of the land to private land development companies that recruited settlers and provided titles. The *municípios* included accounted for over 12 percent of the size of Paraná in 1960.[24] Because it first gained clear legal title to its land before attracting colonists, private land companies may have been able to transfer titles quickly and to avoid conflict and legal disputes that would have resulted in tenure uncertainty.[25] We examine this issue in the following empirical analysis.

Squatting has been more prevalent and has lasted longer in Pará than in Paraná. In 1975, squatters occupied 23.3 percent of the agricultural land in Pará

---

[19] IBGE, *Censo Agropecuário, Paraná* (1950, p. 154; 1960, p. 27). For analysis, see Alston, Libecap, and Schneider (1995b).

[20] Foweraker (1981, pp. 88–92).

[21] Westphalen, Machado, and Balhana (1968).

[22] Nicholls and Paiva (1969, p. 60).

[23] IBGE, *Censo Agropecuário, Paraná* (1970, p. 140). For example, the 1985 census (p. 238) reported 2.9 percent of farm land operated by squatters.

[24] This was calculated using the map in Nicholls and Paiva (1969, p. 28) and the area of the *municípios* within the company's jurisdiction from IBGE, *Anuário Estatístico do Brazil* (1965, pp. 42–3).

[25] Nicholls and Paiva (1969, pp. 27–30), Foweraker (1981, p. 130).

and accounted for 49.2 percent of the farms.[26] Moreover, the shares of farm land and farms operated by squatters have remained high, 11.2 percent and 34.0 percent, respectively, in 1985.[27] Further, the statewide data in the figures mask even more squatting on the frontier, suggesting that the tenuring process has moved more slowly and less completely in that state. As already noted, differences in settlement policies between Pará and Paraná likely explain the differences in the assignment of property rights in the two states. In Pará, more than one land agency has been involved in titling, often with no clear demarcation of authority. In 1965, the federal government initiated Operation Amazonia to settle the region and to secure Brazil's claim to the Amazon. In the 1960s Brazil became concerned that its lack of occupation of the Amazon would lead other countries to claim the region for its potential timber and mineral wealth and farm land. Under the Constitution of 1969, the federal government claimed all lands essential to national security. This action was followed by decree law 1164 in 1971, by which the federal government took control of all land up to 100 km on either side of all roads constructed, under construction, or projected. These areas subsequently were placed under the administration of the federal land colonization agency, INCRA. The public domain transferred from the state to federal government amounted to nearly 75 percent of Pará, leaving the rest of the state for the state land agency, ITERPA. The government of Pará contested the usurpation of its jurisdiction of public land, bringing confusion to claimants and additional delays in the titling process.[28]

Directed colonization programs of the federal government and promises of infrastructure investment further limited the assignment of property rights by encouraging early migration to the Amazon, before land rents had risen to a level that otherwise would have attracted migrants. At the same time, land agency budgets were not augmented to keep pace with the rise in migration. Beginning in 1966 and continuing into the 1970s, the military government provided tax and credit incentives to private firms for investment in the Amazon. These initiatives were joined in the early 1970s with road-building programs, pledges of other infrastructure investment, and directed (subsidized) colonization efforts. INCRA organized colonization projects, especially along the TransAmazon highway, bringing colonists from southern Brazil with pledges of infrastructure and credit. In 1971, the Program for National Integration (PIN) was launched to bring colonists to the Amazon. In Pará, INCRA established three colonization areas: Marabá, Altamira, and Itaituba. A goal of placing 100,000 families, each with 100-hectare plots, in organized colonies and planned urban centers was established.[29] Although this goal was not achieved, a larger number of settlers arrived

---

[26] IBGE, *Censo Agropecuário, Pará* (1975, p. 150).
[27] IBGE, *Censo Agropecuário, Pará* (1985, p. 166).
[28] Schmink and Wood (1992, pp. 62–4).
[29] Fearnside (1986, pp. 19–20).

independent of the formal colonization projects, generally from all over Brazil. Other formal projects for colonization along the TransAmazon and Belém-Brasília highways in Pará included the Program for Redistribution of Land and Stimulus to Agroindustry in the North and Northeast (PROTERRA). In 1974, a policy shift led to greater emphasis on colonization by large ranchers in plots of 500 to 3,000 hectares and less on small holder settlement.[30]

The claims of the many settlers who rushed to the region or who were brought there by official colonization projects flooded the federal agency, INCRA, beyond its capabilities to process them. INCRA, established to administer orderly settlement colonies, was forced to respond to spontaneous migration and informal land claims.[31] INCRA and the state land agency, ITERPA, focused more on directing settlers to particular areas as the two agencies competed for jurisdiction and much less on assigning title. Indeed, settlers were to remain on the land with licenses to occupy before the agencies would return to process title applications. This practice led to a lag between settlement and the assignment of title. With a growing influx of migrants and fluctuating budget appropriations the agencies were severely limited in their ability to provide titles. Although there was considerable migration to the Amazon in the 1970s, most title applications were not processed until after 1980. INCRA's budget for Pará peaked in 1976 and changed as national priorities changed.[32] In 1989, the agency was dissolved and its functions transferred to the Ministry of Agriculture. Later, the agency was reinstated.[33] ITERPA processed title applications according to state election cycles, with officials promising titles in exchange for electoral support.[34]

Among squatters and other small holders in Pará, the lack of title has not contributed extensively to violent disputes, largely because land values have remained comparatively low and individual claim boundaries can be monitored at low cost. Violent land conflicts, however, have occurred between small holders and ranchers, particularly in southeastern Pará in the *município* of Conceição do Araguaia and others near Marabá. Ranchers have received federal subsidies for cattle raising from SUDAM, a federal agency that administered a series of credit benefits and fiscal incentives.[35] The disputes between small holders and ranchers were so intense that land values and investment in the conflict areas were threatened. To mediate conflict and to bypass existing bureaucratic hurdles in order to more rapidly assign title, a temporary federal agency was created, GETAT. GETAT was granted authority to intervene in land disputes, grant titles, and compensate squatters, if they were forced to leave the invasion site, or ranchers, if they lost land to squatters.

---

[30] Fearnside (1986, p. 21).
[31] Mueller (1992, p.6).
[32] Yokota (1981, p. 33), Moran (1984, pp. 290–1), and INCRA *Annual Reports*.
[33] For discussion of the political economy of these actions, see Mueller (1994).
[34] Pinto (1980, p. 187).
[35] Schneider (1994, pp. 2–6).

Statistical analysis of property rights and violence

Elsewhere we have developed a framework for examining the development of property rights to land in Brazil.[36] Here we report the results that relate the assignment of property rights to jurisdictional disputes and violent conflict over land. The basic equation is:

$$\text{Title} = a_1 + a_2 \text{ (change in value)} + a_3 \text{ (size)} +/- a_4 \text{ (jurisdiction)}$$
$$-/+ a_5 \text{ (violence)} - a_6 \text{ (distance)} + a_7 \text{ (characteristics)} + e$$

In general, the demand for title should be a function of expected private net returns, which in turn are due to the increase in land value from having title, less the private costs of obtaining title. Land values will increase with title because of a greater opportunity for investment in land improvements, greater exchange opportunities for land sales, and reduced private enforcement costs. The private costs of securing title will be determined by the requirements of the land laws, such as beneficial use, occupation, boundary marking, and documentation. Costs also will be a function of distance from the farm site to the administrative center that the squatter must travel and any associated group organizational costs and lobby expenses to secure land agency action.

The analysis illustrated in Figure 9-1(b) suggests that the demand for and supply of title will be a function of:

- Distance from the market/administrative center, which will drive up the costs of obtaining title.
- Expected change in land value from having title.
- Jurisdiction – the land agency involved (state or federal in Pará) or whether title was granted by a private land company (Paraná).
- Whether the *município* was characterized by violence.
- Size of the farm.
- Characteristics of the individual farmer.

For the estimation we have the following variables:

- Proportion of *município* farmers with title to their land.
- Change in value from having title.[37]
- Distance from the *município* capital to the state capital (Curitiba or Belém).
- Average farm size in the *município*.
- *Municípios* under private land company jurisdiction in Paraná or under federal jurisdiction in Pará.

---

[36] Alston, Libecap, and Schneider (1995a).

[37] This variable is estimated from a land value equation described in Alston, Libecap, and Schneider (1995a).

- *Municípios* characterized by jurisdictional conflict and violence in Paraná or general violence in Pará.
- For 1980 only in Pará, average age, education, and income in the *município*.[38]

Because private enforcement costs are likely to be higher for large farms or ranches, we expect that larger average farm sizes would increase the demand for title. Jurisdictional conflicts between the state and federal government in the western *municípios* in Paraná likely raised the private costs of obtaining title because it was unclear which government could provide title. There was violent land conflict in those *municípios,* which would increase the demand for clear title. Because the private land companies were residual claimants for increases in land value from providing title, we anticipate that those *municípios* under private jurisdiction would have more titles, on average. In Pará, we expect that the state agency, ITERPA, would be more responsive to local demand for title and provide it more extensively in the *municípios* under its jurisdiction than would the federal agency, INCRA. In the equation, INCRA *municípios* are assigned a dummy variable, one. Additionally, in *municípios* in Pará characterized by violent conflict over land between ranchers and squatters, we expect greater demand for title. Age, as a proxy for experience, education, and income could both increase the demand for title and reduce the private costs of obtaining it. Individuals with greater experience, education, and income may be better able to take advantage of having title, and they may understand the political process and bureaucratic requirements better to secure title at lower private cost.

Econometric results

Table 9-1 presents the estimation results for analyzing property rights and violence in Paraná and Pará for each of the census years. The estimations are performed using OLS.[39] The results reported in Table 9-1 describe the general forces underlying the development of property rights to land and the effects of confused government jurisdiction and violence on the incidence of title in the two Brazilian frontier areas.

With regard to the determinants of private property rights to land, the key change-in-value variable has the predicted positive effect on the proportion of farmers with title in six of the census years in the two states and is significant

---

[38] Before 1980, socioeconomic data are at the state level only and are not by *município*.

[39] We also estimated the title equation, where the proportion of *município* farmers with title is the dependent variable, with a Probit specification. The results were essentially the same as with OLS, and for ease of coefficient interpretation, we chose the OLS specification. In Pará, the *municípios* of Belém, Ananindeua, and Benevides were not used in the analysis because they are primarily urban areas.

Table 1. *Determinants of property rights on the frontier: The role of violence*

Dependent variable: Proportion of farmers with title
Paraná (*t*-statistics in parenthesis)

	Constant	Distance	Farm size	Private company	Government conflict	Change in value	R^2	N
1940	.96 (19.51)	−.0001 −(1.04)	.0002 (1.02)	.02 (.72)	−.16 −(1.01)	.25 (1.04)	.25	49
1950	.93 (36.37)	−.0002 −(1.19)	.0001 (1.86)	−.04 −(.97)	−.27 −(1.53)	.13 (2.12)	.27	80
1960	.93 (48.37)	−.0002 −(1.90)	.0003 (2.34)	−.008 −(.35)	−.34 −(3.45)	.13 (2.97)	.40	162
1970	.93 (40.72)	−.0001 −(.86)	−.0003 −(2.33)	.04 (3.45)	−.02 −(1.47)	−.05 −(2.34)	.13	288

Dependent variable: Proportion of farmers with title
Pará (*t*-statistics in parenthesis)

	Constant	Distance	Farm size	INCRA area	Violent conflict	Change in value	Age	Income	Education	R^2	N
1970	.49 (7.41)	−.0003 −(3.99)	.0001 (1.77)	N.A.	N.A.	8.26 (4.21)	N.A.	N.A.	N.A.	.53	78
1975	.65 (7.08)	−.0003 −(3.90)	.0001 (.89)	−.05 −(.96)	N.A.	−.01 −(.02)	N.A.	N.A.	N.A.	.20	79
1980	−.64 −(1.09)	−.0002 −(1.79)	−.0002 −(2.02)	−.03 −(.47)	.04 (.60)	.03 (.13)	.05 (1.99)	.12 (1.37)	.06 (.74)	.20	79
1985	.46 (5.24)	.0001 (1.12)	.0001 (1.27)	−.03 −(.46)	.0002 (.004)	.51 (2.55)	N.A.	N.A.	N.A.	.11	79

at the .975 level or better for a one-tailed test in four of those years. Jurisdictional conflict in Paraná in the western *municípios* over whether the federal or state government had authorization to issue titles reduced the portion of farmers with title, as would be expected. This condition contributed to violent conflict over land that has been noted in the literature on the region. In Pará, however, there is no difference between the proportion of farmers with title in those *municípios* characterized by violent conflict over land from elsewhere in the state. The federal agency, GETAT, which was created to resolve title disputes and rush the processing of title claims, had obvious effect, at least in terms of the statistical results. Moreover, there is no indication that the *municípios* with violence had a lower proportion of farmers with title than elsewhere in the state. Violence appears to be due to variety of factors, such as the mixing of large and small claimants in the same areas and sharp increases in land values due to new infrastructure investment by the government. We are exploring these issues in on-going research. As hypothesized, distance from the market/administrative center tends to reduce the portion of farmers with title, a finding consistent with the notion that administrative costs rise with remoteness. The generally positive relationship between farm size and title also supports the view that private enforcement costs rise with farm size, increasing the demand for title by large farmers. For the 1980 census in Pará, we have socioeconomic measures by *município*. In the aggregate, higher ages, incomes, and education lead to greater titling. Except for 1970 in Paraná, there is no indication that *municípios* under private company (Paraná) or INCRA (Pará) jurisdiction had a greater portion of farmers with title than elsewhere in the two states.

6   Concluding remarks

In this paper, we have examined the assignment of property rights and violence in two Brazilian states that represent different frontier periods. We are able to follow the emergence of land rents on the frontier and the rise in demand for tenure services. We also are able to examine the supply response by government and the role of politics in determining the supply of tenure. Although frontiers are often associated with violent conflict over property rights to land, violence is not a necessary aspect of the tenure process. As long as tenure institutions are supplied smoothly as land values rise, then settlement of the frontier can be routine with few disputes over property rights. In contrast, where clearly defined tenure is not supplied in a timely manner as rents rise, then violent conflict is a possible outcome. Because tenure services are supplied through the political process, a variety of problems can arise to complicate delivery and encourage violence.

Our analysis indicates that in Brazil the following factors led to localized violence: (1) overlapping government jurisdictions with competing land agencies assigning tenure to the same land; (2) multiple land agencies within the same government with different constituents who are granted title to the same land; (3) government subsidies and other infrastructure programs that unexpectedly and sharply raise potential land values, attracting new claimants; and (4) insufficient agency budgets and staffs to process and police titles.

In an earlier frontier in Paraná, titles were supplied comparatively routinely, especially in the northern *municípios,* as land values rose and demand for tenure services increased between 1940 and 1970. Squatting was less pronounced in Paraná than in Pará. Migration to Paraná came largely from neighboring states, such as São Paulo, through individual decisions to take advantage of rising coffee and land prices. Where there were jurisdictional disputes between the state and federal governments in the western *municípios,* there were violent conflicts over land claims, and titling was less complete. This difference between the northern and western *municípios* of Paraná provides implications for subsequent conditions in Pará, where similar jurisdiction conflicts and conflicts among squatters and ranchers have occurred.

On the more recent Amazon frontier of Pará, migrants were brought to low-valued land in the Amazon (directly or indirectly) by new roads and government subsidized colonization projects. Because of its isolation from the rest of Brazil and the availability of vast amounts of unoccupied land, Amazon land values were much lower than those found during similar frontier periods in Paraná. Without government intervention, migrants likely would have moved to the Amazon later, when expected land rents and the present value of their future net income stream from the land at least equaled their opportunity costs. But government subsidies that either lowered expected costs or increased expected revenues encouraged earlier migration. Moreover, government colonization efforts set in motion a flow of migrants in search of land that the titling agencies could not process expeditiously. Although tenure conditions are not as well defined in Pará as they were in Paraná, low land values and population densities have meant limited conflict over land among small holders. The exception has been in disputes between ranchers with large claims and settlers who have invaded the ranches in southeast Pará. Ranchers were attracted to the region by one federal agency, SUDAM, while small holders were attracted by another, INCRA. The outcome has been violent conflict and confused ownership. As land values rise over time elsewhere in Pará, the potential for tenure uncertainty and violent conflict may increase because of the widespread occupancy of land by squatters and the limited provision of tenuring services by government.

References

Alston, Lee J., Gary D. Libecap, and Robert Schneider, "The Determinants and Impact of Property Rights: Census Data and Survey Results for Land Titles on the Brazilian Frontier," 1995a, working paper, Tucson: Karl Eller Center, University of Arizona.

———, "Property Rights and the Preconditions for Markets: The Case of the Amazon Frontier," *Journal of Institutional and Theoretical Economics,* 1995b, 151(1), 89–107.

Anderson, Terry L. and P.J. Hill, "The Evolution of Property Rights: A Study of the American West," *Journal of Law and Economics,* 1975, 28 (April), 163–80.

———, " The Race for Property Rights," *Journal of Law and Economics,* 1991, 33 (April), 177–97.

Fearnside, Philip M., *Human Carrying Capacity of the Brazilian Rain Forest,* 1986, New York: Columbia University Press.

Feder, Gershon and David Feeny, "Land Tenure and Property Rights: Theory and Implications for Development Policy," *World Bank Economic Review,* 1991, 5 (1), 135–53.

Foweraker, Joseph, *The Struggle for Land: A Political Economy of the Pioneer Frontier in Brazil, 1930 to Present,* 1981, New York: Cambridge University Press.

Hallagan, William S., "Share Contracting for California Gold," *Explorations in Economic History,* 1978, 15, 196–210.

Hardin, Garrett, "The Tragedy of the Commons," *Science,* 1968, 162, 1243–8.

IBGE, *Anuário Estatístico do Brasil,* 1965, 1990, 1991, IBGE: Rio de Janeiro.

———, *Estatísticas Históricas do Brasil,* 1990, IBGE: Rio de Janeiro.

———, *Geografia do Brasil-Região Norte,* 1991, Vol. III, IBGE: Rio de Janeiro.

———, *Censo Agropecuário Paraná,* 1940, 1950, 1960, 1970, IBGE: Rio de Janeiro.

———, *Censo Agropecuário Pará, ,* 1970, 1975, 1980, 1985, IBGE: Rio de Janeiro.

Ianni, Octavio, *Colonização e Contra-Reforma Agrária na Amazônia,* 1979, Petropolis, Brazil: Editora Vozes.

INCRA, *Annual Reports,* 1973–85, INCRA: Brasilia.

Libecap, Gary D., "Economic Variables and the Development of the Law: The Case of Western Mineral Rights," *Journal of Economic History,* 1978, 38, 338–62.

———, "Government Support of Private Claims to Public Minerals: Western Mineral Rights," *Business History Review,* 1979, 53, 364–85.

———, *Contracting for Property Rights,* 1989, New York: Cambridge University Press.

Mahar, Dennis J., *Government Policies and Deforestation in Brazil's Amazon Region,* 1989, Washington D.C.: The World Bank.

Moran, Emilio F., *Developing the Amazon,* 1981, Bloomington: Indiana University Press.

———, "Colonization in the Transamazon and Rondonia," in Marianne Schmink and Charles H. Wood (eds.), *Frontier Expansion in Amazonia,* 1984, Gainesville: University of Florida Press.

———, "Adaptation and Maladaptation in Newly Settled Areas," in Debra A. Schumann and William L. Partridge (eds.), *The Human Ecology of Tropical Land Settlement in Latin America,* 1989a, Boulder: Westview Press.

———, "Government-Directed Settlement in the 1970s: An Assessment of Transamazon Highway Colonization," in Debra A. Schumann and William L. Partridge, (eds.), *The Human Ecology of Tropical Land Settlement in Latin America,* 1989b, Boulder: Westview Press.

Mueller, Bernardo, "The Political Economy of Agrarian Reform in Brazil," PhD Dissertation, 1994, Champaign/Urbana: University of Illinois.

Mueller, Charles, "Frontier Based Agricultural Expansion: The Case of Rondonia," in Francoise Barbira-Scazzocchio (ed)., *Land, People, and Planning in Contemporary Amazonia,* 1980, Cambridge, England: Cambridge University, Center of Latin American Studies, Occasional Publication No. 3.

————, "Colonization Policies, Land Occupation, and Deforestation in the Amazon Countries," 1992, working paper no. 15, Department of Economics, University of Brasília.

Nicholls, William N. and Ruy Miller Paiva, *Ninety-Nine Fazendas: The Structure and Productivity of Brazilian Agriculture, 1963,* 1969, Nashville: Vanderbilt University, Graduate Center for Latin American Studies.

North, Douglass C., *Institutions, Institutional Change, and Economic Performance,* 1990, New York: Cambridge University Press.

Pará Pastoral Land Commission, "People Killed in Land Conflicts," 1989, Belém.

Pinto, Lúcio Flavio, *Amazônia: No Rastro do Saque,* 1980, São Paulo: Hucitec.

Rone, Jermera, *Rural Violence in Brazil,* 1991, New York: Human Rights Watch.

Santos, Roberto, "Law and Social Change: The Problem of Land in the Brazilian Amazon," in Marianne Schmink and Charles H. Wood (eds.), *Frontier Expansion in Amazonia,* 1984, Gainesville: University of Florida Press.

Sawyer, Donald R., "Frontier Expansion and Retraction in Brazil," in Marianne Schmink and Charles H. Wood (eds.), *Frontier Expansion in Amazonia,* 1984, Gainesville: University of Florida Press.

Schmink, Marianne and Charles H. Wood, *Contested Frontiers in Amazonia,* 1992, New York: Columbia University Press.

Schneider, Robert, "Government and the Economy on the Amazon Frontier," 1994, Latin America and Caribbean Technical Department, Regional Studies Program Report No. 34, Washington D.C.: The World Bank.

Umbeck, John, "Might Makes Rights: A Theory of the Foundation and Initial Distribution of Property Rights," *Economic Inquiry,* 1981, 19, 421–37.

Westphalen, M. C., B. Pinheiro Machado, and A. P. Balhana, "Preliminary Note to the Study of the Occupation of Land in Modern Paraná, *Boletim da Universidade Federal do Paraná,* 1968, no. 7, Curitiba.

Wood, Charles and John Wilson, "The Magnitude of Migration to the Brazilian Frontier," in Marianne Schmink and Charles H. Wood (eds.), *Frontier Expansion in Amazonia,* 1984, Gainesville: University of Florida Press.

Yokota, Paulo, "Questão Fundiána Brasileira," 1981, INCRA, Brasilia.

Index